Salt on a
Robin's Tail

An Unlikely Jewish Journey Through
Childhood, Forgiveness, and Hope

A Memoir

Andrea Kott

Blydyn Square Books
Kenilworth, New Jersey

For Sophie and Ben

Blydyn Square Books
Kenilworth, New Jersey

© 2020 by Andrea Kott

ISBN 978-1-7320156-7-8 (paperback)
ISBN 978-1-7320156-8-5 (ebook)

Cover and interior design: Kristin McCarthy

Cover art composition: still life with fruit: Irina Mosina (Shutterstock); menorah: Ursula Page (Shutterstock); robin: Marc Little (Shutterstock); salt shaker: HandmadePictures (Shutterstock).

CIP information available upon request.

Portions of the text originally appeared in the *Tulane Review*, the *Journal of the American Medical Association*, and *Lilith* magazine, and are reprinted with their permission.

Contents

Author's Note

This is a true story, and I have portrayed all of the events, situations, and conversations as accurately as my memory has allowed. Of course, memory fades and age is a prism. Although many of the experiences I describe were clear and accessible, others required some excavation. Thus, in addition to using pseudonyms to protect some people's privacy, I have exercised my author's license to reconstruct chronologies or dialogue that I know, as the owner of this story, honor it.

Prologue

"It won't be long," the nurse said, closing the blinds against the morning sun.

My mother's chest was rising and falling in widening intervals. Her skin was ruddy, her hair matted around her face. She smelled like baby powder.

I had raced in a cab from Manhattan to La Guardia Airport to catch a flight to Florida the day before, minutes after my mother's sister had called from the hospital in Miami. "Get here," was all Aunt Lila said on that early August morning in 1992. Mom had just received the first of two experimental chemotherapy treatments. She was comatose by the time I arrived. I slept in a chair by her bed and awoke the next morning, surprised to find her still breathing. I caressed her arm and kissed her forehead. Then I left.

"I've got to get back to New York," I told Lila in the hospital lobby, expecting her to urge me to stay.

"Do what you have to do," she said.

Mom died the next day. I'd tried to forgive her but I hadn't gotten far enough. If I had, I wouldn't have left her side.

✦ ✦ ✦ ✦ ✦

It would take years for me to forgive my mother for being the parent she had been: depressed, alcoholic, abusive, absent. It would take many more for me to reconcile the angst from having grown up in a home where financial hardship and worry were constant; dislocation was frequent; and emotionally violent eruptions, routine; a home whose brokenness was humiliating enough without us also being Jewish. My stormy life looked nothing like the lives of the kids I grew up with and defied every stereotypical notion I'd had of what being Jewish meant, flooding me with shame and alienating me from my own tradition.

Yes, we were Jewish. And yet, we weren't. There was no mezuzah inside our doorframes or kosher dishes in our kitchen. We served milk with meat, ate deep-fried scallops on Friday nights and bacon on Sunday mornings. During my early childhood, Mom cooked lavishly for the High Holidays. But I didn't get to skip school, and we didn't go to synagogue. I'd never even been inside a synagogue. On the first night of Passover, we attended a Seder, while I ate Wonder Bread French toast throughout the week. During Chanukah we lit the menorah, one candle each night, until all were ablaze—a dramatic and beautiful symbol whose meaning I did not understand. The one Chanukah gift that Mom managed to afford—a Chatty Cathy doll—awaited me on Christmas morning, beneath the "tree" that my brother Steven made from rolled-up pages of *The New York Times*.

The contradiction didn't bother me: the menorah and the newspaper tree. I saw no problem celebrating both holidays, although given a choice, I would have celebrated Christmas. It felt so much more festive than Chanukah. It filled the air with the smell of fresh pine wreaths and trees. It brought twinkling lights and other decorations to stores and streets, and holiday specials to television. It brewed a swelling anticipation that was impossible not to absorb. Even though I was Jewish, I believed that Santa Claus kept his eye on me all year long to see whether I'd been "naughty or nice" and deserving of presents. I loved knowing that he was watching over me. I loved having something to believe in.

My mother wasn't exactly thrilled about my ardor for Christmas. But that didn't stop her from bringing me to see Santa at Alexander's department store, or letting me have a fake tree. It must have seemed like a harmless compromise: a way to stop my nudging, and a surefire recipe for my happiness, however temporary. But I wanted more. I wanted a real tree—I wanted to celebrate Christmas.

"Can we get a tree?"

"No."

"Why?"

"Because we're Jewish."

"So?"

"Jewish people don't have Christmas trees."

"Can we hang lights outside, then?"

"No."

"Why?"

"Jewish people don't hang Christmas lights."

"Everyone has Christmas lights."

"Not Jewish people."

"Maybe no one knows we're Jewish."

"Everyone on our block knows who's Jewish."

"How does everyone know?"

"They just do."

"Are all the houses without Christmas lights Jewish houses? Is that why people know we're Jewish?"

Mom wouldn't answer. I took a quick inventory of our Queens neighborhood. "The Steins are Jewish. Their house is always dark. The Golds', the Rosensteins', and the Weisses' houses are dark. Mrs. Schwartz across the street is Jewish. Her house is dark, too. If we put up Christmas lights, then people won't have to know we're Jewish!"

The logic made perfect sense to me: Christmas decorations of any kind seemed like the perfect cover, like a wig on a balding head. If our house had them, I reasoned, then people would figure we belonged to some denomination of Christianity. And if they figured that, then they wouldn't sneer at us— and we wouldn't have to apologize—for having Christmas decorations. My argument didn't persuade Mom, or perhaps she had simply stopped listening. Either way, she would not relent. I wasn't getting a real Christmas tree, which seemed ridiculous and unfair.

It was also confusing. I was allowed to dip one toe into Christmas but couldn't publicly embrace the holiday because the tradition wasn't ours. Yet, we didn't embrace our own tradition with any kind of enthusiasm.

When the few Jewish holidays that we recognized ended, when the last yahrzeit flame died and the menorah resumed its place behind the gravy boat in the kitchen cabinet, we weren't Jewish anymore. My five-year-old brain couldn't understand why we had to pay attention to being Jewish in the first place. But I ignored the inconsistencies and counted my blessings. I'd gotten a Chatty Cathy doll, after all.

It would be years before I understood that those inconsistencies mirrored my mother's own ambivalence toward Judaism and that her ambivalence, and ultimately her complete disengagement from the tradition, had evolved from a lifetime of disappointment and grief. It wasn't until I reached young adulthood that I began to see how her years of inner turmoil, and her attempts to deaden it, had short-circuited her faith, and how her alienation from Judaism became mine.

PART ONE:

REGO PARK

MY MOTHER, EVELYN, THE ELDEST OF THREE children, grew up in the Canarsie section of Brooklyn. Her parents, Albert and Irene, had immigrated to New York from Hungary a few years before my mother was born in 1920. Like so many Eastern European Jews, my grandparents came to America to escape prejudice and persecution.

They were not religious people. Yet, they were proud to be Jewish and committed to handing down the heritage to their children. They posted a mezuzah on the front door, celebrated all the holidays, and raised my mother, her brother, and her sister to believe in God. For most of her young life, my mother cleaved to these traditions. But a cascade of loss ultimately shattered her faith. It began with the slaughter of extended family in the Holocaust and spiraled with her parents' divorce, the untimely death of her first husband, and her brief and violent marriage to her second husband, my father. Of all these traumatic events, her first husband's death probably devastated her the most. After that, she began to drink.

I don't remember how old I was when I began making the connection between the caramel-colored beverage Mom drank and her disintegrating mood. I don't recall the first time

I realized that her breath, which usually smelled of coffee and cigarettes, began smelling like something else in the late, and sometimes early, afternoon. I don't know when I discovered that just beneath the breakfront drawer, where she stowed a thick bar of Hershey's chocolate, were several bottles of liquor, some light brown, some clear. I don't remember when I began noticing how she struggled to wake up in the morning.

I do remember, from the time I was very young, thinking about God and wanting to know if she believed in Him. And I remember how her answers changed depending on what she was sipping.

"I believe God is in my heart," she would say, sitting with a cup of coffee. When she was nursing a Scotch, however, she'd say, "I used to believe in God. But what kind of God lets a Holocaust happen? Or lets a man in the prime of his life with a wife and two little boys die?"

I wanted to believe in God. It was comforting. But I couldn't grasp the concept of God being in someone's heart. And I didn't want think of Him failing anyone, especially my mother.

In 1963 I was five years old, living with my mother and two brothers in Rego Park, Queens, in a red-brick, two-family house that had belonged to my maternal grandmother, Irene. My mother hadn't grown up in the house. Nor had Grandma Irene and her husband, my grandfather, Albert, ever lived there together. The house had been a gift to my grandmother from her longtime lover, a married Florida real-estate salesman named Abe Gross.

Mom didn't volunteer this—or any autobiographical information—easily. She avoided talking about her past, except for the happy times, of which there were few. "Don't be such a nosey-body," she'd say when I asked why I, unlike any of the kids on our street, lived with just her and why each of my two brothers was almost old enough to be my dad.

"You're too young to understand. I'll explain when you're older." But I probed persistently. By the time I reached my early teens, I'd worn her down.

"You don't stop," she'd say, irritated. And yet, I think part of her wanted me to know our difficult family story. As if delivering tiny drops of nasty medicine, she began parsing out bits of family history, starting with the breakup of her parents' marriage.

"My mother and Abe met at the Hungarian restaurant that she and my father opened on the Upper East Side after leaving Hungary," she began. "It was around 1935. I was about fifteen." She pulled a Kent cigarette from its box, lit it, and took a deep draw.

"Abe was a regular. He ate at the restaurant whenever he came to New York." She blew a stream of gray smoke at the ceiling. "We'd left Canarsie. We were living in a small apartment right above the restaurant. My parents worked until all hours of the night. They didn't want to be traveling back and forth to Brooklyn." She tapped a long ash into a crystal dish. Smoke streamed from her nostrils.

"One day during lunch, my mother went home. She said she didn't feel well. My mother never got sick. Dad went home to check on her. He walked in on them." Mom snuffed out the cigarette, lit another, and drew on it hungrily. "She was awful to him, so cruel. My father was devastated."

My aunt Lila, who was five years old at the time, said she was too young back then to have known how my grandfather learned of Grandma Irene's affair with Abe, and added that Grandma was too smart to have carried on in her own house during the day. "I do remember my father hurling one of my dolls at my mother and yelling, 'Kurva!' which is Hungarian for 'whore.'"

My grandparents divorced when my mother was sixteen years old, and sold the restaurant. My grandfather remarried, and moved with his new wife and baby daughter to Rochester. "He died before I had a chance to see him again," Mom said.

As for Grandma Irene, she moved to an apartment in Astoria with Mom, her brother Doug, and her sister Lila. It was in that apartment, four years later, that my mother would marry the love of her life.

His name was Leslie Neuwirth, and Mom had met him at a Catskills hotel where she, Doug, and Lila had gone with Grandma Irene. Mom was eighteen years old. Leslie was thirty-one. It was 1938. The Nazis weren't in Hungary yet, but there were murmurs of them coming. Leslie had left the country.

Leslie Neuwirth was tall with black, wavy hair. He wore round-rimmed glasses and a thoughtful gaze. He was an engineer. "He was very attractive," Mom said with a coy smile. "Grandma actually met him first, at the pool," Mom told me. "I think she liked him because he was Hungarian and Jewish." She chuckled.

"He was actually quite taken with Lila, if you can believe it. I mean, she was only eight years old. But she was a beautiful child. So, he asked my mother, 'Do you have any more like her at home, maybe a little older?' And Grandma Irene said, 'Well, yes, in fact, I do. I have an older daughter named Evelyn.'"

Mom told the story of her romance with Leslie like a fairy tale. He was the Prince Charming who would carry her away from the pain of her parents' divorce and her father's remarriage. Watching her talk about him was like watching a line of storm clouds drift across the sky, intermittently covering the sun.

She described the beginning of their relationship and her face lit up. "He was heavenly, and very interested in me."

My mother had been a beautiful young woman. Photos from those days show her slender and glamorous in curve-hugging dresses, wide-brimmed hats, and stockings with a thin seam running up the back of each leg. She glowed. As she told the story, however, the light in her eyes faded. "I'd wanted to go to medical school. I'd wanted to be a doctor. But my parents couldn't afford to send me to college. And Leslie wanted to start a family."

In 1940, when Mom was twenty, they married. Mom said Leslie wasn't religious. He didn't care about having a Jewish wedding. But Grandma Irene did. "We couldn't afford a big wedding, so we got married in our apartment, with a rabbi."

After they married, Leslie and Mom moved to a small one-bedroom apartment in Irvington, New Jersey. They paid little attention to Judaism, aside from going to my grandmother's house for dinner on Rosh Hashanah and Yom Kippur. "That's how it was with a lot of Jews who got out of Europe. They didn't want any part of being Jewish anymore. They were just too afraid."

Mom was twenty-two when my brother Roy was born. A year and a half later, she had Steven.

"It was tight with the four of us in that apartment, but it was all we could afford," she said. "Les was working so hard. He was taking care of us, and he was scraping together every spare penny we had to buy his mother and sister out of Hungary." Her eyes brightened as she continued talking. "The boys slept in our room. Roy got the crib. Steven slept in our bottom dresser drawer. Les adored those boys."

When Roy and Steven were seven and five, Leslie got sick. "He started complaining of fatigue. He was gaining weight. But he wasn't eating." Her mouth began to quiver. She pursed her lips to make it stop. She tried to smile. It quivered anyway. Tears rolled down her cheeks. "He had leukemia. Six months later, he was dead."

At age twenty-nine, my mother became a widow. With two small sons, no husband, no job, and only a high school diploma, she had no choice but to move back in with Grandma. Mom never thought she'd live with her mother again once she'd left to get married. "Things happen," she said.

It was 1950, and Grandma no longer lived in Astoria. She lived in Rego Park, in a two-family house that Abe Gross had bought her. "Abe Gross paid cash for that house," Mom recalled. She referred to people by their first and last name when she didn't like them. "How shrewd, keeping Grandma in a two-family house so she could live off the rent from the upstairs tenants and not have to work. Of course, every few months, he flew her down to Florida. In between, he'd fly to New York to see her. He did that until the day she died." She paused and closed her eyes briefly, then snarled, "He kept promising to leave his wife, but he never did."

Meanwhile, Mom needed a way to earn a living. She studied electrolysis and learned to permanently remove facial and body hair with a thin, electrified needle. Then she got a job as an electrologist in an upscale hair salon on Fifth Avenue in Manhattan. She worked long hours. Grandma took care of Roy and Steven.

The tension between Mom and Grandma Irene was constant. "She criticized everything I did," Mom told me. "I'd buy little presents for Roy and Steven on my way home from work. She accused me of spoiling them." She stopped talking to blow her nose and clear her throat. More than twenty years of heavy smoking had given her a phlegmy cough. "They had just lost their father, for God's sake."

I suppose it was grief that made my mother turn to alcohol. She never confessed to me when or why she had begun to drink. I learned the details years later from Aunt Lila, who said, "She always had trouble sleeping, but once Leslie died, her insomnia became unbearable. I guess she thought a little Scotch would help." But one cocktail at night turned into two. Sometimes Mom started as soon as she got home from work. "It drove Grandma Irene crazy," Lila recalled. "She said liquor made your mom sad and ugly. She worried about the boys. Oh, the fights she and Evelyn used to have. . . ."

Mom's drinking wasn't all that she and Grandma fought about. They also battled over sending my brothers to Hebrew school.

"Grandma wanted those boys to know they were Jewish. She wanted them to be proud of it," Mom said. Irene bought Roy a gold Star of David necklace. For Steven, she bought a ceramic pendant with a picture of Moses.

"She wanted each of them to become a bar mitzvah," Mom said. "I didn't see the point. Besides, I couldn't afford it. Grandma said she'd pay for it. I knew the money would come from Abe Gross. But what was I going to do? We were living in her house. She was helping to support us. Well, Abe was, anyway."

So, Mom enrolled my brothers, then eleven and twelve, in Hebrew school. Even though Roy was older than Steven, Mom had persuaded the rabbi to let them become bar mitzvah together. "A few weeks before the ceremony, the rabbi tells me they need extra tutoring, and that it's going to cost more money," Mom said, smashing her cigarette in a pile of ashes. "I couldn't bear the thought of taking one more cent from Abe Gross. I canceled the whole thing." She pressed her palms together, as if in prayer, and rested her face against them. "Your poor brothers. They had worked so hard. They were so disappointed. Grandma never forgave me for that. But I guess I never forgave her for destroying my father."

I never got to know my grandmother; I was just four when she died. The only image I had of her came from the stories my mother and brothers told me, and from pictures. She had an Eastern European peasant woman's build: short, round, and fleshy. Like my mother, she was a heavy smoker. She was also beautiful. Behind her sparkling smile, however, was a searing temper.

"She was a screamer. When she got angry, the only thing to do was get out of her way," Mom said. "She disciplined with the back of her hand, unless a wooden spoon was handy."

Grandma's skin was perpetually bronzed, the result of regular visits to Miami. Once, when I was two, she brought me with her. Mom had a photo of us in bathing suits, standing against a palm tree. I have no memory of that time. Not so of Abe Gross, the man I came to know as Grandpa Abe.

For years after Irene died from lung cancer at age sixty-four, Abe continued to stop by the house when he was in town. He came to see me. Bald and barrel-chested, he always wore a jacket and tie, and a diamond ring on his pudgy pinky finger. He smelled of aftershave and Doublemint gum, which he snapped as he chewed. He'd show up unannounced with a coconut cream pie from Miami in one hand and a stick of gum for me in the other. "He knew how much you loved coconut cream pie," Mom said. Maybe I loved Abe because he was the grandfather I never knew. Or maybe I saw him through my young eyes as the father I longed for, instead of the one I had.

✦　✦　✦　✦　✦

My father was the person my mother wanted to talk about least. He was also the person I wanted to know about most. We had lived together as a family for only a few weeks after I was born. Most of the time, I neither thought nor cared about his absence from my life. But as I got older, and especially as I began spending time with friends' families, I wanted to know why mine had such a cavity, and why my father had no interest in being part of my life. I needed to know if he had ever loved me.

At first, Mom dodged my questions with her stock reply: "I'll explain when you're older." But once I reached middle school, she began surrendering pieces of the story.

"I met Milton Kott around 1955," she began one sunny spring afternoon. She was making a pot of coffee. The radio was playing softly. A cigarette burned in a nearby ashtray. "Grandma introduced us. She had met Milton on a flight back from Miami. She was very excited. She said, 'I met a very handsome man, a bachelor. You should meet him.'" Mom stopped to count, measuring spoonfuls of coffee. "I told her I wasn't ready," she said, staring at the teakettle, waiting for it to whistle. "Leslie had been gone for five years, but Roy and Steven were still young, just twelve and thirteen. Grandma was pushing me. She said it was time for me to meet someone."

Like Mom, my father had been born and raised in Brooklyn, near the beach in Coney Island. The son of Russian Jewish immigrants, he never went to college. Instead, he turned his passion for fishing into his livelihood, and opened what became a very successful sports-fishing supply store on the Lower East Side. Mom was thirty-five when they met; Milton was nearly fifty. He had never married.

"I never asked why," Mom said, pouring boiling water into the top half of the aluminum drip coffee pot. "I was attracted to him." He was tall and solid; his hair and teeth were white flashes against his deep tan. "He could be very charming," Mom said, sitting down with a cup of steaming black coffee. "He could also be very cruel."

Whenever Mom talked about Milton, she would shudder, as if suddenly chilled. She'd cough and clear her throat, and shift in her chair. Her eyes would dart around the room. She'd stare at her hands, hunting for a fingernail long enough to bite.

Their romance was a whirlwind.

"He swept me off my feet," she said. "He bought Roy and Steven their own fishing rods. He told me he loved me." They dated for six months. Then, all of a sudden, Milton dropped out of her life. "I was waiting for him to pick me up. We had dinner reservations," Mom said, pouring another cup of coffee.

"I waited and waited. He never showed. He didn't call. He didn't write. He just disappeared. I felt crushed."

A year passed. Then, one day while shopping in Macy's, Mom spotted Milton on the escalator. She was going up. He was going down. "He practically leaped over the railing to get to me," she said, unwrapping a carton of Kents. "He started apologizing. I got off the escalator and started walking. He walked right next to me. He said, 'Oh, Evy, I'm so sorry, I'm so sorry.' He said he got scared. He told me how much he missed me. He said he couldn't live without me."

They married in a synagogue in 1956. In one wedding picture, Milton is walking down the aisle, and in another picture are my brothers. They wore yarmulkes. There were no other signs that it was a Jewish wedding—no shots of Mom and Milton under a chuppah, or of Milton ceremoniously stepping on a wineglass. Mom was the only one in any of the pictures who was smiling.

"Grandma wasn't happy," she said, lighting a cigarette. "She never got over Milton dropping out of my life. She said I was making a giant mistake. I refused to believe her. I begged her to give Milton a second chance. I told her he wanted to adopt Roy and Steven, and that he was going to take very care good of us. I told her he wanted us to be a family."

Grandma Irene wasn't the only family member who didn't want Mom to marry Milton. Lila and her husband, my uncle Eli, told me about their concerns many years later. "We warned her. No, we begged her not to marry him," Lila recalled.

Mom said that on her wedding night she feared her family had been right. "It was my time of the month," she said, flicking a nonexistent ash from her cigarette. "What rotten timing. You know what your father said? He said, 'You disgust me.' Our first night of being husband and wife, and we slept on opposite sides of the bed."

If there was any topic that made my mother uncomfortable, it was sex. At some point in her life, it must have mattered to her. After all, she'd made a point of emphasizing how attracted she had been to Leslie and Milton. I have photos of her in her twenties and early thirties, looking alluring in clingy dresses and short shorts, outfits that I can only imagine she chose because she was sexual, yet this was not the mother I ever knew. From my earliest memories, my mother recoiled from any discussion of sex or sexuality. Even once I'd reached high school and began asking her about it, she would turn her head, as if to avoid a foul odor. The story she picked up then gave me some indication why.

"Milton built an extravagant house on Long Island. The boys and I moved in. From the very beginning, I knew something was wrong." She put a fresh cigarette between her lips and struck several matches before one finally lit. "He'd pretend to wrestle with them, and when he got them on the ground, he'd climb on top of them." Her cheeks caved in as she drew on the cigarette. She blew the smoke out hard. "They complained that he kept trying to grab them in their crotch."

Milton would be funny one minute and menacing the next. "His idea of fun was standing your brothers against an archery target and aiming a bow and arrow at them. They tried to play along. They didn't want to make him mad. They didn't want to add to my troubles." Her eyes welled. "When I saw them standing frozen against those targets, terrified and trembling, I screamed."

Milton laughed.

"He said, 'What's the big deal, Evelyn? It's only a Goddamn game!' From then on, I made your brothers sleep with baseball bats under their beds."

Unfortunately, those bats didn't protect Mom during the night. "There were things he wanted me to do in bed . . . with one of his business partners . . . while he watched. . . ." More tears. The cigarette burned itself out.

Mom was determined to make her marriage work, and she thought living with Milton—without the distraction of Roy and Steven—would help. On the advice of a family friend, she sent them to an all-boy boarding school in Hershey, Pennsylvania, for two years. "Milton and I needed to work things out," she said.

Instead of being a regular boarding school, however, "Hershey" turned out to be a home for abandoned and wayward boys. "It was an orphanage," Aunt Lila exclaimed, sounding pained so many years later. "I was furious when your mother sent the boys there. They could have stayed with me!"

My mother had no idea what kind of place Hershey was. "Roy and Steven were the only Jewish boys there, and the others beat them for it," she said, her eyes downcast. "They tortured them. They threw them over the fence that surrounded the pigpen, right into the slop and manure." She grew tearful. "Roy and Steven begged me to take them home. But I was trying so hard to make my marriage to work. I told them, 'The taunting will stop. You'll adjust.' They had to."

Milton promised my mother that their life together would be better if he had a child of his own. Conceiving me, in other words, had not been her first choice. She folded her hands on top of the table and took a breath, as if to prepare us both.

"You were born during a blizzard," she began. "It was 1958, one of the snowiest winters Long Island had ever had. I had just brought you home from the hospital. The house was freezing, so I turned up the heat. Milton became furious. He was already angry about my having sent the boys winter jackets at school. He said I was spending all his money." She closed her eyes, combed her fingers through her hair, and cleared her throat.

"He went crazy. He said, 'You think it's cold in here? I should throw you outside so you know what cold feels like.'

I must have said something back, although I can't remember what. Then, out of nowhere, he grabbed a pot of hot coffee and threw it at me. I had you in my arms." She cradled her head in her hands. When she looked at me again, her eyes were wet. "The next day, I packed you up and we went to Grandma Irene's. I thought, 'If I could only figure out what I was doing to trigger Milton's outbursts, I could make them stop.'" She shook her head slowly. "I was being tortured and blaming myself for it. I felt like such a failure. What little self-esteem I'd had was destroyed. I was so shattered by the time we got to Grandma's, so full of fear and self-doubt that I didn't know which way to turn the gas jet on the stove to boil water."

Mom had finished her coffee and almost a full pack of cigarettes. She sat straight-backed, staring at her hands gripping each other on the table. I understood then why she had avoided speaking about my father. Even though the abuse she endured had occurred fifteen years earlier, she still seemed petrified.

✦ ✦ ✦ ✦ ✦

At Grandma's, Mom tried to start working again. She began building a private electrolysis practice. But she was in tatters. "Every time the doorbell rang, I went into a panic. I couldn't sleep. I couldn't stop crying. Grandma was no help. She kept criticizing me. She said, 'How are you going to take care of three children in the shape you're in?' She was right. I didn't know if I was coming or going."

Mom's family and friends could see that she was too jangled to care for me. Just after my first birthday, she asked Lila if I could live with her and her family on Long Island for a little while. "Just until I got back on my feet," Mom explained. She sent Roy and Steven, who had just returned from Hershey, to live on Long Island, alternating between the home of her best friend, Zelda, and Aunt Lila's house.

These arrangements were supposed to be temporary, lasting a month, maybe two. But one month turned into six, six months into a year, and one year into two. Roy and Steven returned to Rego Park in time to attend and graduate from Forest Hills High School. As for me: I lived with Aunt Lila for more than three years. "You called us Mommy Lila and Daddy Eli," Lila recalled, years later. "To me, you were our daughter, not our niece. You were so happy living with us." She said my mother never visited. "I told her it would be too confusing for you."

Back in Grandma Irene's house in Rego Park, Mom was struggling. She was trying to earn enough money to send Roy and Steven to college, and to support all of us, even though I was still living with Lila. Milton wasn't paying any alimony or child support. "He said that since Lila and Eli were taking such good care of you, there was no reason to give me money." She took him to court.

"She was beside herself," Lila told me. "Grandma Irene would tell me what a nervous wreck she was—not sleeping, drinking too much. What your father did to her, let me tell you. . . ."

By the time I was nearly four, Mom had made no move to take me back. "I called her," Lila said. "I said, 'Evy, it's been three years. It's time to take her home.' What a mistake that was. I never forgave myself for giving you back."

In 1962, I returned to Grandma Irene's house. She had died two years earlier. Roy and Steven were both attending the City University of New York, and working part-time. I don't remember ever having lived with Lila and Eli, or returning to Rego Park. But I remember our house because it was the last and only place where Mom, my brothers, and I lived together as a family.

MY MOTHER WAS MANY THINGS: TRAUMATIZED as a child and an adult, a widow, a battered wife. She was anxious and depressed. At the same time, she was an elegant woman who took pride in her appearance and cared deeply about family and friends. She was a fabulous cook. She loved a good joke. And, in spite of all her losses, she was a glass-half-full type, determined that life could only get better. "Tomorrow is a new day," she'd chirp, even if she did it through a forced smile. She was adamant about hiding her pain, especially from me, and she did whatever she could, including drinking too much, toward that end.

After Grandma Irene died, we continued to live in her house in Rego Park. The house looked like all the others on our tree-lined block, with a scrap of front lawn and a red-brick path leading to a stoop where we kept a gray metal milk box. It had a separate apartment upstairs that Rose and Harry Weiser rented. The Weisers had been close friends of Grandma Irene's. I knew them as Aunt Rose and Uncle Harry. On mornings when Mom couldn't get out of bed, I'd climb the stairs to their apartment, pajama-clad and with a box of Cocoa Puffs tucked under my arm, to ask them to make me breakfast.

The main floor where we lived had two bedrooms. Mom used Grandma's old room as an electrolysis studio. She had opened her private practice after a few years of working at the Fifth Avenue salon, drawing on her city clientele. Word of mouth brought in more clients, mostly women.

"I had a customer once who asked me to tweeze her pubic hair in the shape of a heart," my mother recalled years later. "Can you imagine? A heart? There?" She chuckled at the memory, and at the next one: "I did have a male customer once," she said, bashfully cupping her hand over her widening grin. "He wanted all the hair off his face and his legs!" She was laughing hard now, tears streaming down her cheeks. "I never asked why he wanted all that hair removed," she said, wiping her eyes. "But week after week he came for treatments until all that hair was gone."

So many of Mom's memories were tragic that it was a rare treat when she touched one that tickled. She had a dry wit, and though demure, she didn't mind a good dirty joke.

"What's funny?" I'd ask when she'd convulse with laughter. "What's funny?" I'd demand, eager for a piece of the action.

"I'll explain when you're older," she'd gasp, catching her breath. I hated the brush-off but loved seeing her look so happy. It wasn't a side of her that I saw often. What I usually saw was her anxiety and sadness, which, I would later learn, she drowned in booze at night.

✦ ✦ ✦ ✦ ✦

Mom's electrolysis studio could have been my room, but I had a habit of imagining monsters lurking under the bed. So, I shared the adjacent master bedroom—and a king-size bed—with her. When nightmares woke me in the middle of the night, it was a relief to see her lying there smoking, the tip of her cigarette glowing in the dark.

In that bedroom, I watched Mom dress, and it was there that I became most enamored with her. She was small and plump when she wasn't starving herself into thinness. Her complexion was rosy. When she smiled, her hazel eyes crinkled at the corners. I'd lie on our bed, waiting for her to come out of the shower, my eyes following her every move. She'd light a cigarette, hold it between her lips, and douse herself with perfume.

"A woman is never fully dressed until she puts on toilet water," she'd explain, splashing the scent on her neck, arms, belly, and legs, and then on me.

"Eeewwww. Is that water from the toilet?"

"No, monkey. Eau de toilette." Her drawers clattered with empty Arpège and L'Air du Temps bottles that she tucked between her clothes.

Once she finished saturating herself, she'd pull up her stockings, fasten her garters, apply her makeup, slip into a dress and pointy-toed, spike-heeled shoes, clasp a strand of pearls around her neck, grab her coat and pocketbook, and she was out the door where a yellow cab waited.

"Be good, monkey," she'd instruct, giving me a quick kiss. I'd close my eyes and breathe her in, perfume and cigarettes, and watch her drive away.

✦ ✦ ✦ ✦ ✦

The dinette, which adjoined the kitchen, was where we ate. My mother was a phenomenal cook. Everything she made, even the farina that she coaxed me to eat by covering it with shavings of Hershey's chocolate, was scrumptious. She lived to feed people. For her, food was two-way love. There was no greater demonstration of her care than spending all day preparing Hungarian goulash or chicken paprikash for someone. And nothing filled her heart like seeing people eat her cooking until they could no longer breathe.

Every occasion was a reason to eat. On Sundays it was visits with Mom's Hungarian aunts and uncles—my great-aunts and great-uncles—Vera and Margaret, and their husbands, Yawshee and El. They'd come for coffee and cake in the late afternoon, blowing into the house like a gale-force wind, all speaking in Hungarian at once, carrying white bakery boxes tied with red string, taking turns pinching and twisting my cheeks like taffy.

Mom relished these visits. Her aunts and uncles loved her like the parents she no longer had. They were her most important and trusted support system.

They were also the only members of her family who had survived the Holocaust. At age five, I had not yet heard this word. Even by the time I was ten and curious to know why our family was so small, Mom tried not elaborate.

"Most of our family died during the war," she would offer.

"Why?"

"Because a very sick man named Hitler decided to kill all the Jews in Hungary and the rest of Europe."

I couldn't wrap my mind around it. How could one person manage to kill every single Jewish person in a whole country?

"Why?" I persisted.

"He blamed the Jews for everything that was wrong in the world, and he convinced others to blame them."

"How did Aunt Vera and Uncle Yawshee and Aunt Margaret and Uncle El get out of Hungary?"

"I don't know, sweetie." She stopped talking and looked at me as if struggling to make a decision. "You know," she said hesitantly, "Aunt Vera had a son. She saw him shot right before her eyes."

This story frightened me. I was too young to comprehend the enormity of the atrocity. Yet, somewhere deep inside me, the first seeds of my ambivalence about being Jewish had begun taking root. How could I have not felt ambivalent or just plain confused about being Jewish even at such a young age? At one moment, Mom was recounting the story of a cousin's murder during the Shoah. At another, she was joyfully cooking feasts for Rosh Hashanah and Yom Kippur.

She wasn't religious, and didn't approach these traditions with piousness. But she'd grown up with them and held them close, like cherished mementoes of better days, before her parents' split, before she'd lost one husband and fled from another. I think the comfort she found was in ritual rather than actual belief: in shopping and preparing, draping the perfect lace cloth over the table, arranging the fancy china bowls and crystal dishes, lighting the candles. All of this seemed to transport her to another place and time, distracting her from the present.

The part of these holidays that mattered most to her was the food. Ever worried about her weight, Mom ate like a bird. Still, she'd spend days cooking, all for the supreme pleasure of feeding others, especially me.

In the dinette, she and I celebrated the High Holidays over homemade chicken soup, chicken in béchamel sauce, egg noodles, cucumber salad, challah, and cake. Roy and Steven never joined us. They were rarely home for family meals of any kind. Both were busy in college and working part-time, although Roy joined the navy after his sophomore year. My great-aunts and their husbands didn't join us, either. Mom said they were no longer interested in the holidays—all except Uncle El, who never abandoned his Jewish orthodoxy and spent part of every day in synagogue.

As a young child, my understanding of the High Holidays was limited. In the most cursory way, Mom had explained that Rosh Hashanah was the Jewish New Year, and the more sugar-dipped challah we ate, the sweeter the next year would be. Yom Kippur, on the other hand, was the day when we apologized to God for anything we had done wrong and remembered loved ones who had died. Through my child lens, I saw Rosh Hashanah as the happy holiday and Yom Kippur as the sad one. Yom Kippur was also the day when my Jewish friends fasted. We didn't. My mother prohibited it but didn't explain why. Being denied participation in this symbolically important ritual made me feel like an outsider, less than Jewish.

Not feeling fully Jewish, and not being Christian, left me in limbo. I couldn't fast and I couldn't have a Christmas tree. I had no tradition to own; I belonged nowhere.

Still, I loved the High Holidays because they suspended time. Mom didn't work. She didn't talk on the phone. She didn't fight with Steven. She wasn't especially happy, but she became contemplative. She cooked. She polished the silver. She lit candles. She prayed. Our house was calm. These days turned my world into an oasis of tranquility. For that reason alone, they felt precious.

Mom never went so far as to call the High Holidays holy, but I could tell by the way she bowed her head and wept after lighting the yahrzeit candles that they were. The candles sat high on a counter, out of my reach. They burned from sundown before Yom Kippur to sundown the next day. Mom said each candle represented someone she loved—her mother, her father, and her first husband, my brothers' father—who could see them burning from heaven. She said that having the candles burn was like having them pay us a visit. Nevertheless, once they began to flicker and sizzle in pools of melted wax, I saw no harm in blowing them out.

"Don't blow them OUT!" Mom would gasp, grabbing a book of matches and relighting each wick. "They have to burn out on their own." She wasn't angry. She was sad. I felt sick with guilt, wondering if I had time for one more apology to God before the sun went down and the holiday ended.

I never wanted the High Holidays to end. I didn't want Mom's serenity or the peacefulness at home to vanish. I especially didn't want to have to take off my Star of David. These were the only days when Mom let me wear the gold and silver Star of David necklace that Grandma Irene had had engraved with my initials. During the rest of the year, she kept the necklace wrapped in tissue paper, tucked into a dark blue velvet box that she hid in the back of her sweater drawer.

"It's not necessary to advertise that you're Jewish," she would say if I asked to wear it on an ordinary day. "Wearing it on the holidays is enough."

Being forbidden from fasting was one thing. But being cautioned against wearing my Star of David was something else altogether. The warning made me uneasy. Why can't I let people know that I'm Jewish? Why is it okay to be Jewish on some days and not others? Steven never took off his Moses pendant, although he wore it beneath his undershirt. Did Mom let him wear his pendant as long as he kept it hidden? I never saw Roy wear his Star of David. But by the time I was five, I wasn't seeing enough of Roy to ask him about it.

In 1963, Roy joined the navy. He had been attending Queens College but joined the service so he could take advantage of the GI Bill and later go to the University of Michigan. Once Roy left home, he never moved back. He hardly ever visited. When he did, he and Mom would argue, loudly enough for me to hear behind closed doors.

"You don't call enough."

"I live on a ship, Mom."

"You should call. For Andrea. She needs *you*."

"No, Mom. She needs *you*."

"She needs a man in her life."

I wasn't aware of needing a man in my life, per se; I did, however, need someone to look up to.

Roy was striking like his father: lean and swarthy, with an angular face, straight black hair, and dark brown eyes. Dressed in crisp navy blues or whites or khakis, he took my breath away. I didn't just look up to him. I idolized him. Such reverence was probably illogical, since he was gone more than he was home, incommunicado for months at a time. He was completely disengaged from the daily realities of life with Mom. He never disciplined me. He never lost his temper. He simply beamed all of his goodness on me. He treated my friends and me to pizza. He bought me my first Beatles' record. He taught me the Lindy and how to ride a two-wheeler, furiously gripping the seat as he ran alongside. In the bubble of our relationship, his love was unconditional, and I glorified him. Long before I saw the popularized Western depiction of God as an old, long-white-haired-and-bearded man in robes, I envisioned Him as a composite of my three favorite handsome men: Ken (Barbie's boyfriend), Paul McCartney, and my brother Roy.

Because Roy's visits were rare, Mom treated them like holidays. When she knew he was coming, she'd spend the day cooking and cleaning. She'd let me stay home from school. We'd have our hair done. Then, more often than not, and always at the last minute, Roy would cancel. Sometimes he just never showed up. The disappointment, which had me in tears for days, could easily have destroyed my adoration for Roy. But it didn't. If anything, it made me idolize him more, because when he finally did appear, usually unannounced and in the middle of the night, it felt like a miracle.

Neither the doorbell nor the sound of Mom's exclamations would awaken me. Rather, the aroma of broiling steak and sizzling French fries that Mom, in her robe and slippers, would immediately start cooking, pulled me bleary-eyed into the dinette.

"Hey, hey, look who's here!" Roy would cheer.

As soon as I saw him, I would charge onto his lap and lock my arms around his neck. His uniform jacket would be draped over a chair, his shiny officer's shoes kicked off, his shirt unbuttoned. He'd take his cap from the chair post, plop it on my head, and offer me a fry.

Our time together was always too brief. After a day or two, when his jacket hung in the hallway, I knew it was time for him to leave.

"No teeeerz," he would say as soon he saw my bottom lip quiver. Then he'd kneel down and whisper in my ear, "Take care of Mommy." I'd bury my face in his neck, soaking his stiff jacket collar with my tears. He didn't say when he'd be back. He'd promise to call. He'd promise to write. But he never did.

✦ ✦ ✦ ✦ ✦

Unlike Roy, Steven was a constant presence in my life. He lived at home, where he spent most of his time in the basement doing homework. Steven attended Hunter College in the Bronx. At night and on weekends, he stocked shelves at the Associated Supermarket on Queens Boulevard to earn money for tuition. Thick and muscular, with a full face and a frizzy globe of light-brown hair, Steven didn't look anything like my image of God. Nevertheless, I revered him. I also feared him.

I knew that Steven loved me. I also knew that his acceptance was not unconditional. Because he was entrenched in our family life, and because he helped take care of me, he assumed something of an authoritarian role. If I back-talked or disobeyed Mom, he scolded me. If I whined or nudged, he delivered a glare that made me wither.

And yet, as Roy was my source of mercy, Steven was my source of strength. When Mom's mood swings turned my world upside down, Steven was my pillar. When random feelings confused or overwhelmed me, he was my voice of reason.

One cold, gray autumn day, I heard the soft bleat of a trumpet and the roll of drums coming from the basement. Inexplicably, I began to weep. It was La Marseillaise, the victory march from Tchaikovsky's *1812 Overture*.

"What's up, cookie?" Steven asked. "Why the tears? C'mere." He pushed aside his homework, and pulled me onto his lap. His blue and white Moses pendant rested on top of his white undershirt.

"Who is this?" I asked, running my fingertip over the picture of the white-haired man holding a tablet, wondering if this is what God looks like. I was already crestfallen at the thought of having to discard my debonair image of Him.

"Moses."

I felt relieved. I didn't know anything about Moses or the Ten Commandments, but the pendant, with its minute Hebrew lettering, fascinated me.

"Why do you wear it?" I hoped he'd say something about not wanting to hide being Jewish.

"Because Grandma Irene gave it to me."

"Is that the only reason?"

"Yes."

The answer disappointed me. It was so finite. It left no room for questions or discussion. About God. Or faith. The Moses necklace was Steven's link to a memory. He wore it, just as my mother ritually cooked for the High Holidays, for comfort, not as an act of faith; it had nothing to do with being Jewish. For him, Mom, and Roy, Judaism was merely a consequence of having been born; yet, it was inconsequential. It deprived me of a Christmas tree but offered nothing. How could I forge an identity or find meaning in something that my family found meaningless?

I turned my attention to the overture, which Steven started from the beginning. The opening notes were somber and slow. As the music quickened, he began weaving a tale about a war between a good army and a bad army. He described battles as the timpani thundered, celebrations as tambourines jingled, and victory as bells clanged. I had no clue that he was inventing the story on the spot. Decades later, I would learn that the *1812 Overture* actually commemorated Russia's defeat of Napoleon's troops. At that moment in the basement, however, Steven created a context for the emotions that had mysteriously consumed me, a story of good triumphing over evil. My tears didn't stop, but they didn't bewilder me anymore, either.

During those years, depression slowly began to immobilize Mom. Her bouts of despondency grew more frequent. She was increasingly quiet, withdrawn, and remote. She displayed no interest in engaging with me. She didn't carve out time for us to read or play together. Even when she was sitting by herself, having a cigarette and a cup of coffee, her hushed demeanor screamed, "Do not disturb," which I, in my five-year-old quest for love and attention, ignored.

"I want to be with you."

"Go out and play. It's a beautiful day. The sun is shining."

"It's cold."

"It's crisp."

"There's nothing to do."

"Jump in the leaves!"

"It's cold!"

"It's a gorgeous fall day! Bundle up and GO OUTSIDE!"

As a last resort, I'd climb onto her lap, and like a baby marsupial, try burrowing into her perfumed softness. "Get OFF me!" she'd hiss, forcing me back to my feet.

All these years later, I can still feel the pain of her rejection and the loneliness that plagued me, which would later morph into depression. I'm sure Steven noticed my sadness. This, I'm also sure, is what drove him to instill in me the kind of emotional self-sufficiency that Mom lacked. He had no patience for my gloom. When I voiced self-doubt or fear, even at the age of five, he insisted that I confront it. Worse than failing, he said, was not to give something a try. Eager for his approval, I agreed to ride the fearsome Cyclone in Coney Island.

"Ready?" he said, as a man clamped the padded safety bar across our laps. The roller-coaster car jerked. Then, it began its ascent, click-click-click up the rickety tracks, tilting us onto our backs. As we inched skyward, the people below disappeared. At the top, we hovered.

"Don't look down," Steven advised. He gripped my hand. "Hold on."

WHOOSH, we plunged. My stomach shot up into my throat. Had we fallen off the tracks already? Steven's face was a blur. Everything was a blur. Fighting gravity, I wedged myself inside the crook of his arm.

"Isn't this great?" he yelled, pulling me next to him.

Terror seized me. We'd been on the ride for only seconds and I wanted out. The car sped and lurched and sped again. Its wheels scraped along the wood and metal roadway, groaning with every turn. I shut my eyes, waiting for a crash. We whipped around a corner, hit a dip, and started climbing again.

"You okay?" he asked.

We rose and plunged, snapped around another bend, then rose and plunged again. Finally, we slowed on a straightaway. The car stopped. Steven lifted me out of the seat. Relief poured out of me in an explosion of tears.

"Are you out of your MIND?" Mom screamed when Steven told her he'd taken me on the ride. "She's FIVE YEARS OLD!"

"She's fine," he snapped. "Sure, she was scared. But it didn't stop her. That's what matters."

Steven would never have endangered me. In many ways, he protected me more than Mom, who was incapacitated by depression and fear, the very things he taught me to conquer.

✦ ✦ ✦ ✦ ✦

Of all the rooms in the house in Rego Park, the living room was my favorite. This was where I spent luxurious hours watching *Mister Ed, Winchell-Mahoney Time, The Soupy Sales Show*, and, my all-time favorite, *Wonderama*, the educational kids' show that I watched religiously every Sunday morning. It was the room that housed the plush maroon velvet couch that Mom turned into a bed after I'd had my tonsils removed, where she tucked me under her best down quilt and propped me up with pillows so I could watch TV all day while she brought me bowls of Jell-O and ice cream. It was my favorite room, until it became the place where I endured visitations with my father, which family court ordered in exchange for his child-support payments. From the time I was five, when these court-ordered visits began, until the time I was nine, when Milton stopped coming, I could count on one hand the number of times he showed up.

"He told the judge that he wouldn't pay a penny of child support unless he could see you," Mom explained years later. "I said he could see you any time he wanted. He just didn't want to."

Although Mom hadn't yet disclosed any of her nightmarish experiences with Milton, I had already absorbed her fear of him. It would have been impossible not to. On Sunday mornings, awaiting his arrival, she'd smoke cigarette after cigarette and gnaw her bitten-down fingernails. Even if the doorbell rang unexpectedly on any other day, her eyes would pop open as if she'd seen a ghost, and she'd instruct me to peek between the venetian blinds to see who it was while she hid in the bedroom.

By the time I actually met Milton—years after Mom had fled the house in Long Island—I was terrified.

How I hated Sunday mornings. The thought of sitting in the same room with my father soured my stomach. Just hearing his name filled me with dread. I never spoke it. I never called him "Daddy." The word felt like a dead bug in my mouth. I never called him anything.

"Where's your mudda?" he would say the minute I opened the front door. I'd scurry ahead so he couldn't hug me, and dash back to my seat next to Mom. His visits usually coincided with *Wonderama*. Mom and I would sit glued to each other on one chair staring at the television. Milton would sit on another. No one spoke. He would make funny faces, tug on his earlobes, and stick out his tongue, then press on his nose and blow raspberries—anything to get my attention. I'd ignore him, keeping my eyes fixed on the TV screen. Eventually, he'd stop. Then he'd grumble, "I didn't come here to watch television."

One Sunday morning just after my fifth birthday, Milton said, "Hey, Andrea, why don't you and I take a ride down to Parson's toy store and buy you a new bicycle?"

The offer was too exciting to ignore. I begged Mom to let me go. "Have her back here in half an hour," she commanded.

At the store, I roamed the toy-strewn aisles while Milton chatted with the store's owner. After a while, I returned to my father and tugged on his sleeve. "C'mon, Daddy," I said, forcing myself to try the word. "Let's get me a bicycle."

Milton smacked his open hand on the counter. "First of all," he bellowed, "you interrupted me." His black, bushy eyebrows knitted together as he glared. "Don't you know how to say 'excuse me'? Doesn't your mother teach you any manners?"

I could feel my heart thud through my jacket.

"Second," he continued, jangling his car keys in his pocket, "your mother has all the money. Let her buy you a bicycle."

He rushed me out of the store and into his car. I burrowed myself deep into the Cadillac's soft leather seat, and pressed my face against the window, watching rain stream down the glass. Tears clogged my throat.

"You're a liar," I heard Mom hiss from the kitchen.

"I'm a liar? Who's a liar? I'm looking around this house, and I'm thinking, 'She doesn't need my money. She's trying to take me for a ride.'"

"This house was my mother's and you know it. I take care of Andrea alone. I DO need help."

"I'll say you need help."

"You're lousy. You're a lousy, good for nothing—"

"You watch yourself, or I'll slap your face."

"You wouldn't dare."

"Don't dare me. . . ."

Their voices grew loud and fierce, pulling me away from the television and under a nearby table where I crouched. I thought about running up to Aunt Rose and Uncle Harry's, but I was frozen. What if he hits her?

He didn't. He just stormed out, slamming the door behind him.

For days after one of Milton's visits, I'd have trouble sleeping. Nightmares about monsters would jolt me awake, and I'd shimmy over to Mom's side of the bed, crawl under her covers, and press close to her. Meanwhile, she would turn glum. She'd spend hours on the phone, her stream of Hungarian punctuated with "Andrea" or "Milton Kott."

Like an electric current, her anxiety ran through the house. Sometimes it sparked fights with Steven, who would explode at her for acting feeble, reducing her to a puddle of tears. Very occasionally, she would turn on me. The smallest act of disobedience could set her ablaze, like the time I called her stupid. She had been using a sewing needle to dig a splinter out of my finger and accidentally gouged me.

"Owww, stupid!" I muttered under my breath, certain she couldn't hear me. She clamped her hand on my arm, tore me off the chair, dragged me into the bathroom, and shoved an entire bar of Ivory soap into my mouth. Such a display of excessive strictness was a sure sign that my mother's last nerve was frayed.

Eventually, our tensions over Milton's visit would fade. Mom would calm down. I'd sleep better. Milton would stop calling. He'd stop visiting. He'd also stop sending child support.

"How am I going to make ends meet?" I'd overhear Mom asking Steven. "There's just not enough money coming into this house."

"I don't know what to tell you, Mom," Steven would snap. "Take him back to court."

"I don't know if I can go through it anymore."

But she did, and the cycle would start all over again.

Mom and Milton were legally separated, but didn't divorce until I was in high school. I found this odd but never asked Mom to explain. Unrealistic though it was, I liked to imagine that beneath my father's menacing and nasty demeanor, he actually loved me and wanted to forge some kind of relationship. Sometimes I wondered if Mom had deliberately postponed divorce and held out hope, however far-fetched, that one day Milton would revert back to the charming and romantic man she had first met and we could be a happy family.

✦ ✦ ✦ ✦ ✦

Mom was a great one for hoping. That was the paradox about her: Despite the years of heartbreak and horror she had endured, and despite her lengthening bouts of despair, she had an inner reservoir of faith. It wasn't religious faith. She had abandoned that after her first husband died. "God let me down" is all she ever said. It was pure doggedness. She had become an electrologist, built a business, and supported our family, albeit barely. She even managed to send my brothers to college. At times when depression and her growing dependence on alcohol made it impossible for her to work or find a job, or after a night of lying awake and smoking cigarettes, she'd still eke out a smile and say, "Tomorrow's another day." She said this as if the sun's rising were her guarantee that life's painful patches would pass, and that she would prevail. It was a comforting bromide, one I readily embraced in my search for absolutes. It was like believing in Santa Claus, or God.

If I was lucky, and Mom was in a hopeful mood, she'd press a salt shaker into my hand. "Go outside and play!" she'd instruct, emerging from her electrolysis room to escort a freshly tweezed customer out the door.

"No one's around," I'd whine.

"Why don't you try to catch a robin? If you sprinkle salt on its tail, it will stand still for you."

At first, the notion seemed ludicrous. How could I ever get close enough to a robin to sprinkle salt on its tail? Yet, Mom spoke with such zeal and certitude that I couldn't possibly doubt her. Besides, the clandestine way in which she presented this challenge was irresistibly intriguing. She would close my fingers around the salt shaker, as if entrusting me with its magic powers. Then, she would tilt her head close to mine, peer deeply into my eyes, and whisper like we were co-conspirators.

"You have to tiptoe. You have to be verrry quiet." With a wink, she'd shoo me outside.

On a mission, I would skip down the stoop steps and peel my eyes for robins. As soon as one landed, I'd sneak toward it, careful to hide the salt shaker behind my back. No sooner would I extend my arm than the bird would fly away.

When the next robin landed, I'd take wide, stealthy steps and furiously spray the air with salt. Up and down the block I would run, feverishly flinging salt until I was breathless. After an hour or more, I would shuffle home defeated, my empty shaker in hand, my head hung low.

"Why the sour puss?" Mom would ask.

"I didn't catch one robin. I didn't even get close."

"Next time you will," she promised. "How about a treatment?" she'd ask, and invite me onto her electrolysis table, where she would zap an inconsequential hair from one of my eyebrows. This was the invitation I waited for whenever she finished working. It meant that she was in good spirits, and had enough energy to focus on just me. I treasured this.

Mom's hopefulness was erratic, like all her behavior. At one minute she'd be singing along as Frank Sinatra crooned "High Hopes" on the radio; the next minute, she'd be staring vacantly, gnawing at her red, puffy cuticles, a cigarette burning in a nearby ashtray, a cup of coffee turning cold. As I got older and her drinking increased, the shifts in her mood intensified. The poise and positivity she exuded in the morning would vanish by the end of the day. With only a few sips of Scotch in her, she would turn woozy and morose.

Life was a seesaw. When Mom was happy, I was happy. When she smiled, her cheeks turned rosy and plump. Her eyes sparkled. When she laughed, she'd throw back her head and roar with delight. And when she beamed her smile on me, I felt like the most loved child in the world. But when she was sad, she grew prickly and remote. Her cheeks deflated. Her mouth drooped. Her eyes dimmed. She could look straight at me and neither see nor hear me. Every dismissal strengthened my need to be close to her. And every display of my neediness aggravated her. Then, instead of feeling like the most loved child in the world, I felt wretched.

Had I regarded God as a source of spiritual love and fortitude rather than as a movie star who lived in the clouds, I might have found the emotional muscle I needed to withstand Mom's shunning. But for most of my young life, my feelings about God and faith remained uninformed and unexplored. I certainly had no sense that I deserved anything more. My self-worth reflected the way my mother treated me. I was determined, therefore, to do everything in my power to please her, which frequently meant staying out of her way.

Never knowing whether Mom would be icy or kind kept me on edge. I would try to forecast, but the only thing I could count on was her volatility. Worry chewed at me. I felt nervous much of the time. I was unsure of her love. In time, I became unsure of myself, of everything. Had I been raised in a religious household, such aching insecurity might have driven me to seek reassurance or perhaps a higher love in God. But my sense of God was not spiritual. I believed in Him the way I believed in the Tooth Fairy. I didn't think of turning to Him or to Judaism for solace or security. I used another strategy to secure myself.

Subconsciously, I began compartmentalizing life with my mother into two zones, black or white: black for sad, white for happy. This, I learned much later, is one way that children of alcoholics anchor themselves. At the age of five, I was painfully aware of my Mom's mood swings, though the source of those mood swings was not yet apparent to me— the image of her brooding over a cocktail, her breath rank, had not yet permanently etched itself into my mind. Fielding her ever-changing behavior kept me on my toes, alert for surprises, constantly set to tilt toward one extreme or the other. Living in this skewed state kept life simple. There were, after all, only two types of experiences I could ever anticipate: ghastly or glorious, and within these confines, I could predict and navigate the landmines ahead. I liked knowing what to expect, even if it was misery. What I hated were the emotional surprises.

✦ ✦ ✦ ✦ ✦

The times that Mom was truly happiest were at the beach. The ocean was the one place where she seemed able to escape the fear and despair that plagued her. "YOW!" she'd yell as the cold sea slapped her legs. "Jump!" she'd shout, holding my hand as we rose and fell with the swells.

When beach days ended, our joy waned. Max, the beloved neighborhood ice-cream man, stopped coming around. There were no more robins to chase. Still, there was the thrill of jumping into waist-high piles of leaves. There were crisp, tart Macintosh apples. And there were the High Holidays.

Because Mom and I celebrated the High Holidays alone, I never thought of them as events to share. Like my Star of David or being Jewish, they were parts of our life to keep private. I wondered how other Jewish families on our street celebrated these holidays. I knew that the Pashkes went to synagogue because I would see them walking to and from services.

Amy Pashke was one of my two best friends. She lived at the end of the block, on the top floor of a two-family house. Her parents were from Israel. Both had served in the Israeli Army. Her dad wore a chai around his neck. Her mother wore a gold Jewish star. They were observant Jews. Amy had to stop playing at sundown on Friday nights. On Saturdays, Rosh Hashanah, and Yom Kippur, she had to dress up and sit in synagogue for hours.

The house that the Pashkes lived in belonged to the Imbrolios. Joey Imbrolio was my other best friend. His family lived downstairs from Amy's. Joey's parents were from Italy. They were also religious. His mother wore a gold cross with Jesus nailed to it around her neck. His father wore a gold medallion with a picture of St. Christopher. Every Sunday morning, Joey went to church with his parents. In the afternoon, and on Christmas, his large extended family of grandparents, aunts, uncles, and cousins came to his house for dinner. There were so many of them that their cars took up both sides of our block.

"Why don't we have a big family?" I asked whenever Joey's family came to visit, hoping for a less gruesome answer. But the answer never changed, nor did Mom's presentation. Although the Holocaust had ended nearly twenty years earlier, she talked about it the way she talked about my father: with raw bitterness, as if it were a looming danger.

I envied Amy and Joey for more than their religious upbringing. I envied them for having two parents and for having mothers who didn't have to work or weren't always telling them to get out of their way.

Sometimes Amy, Joey, and I compared stories about our families' traditions. Amy said synagogue was boring. She said she hated having to be home on Friday nights before sundown. Joey didn't talk much about church. He mostly talked about all the things he wanted for Christmas.

"Joey says that Christmas is Jesus's birthday," I shared with Mom on a winter night a few weeks before Christmas. "He says Jesus is God. He says the Father and the Holy Spirit are God, too. He says all three of them are one God."

Joey and I both believed in a God that consisted of three beings. His were the Father, the Son, and the Holy Spirit. Mine were a Ken doll, Paul McCartney, and my brother Roy. Thinking about it, I realized that we really weren't so different from one another; I could have been Catholic just as easily as Jewish.

"Joey says God lives in heaven. He says God can look down and see what we're doing all the time."

"God lives everywhere," Mom said. "He is anywhere you want Him to be." No matter how often she asserted this, I found it baffling.

"Do you believe in God?"

"I believe in a God in my heart."

"In your heart?"

She laid her opened hand on her chest. "Right here."

"Is He there for me, too?"

"He is wherever you want Him to be."

None of it made sense.

"Do you pray to God?" I asked.

"Sometimes."

"Maybe if you had prayed harder, God wouldn't have let you marry Milton."

"If I hadn't married Milton," she said, kissing the top of my head, "I would never have had you."

✦　✦　✦　✦　✦

Unless Mom and I were expecting or recovering from one of Milton's visits, I didn't give him much thought. Perhaps I made a conscious effort to banish him from my mind. Or perhaps I eventually came to believe what I had begun telling anyone who asked: I had no father. I tried tricking myself into believing that I didn't feel sad about this, that I was the luckiest kid in the world because I had something better than a father: I had two brothers who were practically old enough to be my father, but who were much nicer and more fun (and handsome) than any of the dads I knew. But deep down, I didn't feel lucky. I wanted a dad like everyone else.

I also didn't feel lucky to be Jewish, especially during Passover. This was one holiday that made being Jewish feel like rotten luck.

Though Mom had given me a bare-bones explanation of the High Holidays, she never explained anything about Passover. I had no clue why we ate matzo instead of bread for eight days, or what Seders were for, or why we had to sit through such an interminable one before we could eat dinner, or, for that matter, why we had to sit through one at all. What I knew was that Passover was a punishing marathon of incomprehensible Hebrew liturgy and food deprivation.

Seders took place in Williamsburg, Brooklyn, at Aunt Margaret and Uncle El's apartment. They lived in a dilapidated tenement with a spiral staircase that creaked and swayed with every step up to their second-floor flat. Their front door opened into a grand, high-ceilinged living room that overlooked the street. Unlike most living rooms, however, this one did not have sofas or chairs or even a television set. What it had was an exhaustive array of professional hair-salon equipment: a large porcelain sink, a big clunky hair dryer, and swiveling haircutting chairs. The works. That's because it was, in fact, a full-service beauty parlor and Margaret, a beautician, was its proprietor. On the landing just outside their threshold, I could smell the distinct aromas of chicken paprikash, matzo ball soup, and hairspray.

The Seder table was always exquisitely set, with a white lace cloth, delicate china, crystal goblets, and a Haggadah on every plate. The table extended from the front door of the apartment to the floor-to-ceiling windows at the far end of the room. It was here that I was forced to sit for a brief eternity, listening to my stomach rumble while Uncle El droned Hebrew prayers in a voice that was perpetually thick with phlegm.

Because El spoke barely any English, he and I didn't communicate much. In his own way, however, he showed me affection. As soon as he saw me, he would bend down to give me a hug and kiss, scratching my soft cheek with his whiskers, and leaving a tiny trail of spittle on my face. Despite this display of warmth, El scared me, especially at Passover. An Orthodox Jew, he took Seders very seriously. He permitted no questions or talking. Not even a whisper. If anyone uttered the slightest sound, yawned, coughed, or even shifted in a chair, he would silence himself, raise his head slowly, and glare. Then he'd clear his throat, spit something sizable into a handkerchief, and resume reading.

Neither Roy nor Steven attended the Seder. Roy was still in the navy. Steven was usually working. My great-aunt Vera and great-uncle Yawshee came; so did upstairs neighbors who weren't Jewish but had a daughter named Catherine. Catherine and I were the same age and liked to play together, but we never got to play for long because by the time she and her parents arrived, El commanded everyone to take their seats.

As soon as he began reading, I was bored. Anything would have been more interesting than listening to him drone on in Hebrew. Needless to say, everything distracted me: my growling stomach, the smell of homemade chicken soup, and the stack of matzos on the table.

Hungry and antsy, I leaned back to see if I could reach the neck rest in the hair-washing sink.

"Sit up," Mom scolded.

"Can I have a piece of matzo?" I whispered.

"Shhhh!"

"When's matzo ball soup coming?"

"Shhhhhhhhhh!"

"I'm starving."

"Pssst!" While El gave us his evil eye, Mom exercised her last resort: mixing me a Manischewitz spritzer, a bubbly cocktail made from the sweet Passover wine and seltzer. Her goal was twofold: to still my hunger pangs, and, with a little alcohol, to settle me down. The problem with making a spritzer was the near-impossibility of soundlessly pumping seltzer. Mom simply couldn't draw the bubbly water into my glass quietly enough for El, who would again stop reading, shoot her his trademark glower, wait for her to finish making my drink, and then pick up where he left off. After a couple of spritzers, which I downed like lemonade, I'd float far away from the Seder table as El's voice faded gently into the background. After dinner but before the Seder was over, Mom would give me permission to stretch out on a couch in the next room, where I fell asleep.

Passover was one of two holidays that made me hate being Jewish. Christmas was the other.

My love of Christmas was about more than the festivities. I wanted something that other kids on my street had: I wanted the ritual of religious tradition that brought their families together and held them close. Mom couldn't conjure such closeness at Christmas or any other time. She couldn't heal our fractured bonds or transform herself into an emotionally whole and available parent. So, she did the next best thing. She took me to Rockefeller Center to marvel at the giant tree. She treated me to the Rockettes' Christmas extravaganza at Radio City Music Hall. She waited without complaint in line at Alexander's so I could sit on Santa's lap. And she brought me to FAO Schwarz.

Like Mom, Steven tried appeasing me with a newspaper Christmas tree. He rolled pages from *The New York Times* into cones. The tightest cone was the trunk of the tree. Over the trunk, he layered one cone, then another and another, making each one progressively looser and splaying their bottoms. Then, he cinched the layers together at the top and propped the tree against a chair to prevent it from toppling over.

Though heartfelt, these efforts never produced what I truly craved—a stable and loving family united by a religious tradition. Though at five I fixated on the trappings and festivities of Christmas, what I truly yearned for was something deeper, which no amount of decoration could satisfy. I wanted a peaceful, secure home life. And I wanted a spiritual relationship with God.

✦ ✦ ✦ ✦ ✦

I hoped that the New Year, 1964, was going to be a good one. I finally owned a Chatty Cathy doll, and in March, I would turn six, a much weightier age than five. I was in the final stretch of kindergarten, and in the summer, I would be going to day camp, and in the fall, first grade.

In spite of my optimism, life hadn't really changed. Mom's moods still seesawed, although they seemed more down than up. I knew she was having trouble sleeping because the smell of her cigarette would awaken me in the middle of the night. She still spent a lot of time on the phone, speaking Hungarian. And she and Steven continued to fight frequently. Even though they'd order me out of the room, I'd overhear bits and pieces of their arguments:

"I'm twenty-one years old," Steven would say. "I'm too old to be living with my mother."

"But who will help me take care of Andrea?"

"What do you mean, who will help you? You're her mother, for Christ's sake!"

"I know I'm her mother! But I need help!"

"I can't help you anymore, Mom. I've got to start living my own life!"

"What will I do without you?"

"You will take care of Andrea, Mom."

"How can I? I can't do it alone. I need you. I need your help."

"I'm your son, Mom. I need a life of my own."

Still, I was figuring out how to take care of myself. I was getting good at taking the emotional temperature at home and recognizing when I could be close to Mom or when I was better off making myself scarce. When she was cranky or sad, I would find someone to play with, or grab the salt shaker and chase robins. I knew that asking for her company would only make her mad, so I was learning to stifle the yearning inside me. Television and food were great distractions. They filled me up, at least for a while.

Not that I was lonely all the time. After all, I had plenty of friends. I lived on a block full of caring neighbors who kept an eye on me while I played outside and while Mom worked; they were people who had watched me grow up and had known my mother and my grandmother long before I was born. I took deep comfort in this familiarity, in having lived in one place for so long that I knew all the streets and sidewalk cracks by heart. I had a school that I liked and a house that I loved. Plus, I had Max, the ice-cream man. In spite of the struggles at home, even in spite of the occasional, awful visits with my father, life was good in Rego Park. It was a wonderful place to call home.

In the summer of that year, Mom put the house on the market. It hadn't been her choice. Grandma Irene had willed the house to Mom, Doug, and Lila, and although the will had stipulated that Mom could live there indefinitely and rent-free, it became clear to her siblings that she wouldn't be able to afford its upkeep. When Grandma was alive, Abe Gross had paid for the plumber, the gardener, and everything that needed fixing. "He took care of Grandma for twenty-three years until her death, and he paid for everything," Lila told me years later. A few months after Grandma died, he stopped.

"The rent from the Weisers was supposed to pay for things like real-estate taxes and maintaining the house," Lila said. "We told your mother, 'Evy, put the money away so you'll have it if something in the house breaks.' But she spent it on other things, like flying Roy home from the navy. And liquor."

Lila, Eli, and Doug insisted that Mom sell the house. "Eli and I didn't have the means to take care of that house. Neither did Doug." When Lila and Eli decided to move to Florida, they invited Mom to join them. "We said, 'Come with us to Florida, Evy, we can all live together, but she wouldn't move,'" Lila recounted.

My mother's version of this story, though similar, echoed resentment: "I explained how attached you were to the house, and how it was the only home you'd ever known. How you had so many friends in the neighborhood and were about to start first grade." Her anger sounded fresh. "Eli said I couldn't afford to keep up the house. He said his dry-cleaning business wasn't doing well and he and Lila wouldn't be able to lend me money when things started falling apart. He said, 'Let's sell it now, while it's in decent shape and we can get a good price for it.' We. Can you imagine? It wasn't even his house, for God's sake."

By August 1964, Mom had sold the house. "Doug and I each gave her part of our share of the money from the sale to help her move," Lila said. Yet, neither the logic behind selling the house nor Lila's and Doug's financial help appeased my mother. Although she stayed in touch with Doug, who moved to California, she cut Lila and Eli out of her life. "I think she felt rejected when Eli and I moved to Florida," Lila reasoned. "She'd already suffered so much rejection. She felt rejected when our parents divorced, when Leslie died, and when her marriage to your father failed. Our moving was the last straw." It must have been. Mom didn't speak to Lila or Eli for the next fifteen years.

Mom didn't tell me that she'd sold the house. I found out one afternoon when I came home from camp and saw empty cartons strewn around the living room. Mom was in the kitchen, humming along with Frank Sinatra, wrapping dishes in newspaper.

"Hi, sweetie! How was camp?"

"What are the boxes for? Why are you wrapping dishes?"

"We're moving. Did you have fun at camp?"

I felt as if someone had punched me in the stomach. "Moving? Why?"

"I sold the house." Mom was digging through my camp bag. "Let's hang up your wet bathing suit."

When I'd left for camp that morning, the house had been mine. Now it wasn't. Now someone else owned it. Someone else was going to live here, play in my basement, eat where I ate, sleep in my room. Who cared about my bathing suit?

"You sold the house? Why?" Tears stung my eyes.

"I had to, doll. It was time."

How could it be time to leave the place I loved?

"Where are we going to live?"

"In an apartment."

"An apartment?"

"In Forest Hills."

"Where's Forest Hills?"

"It's close, just fifteen minutes away."

"Can I go to my same school at least? What about first grade?"

"You're going to go to P.S. 196. It's a wonderful school."

I hoped I was having a nightmare. Please, God, wake me up.

"But what about my friends? What about Amy and Joey?"

"You'll make new friends. And we'll come back to visit."

"I don't want new friends. I want the same friends I have now!" I was crying and I didn't care. "What about Max?"

"I'm sure our new neighborhood has a Good Humor man."

"What about Steven? Is Steven coming?"

"Yes, Steven is coming. We'll all be together. Everything's going to be fine, sweetie. I promise."

I wanted to believe her, the way I did about the robins and the salt. But I was too crushed to think about anything beside the fact that I was about to leave everything I had ever known and loved.

PART TWO:

FOREST HILLS, 1966

AS THE CROW FLIES, FOREST HILLS WASN'T far from Rego Park—just a few minutes up Queens Boulevard. But it felt like another world.

Our apartment was on 110th Street and 71st Road, in a six-story brick building on a tree-lined street a few blocks away from the tennis courts that once housed the U.S. Open. The building had two wings, each with its own elevator, laundry room, and milk machine that dispensed chilled quarts of milk, plain or chocolate, for a quarter. It was an average building as far as apartment houses go, except for the lobby, which was palatial, with highly polished marble floors, mirrored walls, potted fichus trees, and a nymph-shaped granite fountain that dribbled water from its mouth.

Manning the building's lead-glass double-front doors was Victor the doorman. Victor was probably in his sixties, but to my six-year-old eyes he looked ancient. Liver spots speckled the wrinkly skin on his face and hands. His silver hair was thin. He reminded me of Max the ice-cream man, except that instead of wearing a crumpled white shirt and pants, he wore a crisp navy-blue uniform with epaulets on his jacket and a matching cap with a patent-leather visor. Victor was always doing something around the building: polishing the mirrors, watering the plants, or sweeping the sidewalk. During the nice weather he'd stand out front and smoke. He'd hold his cigarette down by his side and sneak quick puffs, blowing smoke from the corner of his mouth toward the ground behind him. As soon as someone approached, he would drop the cigarette, step on it, and gallantly open the door.

No matter what kind of day I was having, I could count on Victor for chitchat. "How's it going up there in 5G?" he'd ask in his raspy smoker's voice. "You're next to Mrs. Lewis in 5F, isn't that right? Her husband's some kind of radio star. Keep your eyes out for the Friedman girl in 6C. She's about your age, I think. Lemme know if there's anything I can do for you or your mom. Whatever it is, you just ask ole Vic."

When we moved to Forest Hills, I thought I'd miss the house in Rego Park. But living in an apartment turned out to be an adventure. I could talk to Mom from the intercom in the lobby, ride up and down the elevator, and race down the long hallway to our apartment. I could look through the tiny peephole in the center of our heavy steel door to see who was on the other side. I could drop a bag of garbage down the incinerator chute as easily as mailing a letter. Best of all, I could get a frosty quart of chocolate milk from the machine in the basement. Nevertheless, I missed my friends in Rego Park and clung tightly to Mom. Had it been up to me, I would have stayed home with her all day. But I had to go to school.

Mom had tried to time our move so that I'd be able to start first grade at P.S. 196 on the first day of the school year. But I didn't make it on the first day, or the second. Indeed, riding the Cyclone in Coney Island felt effortless compared to the prospect of starting first grade in a school where I would know no one. Mom didn't push me, at first. Either she was trying to be kind, or she took seriously my fabricated complaints about feeling nauseated, or she was simply too overwhelmed with her own struggles to engage in battle with me. By the third day, however, she and Steven forced me to go to school.

"Eat a little something," she coaxed as she packed my lunch.

"I can't, I'm not hungry," I said, staring at an English muffin slathered in apricot jam.

"You'll be hungry later."

"I won't be hungry. I'm sick. I'm going to throw up."

"You're not sick, and you're going. C'mon now. We're going to be late."

Mom's patience was thinning. She had to get to work, but I wouldn't budge. The more I begged to stay home, the louder she yelled and the more my stomach somersaulted. It was just past 7:30 on a Wednesday morning. Steven walked into the room, wearing a jacket and tie. He had to get to work, too.

"You're not sick, Andrea," he said, flatly. "You're going to school."

"I can't go."

I moved toward him, hoping for a hug, but he gripped my shoulders and held me at arm's length in front of him.

"You have to go to school."

"I don't want to go!"

"Mom has to go to work. I have to go to work. Stop giving us such a hard time. You have to go."

"I can't. I don't feel well!"

"ANDREA!" He dug his fingers into my flesh and shook me twice, stunning me into silence. "You're going to school," he said, smoothing his shirt and tie, "and that's final."

Leaving my mother's side wrenched my heart, at least while I was very young. On the first day of kindergarten in Rego Park, my teacher had had to peel me off of her like plastic wrap from a candied apple. No sooner would the teacher pry one of my hands loose than I would clamp onto Mom with the other, shrieking for her to take me home. The first day of summer camp had been no different. The only thing more powerful than my fear of separation was the lure of a shiny new bicycle, which had persuaded me to accompany my father to Parson's toy store. Once I returned from that disastrous outing, I latched onto my mother more furiously than ever.

What was I latching onto? Certainly not someone who offered any reliable sense of security or succor. My mother was never that person. Still, I needed her. I didn't have a loving father and had no connection to his parents or anyone else on his side of the family. My maternal grandparents were dead. I had no young, happy relatives or close family friends nearby. One brother was absent. The other, Steven, I leaned on heavily. But as his life took shape, and as his relationship with Mom withered, he became increasingly scarce. Inadequate though she was, my mother was all I had.

Together, she and I walked the two blocks to P.S. 196.

"You're pulling me," I cried, skipping alongside her every few steps to keep up, my hand in her vise-like grip.

"We're late."

The school's hallways smelled of freshly waxed linoleum and wood. Mrs. Green wore a short, knit dress with a chain belt, fishnet stockings, and spike heels. Her beehive hairdo and false eyelashes were inky black. Her white lipstick shimmered. She was as beautiful as the dancers on *American Bandstand*. I loved her instantly.

"A little late, aren't we?" she said as she put her arm around my shoulders, enveloping me in a cloud of Emeraude. "Girls and boys!" she yelled. "This is Andrea. Please make her feel welcome."

All eyes followed me as I took my seat. I clasped my hands tightly on top of the desk, burning inside my new dress, my toes curling inside my saddle shoes, trying to ignore the whispers.

"I hear tawwwking," Mrs. Green in a menacing singsong. A hush swallowed the room.

Mrs. Green tolerated no misbehavior or what she called stupid mistakes. The smallest blunders infuriated her. She wasn't just impatient. She had a mean streak. It wouldn't be long before the crush I had on her morphed into fright, or before the nervousness that had begun plaguing me back in Rego Park completely paralyzed me in my first-grade classroom.

Several weeks after I'd arrived at P.S. 196, Mrs. Green began teaching addition and subtraction. One day, she handed out sheets of membrane-thin yellow paper and directed us to fold our paper into eight squares. Then, she dictated eight addition and subtraction problems, one for each square. She spoke fast. As soon as I started copying down one problem, she was onto the next. I glanced at my neighbor's paper and saw that I had written the wrong problem in the wrong square. My body began to quake. My hands grew sticky with sweat. Furiously, I began erasing. My paper ripped. All I could think about was how much I wanted to go home.

"What is it now, Andrea?" Mrs. Green snapped, seeing my half-raised hand.

"My paper tore."

"All by itself? Your paper just tore ALL BY ITSELF?"

Snickers rippled the air. I winced. Hold your breath. Don't cry.

She leaned over and slapped a clean piece of paper on the table in front of me. That's when I saw it: a gold Star of David dangling from a delicate chain around her neck. She's Jewish. I fixed my eyes on the Jewish star. She's wearing a Jewish star and it's not even a holiday.

Mrs. Green was still yelling but her voice faded as I drifted back to High Holiday dinners in Rego Park. I saw myself setting the table. I saw Mom lighting the yahrzeit candles. I replayed the story of Aunt Vera losing her son. Where is my star? Has Mom unpacked it yet? I hadn't worn my Jewish star since the last year's holidays. When are the holidays? Did we miss them? Did Mom forget?

We had, in fact, missed the holidays that year. Had I not spotted Mrs. Green's necklace, I would not have given them a second thought. But I was thinking about them now: about chicken soup and challah dipped in sugar, about Mom cooking and praying, about how serene she became, and about how life during those few holy days took a peaceful pause.

"Andrea, wake UP!" Mrs. Green screamed. My stomach shot up into my throat. She towered over me, spitting out instructions to redo the assignment. I steeled myself. Once, twice, and again I folded the flimsy yellow paper. I copied down the problems, one in each square. Please, God, let me do this right. Please make Mrs. Green stop yelling. I spied her Jewish star again. Even as my body pulsed with fear, I felt oddly at home.

Like Mom, Mrs. Green both attracted and frightened me. Her Jewish star drew me in, while her flares of anger cowed me. She'd flip without warning, tender one moment, scary the next. Her volatility, though it kept me on edge, felt comfortable because it was familiar.

"Mrs. Green's Jewish!" I told Mom at lunchtime. She had a bowl of hot farina waiting for me when I got home. I hated farina, unless Mom made it. She unwrapped the giant Hershey's bar that she kept in the breakfront drawer and, using the edge of a knife, she shaved bits of chocolate onto the steaming cereal. I scooped up just enough cereal to capture all the melted chocolate. Then, Mom sprinkled on more until I finished the bowl. "Can we buy her a Chanukah present?"

Mom bought Mrs. Green a set of linen placemats and wrapped them in blue and white Chanukah paper. On the last day of school before winter vacation, I gave her the gift.

"Sweetie, you didn't have to do that," Mrs. Green said, pulling me in for a hug. "You're Jewish too, yes?"

I nodded. How could she tell?

"Well, I hope you have a very happy Chanukah."

I had no reason to believe I would.

Chanukah came a few days before Christmas, but the only decorations I saw on our street were menorahs. There was a menorah in every apartment window and even in our building lobby. Mom hadn't mentioned Chanukah. She hadn't bought any Chanukah candles. She had unpacked our menorah, though, and stashed it on the highest shelf of the breakfront, behind the gravy boat. Once again, Steven made me a newspaper Christmas tree. I found a hat and matching pair of mittens underneath it on Christmas morning.

✦　✦　✦　✦　✦

By the time Christmas arrived, I was beginning to feel comfortable in Forest Hills. I didn't have a lot of friends, but I liked school. I had even gotten used to Mrs. Green's screaming, although she wasn't screaming at me much anymore, which was sweet relief, since there was more than a little screaming going on at home.

Mom was still practicing electrolysis when we moved to Forest Hills. She saw customers in the salon in the city two days a week. On the other days, she saw customers at home. Money was tight. I knew this because I overheard arguments she and Steven had at night when they thought I was sleeping.

"You have to find work, Mom."

"I have work," she said, her volume rising.

"I mean a full-time job, Mom! You need a full-time job! I don't make enough at the publishing house to keep helping you out!"

"Who will take care of Andrea?"

"Andrea will be fine. She doesn't have to come home for lunch. She can eat at school."

"But at the end of the day? Who will be here to take care of her?"

"Give her a key. She can let herself in and wait for you to get home. Just find a job!"

The screaming fights between Mom and Steven—the two people I depended on for safety—rocked what little stability I'd begun to feel in my new home.

So did Mom's drinking.

Before moving to Forest Hills, I had never seen Mom drink. But once we moved, I began noticing the occasional cocktails she'd have in the late afternoon. Even though I was only six years old, I noticed how just a sip or two of liquor transformed her from an elegant woman to a slurring, blurry-eyed stranger. Her mouth would collapse, her eyes would turn fuzzy; her words would sound fuzzy, too. And her mood would sour. She'd pick a fight about anything. I didn't know what was going on at first. I figured she was tired or sick. Then one evening before dinner, I caught a whiff of her breath. It didn't smell like coffee. It smelled like the Manischewitz spritzers I drank at Passover, only rancid.

I felt dismayed and disgusted. Here was the person I had once revered, whose tenderness, meager as it was, I craved. Drinking obliterated whatever softness she possessed. It made her hard, ugly, and completely unreachable. I needed her so badly, but when she drank, I felt deserted. I hated her for that. I was too young and scared to articulate my anger, but in my clumsy, childlike way, I tried desperately to reach her:

"What are you looking at?" she would sneer.

"Your eyes look funny. Like you need to go to sleep."

"I don't NEED to go to SLEEP."

"You look tired. . . ."

"I'm not TIRED."

"And you sound funny. Your words are fuzzy. . . ."

"That's enough."

"Mommy, when you drink, you're—"

"That's ENOUGH."

"...different..."

"I SAID that's ENOUGH!"

"Your face gets all twisted—"

"You'd better stop..."

"...and your eyes..."

"I said STOP!"

"...like they're closing..."

"Andrea, I SWEAR you'd better STOP WHILE YOU'RE AHEAD!"

At times like this, my mother terrified me. But my need for her kept me from backing down. I'd risk her fury, even the back of her hand, for the chance to win her love.

✦ ✦ ✦ ✦ ✦

Just after New Year's in 1965, Mom found a job at Bloomingdale's selling sweaters during the after-Christmas sale. It was only part-time, but it brought in extra cash and allowed her to continue seeing electrolysis customers at the salon and at home. Being busy made her happy. And when she was happy, she drank less—at least when I was around.

Mom's job entitled her to an employee discount, which came in handy, especially on my seventh birthday. Birthdays were big in our family. No matter how distressed Mom was or how little money we had, she did everything possible to make them special. Just before midnight on March 12, minutes before I officially turned seven, I awoke from a restless sleep, too excited to settle down. Mom wasn't asleep next to me. From the hallway I saw lights on. Then I heard, "Heeeere's Johnny!"

I got out of bed and crept into the living room. She wasn't watching TV. She was sitting at the dining room table, smoking a cigarette and having a cup of coffee. Out of the corner of my eye, I saw Bloomingdale's shopping bags and piles of tissue paper scattered on the floor. Draped over both living room chairs were brand-new dresses, each one prettier than the last. One had short sleeves, another had long sleeves; one had a sash and another, a pleated skirt. My favorite had a flower at the waist. I stood with both hands covering my gaping mouth. Part of me was thrilled. Part of me was sad for having spoiled my own birthday surprise. I feared that Mom would be angry. She looked up and smiled.

"Happy birthday, monkey!"

"It's not my birthday yet."

"It's almost your birthday." She checked her watch. "It's 11:45. We can cheat a little." She nodded at the dresses. "Wanna try them on?"

I flung off my pajamas and held up my arms as she slipped each dress over my head, pulled it off, and slipped on another. None of them fit.

"Don't worry, sweetie," she said, seeing my eyes well up. "You are growing overnight these days. I swear you're taller today than you were yesterday."

I was also fatter. To her credit, Mom was careful not to mention that. I was already an anxious kid.

"I'll exchange them first thing in the morning." She tucked me back into bed, and kissed me goodnight. "Hey, you know what?" she announced before leaving the room. "It's after midnight. You are officially seven years old!" She kissed me again and hugged me tight. "See you in the morning, Birthday Girl!"

Unable to sleep, I lay there, listening to her wrap the dresses in tissue paper and return them to their bags. My birthday felt finished. I had ruined it. Tears streamed sideways toward my ears, dampening my pillow. From the living room, I heard the *Tonight Show* theme song and the clink of ice cubes falling into a glass.

✦ ✦ ✦ ✦ ✦

June came. The mild, late spring air was sweet with the perfume of bursting tree blossoms. The end of my first year at P.S. 196 was near. Mrs. Green announced our final project: Everyone would make a Father's Day card.

"Go home and ask your mother for any pictures that you might like to add to your card," she instructed, "but don't let your dad find out!"

That night, I asked Mom, "What should I do? What do I say when kids ask me why I'm not making a card?"

"Say your father is dead."

"Is he dead?"

"He might as well be."

The next day, Mrs. Green placed a package of construction paper, a bucket of magic markers, a bag of felt, tubes of glitter, and a bottle of Elmer's glue on each table. I approached her.

"What is it, Andrea?"

"I don't have a father," I whispered.

She put her arm around my waist. "Well, of course you have a father. Everyone has a father."

I stared at her. I felt angry and sad.

"Is there anyone else you could make a card for?"

"I have two big brothers, Roy and Steven."

"Okay, then! So, you'll make a Brothers' Day card!"

On a piece of pale blue construction paper, I penned "Happy Brothers' Day!" in Elmer's glue. Then, I carefully sprinkled gold glitter on top of each letter. I was admiring my artwork, when someone behind me said, "Happy Brothers' Day? What's Brothers' Day?"

One by one, my classmates craned their necks to look at my card. "Brothers' Day? That's weird! Why aren't you making a Father's Day card?"

I placed the card on my lap and focused on its glittery letters. I bit down hard on my tongue to keep from crying. The drying glue felt cold on my thighs.

Steven loved the card. I wanted to send it to Roy, but Mom said all the glitter would come off in the mail. "You can give it to him when he comes home," she told me.

I couldn't remember the last time I'd seen Roy. He'd called during Christmas and said he was planning to visit soon. He hadn't called since.

Mom tucked the card into a big tan envelope and put it in a large white box from Lord & Taylor that she kept on the top shelf of the bedroom closet. The box bulged with photographs.

"Can I look at the pictures?" I asked before she returned the box to the shelf.

"Don't make a mess."

I climbed onto the bed and opened the box. The photos lay in scattered mounds. Some were yellowed and stuck together, their corners bent; others were crammed into coffee-stained envelopes with faded addresses. They spanned decades, from Mom's childhood in Brooklyn to her life with my brothers and me in Rego Park.

I emptied pictures from an envelope. There was Mom, chubby and smiling as a young child, thinner and somber at sixteen, swathed in a white chiffon high school graduation dress. With age she became severely thin—the result, she would admit, of anorexia. But how svelte and happy she looked at twenty in a body-hugging tea dress and wide-brimmed hat, dancing with her first husband, Leslie.

I dumped more pictures onto the bed and found one of her at home, standing next to Leslie, with my brothers in the foreground. Everyone was smiling, including six-year-old, gap-toothed Roy.

"He used to hit us," recounted Roy, who only ever described his father as a disciplinarian.

My mother agreed. "Leslie was very strict." But with her, she'd note, he was tender.

One year after that photo was taken, they were a family of three.

More photos. Roy and Steven were a year older and in Miami with Mom, who wore a pink strapless two-piece that set off her bronzed skin and dyed-blond hair. Her bones jutted out. At the bottom of the box was a white, clear-plastic-covered wedding album from Mom's 1956 marriage to my father. She glowed in a pale blue, short-sleeved beaded satin dress that hugged her narrow hips and had a ribbon beneath the wide décolletage. A matching blue-veiled hat topped her yellow pin curls. She wore pearls around her neck and on her ears. Her left arm embraced Grandma Irene. Her right hand loosely held a bouquet.

Roy and Steven walked down the synagogue's red-carpeted aisle in suits that swallowed them. Their heads tilted forward slightly, revealing Hebrew letters on their yarmulkes. Their mouths parted slightly, their eyes cast downward.

In one picture, Milton appeared alone and solemn, walking down the aisle in a baggy suit and satin yarmulke. In another, he and Mom were smiling, their faces squeezed into the sliver of space that would vanish once they closed the door that had a "Do Not Disturb" sign hanging from its knob.

"Say he's dead." Mom's words echoed in my ears.

From every envelope I pulled photos of Mom smiling, looking happy. Not one photo, including those from her early widowhood, captured her sorrow or stress. They all showed her at her best and most beautiful. It was a skewed portrait of her life, one that she had memorialized in a box. I wondered, as booze and depression fattened and fatigued her, if she clung to the images of who she'd been, so as to avoid seeing the woman she'd become: broken and afraid, someone who needed two double Scotches to fall asleep and was too emotionally crippled to take care of her children.

✦ ✦ ✦ ✦ ✦

Mom's job at Bloomingdale's turned me into a latchkey kid. If it was nice outside and I had no homework to do, I'd grab the salt shaker and try to catch robins in front of our building. I hadn't caught one yet, but Mom told me to keep trying. She said she never wanted me to give up.

"Whatcha got there?" Victor the doorman asked.

"Salt. If you shake salt on a robin's tail, it will stand still for you."

"Nonsense."

"It's not nonsense. My mom said it's true."

"Oh, did she? Have you ever gotten close enough to a robin to make it stand still?"

"Not yet, but I will. My mom said I just have to keep trying."

"Don't hold your breath, kiddo."

✦ ✦ ✦ ✦ ✦

With the money she made working at Bloomingdale's and seeing electrolysis customers, Mom was able to send me to day camp that summer. She would put me on the camp bus at seven-thirty in the morning, rush to work, and make it home in time to meet me by five. On the days that she worked late or had an appointment in the city, she would ask Victor to get me off the bus. She didn't say what her twice-weekly appointments were about, just that they were personal.

Somehow, Mom managed to scrounge together enough money for occasional luxuries, like Broadway musicals. Mom loved musicals. She loved all music. So did Steven. To them, music was another piece of my education. On Sunday afternoons, they would take turns spinning their favorite soundtracks on the turntable: *Fiddler on the Roof, Annie Get Your Gun, My Fair Lady, West Side Story, The King and I*—we had them all. In time, I knew all the words to every song from every one of those shows.

After the Broadway tunes, Steven would put classical music on the record player, operas and overtures by Verdi, Mozart, Beethoven, and Tchaikovsky. He always played my favorite, the *1812 Overture*. For Mom, he played Beethoven's Sixth Symphony, and for himself, Beethoven's Fifth. He'd stand behind me, take my arms in his hands, and together we would conduct the orchestra, slicing the air with our imaginary batons. Ba-ba-ba-bummmmm!

Mom would come out of the kitchen and tap her foot as Steven and I air-conducted the symphony. Her face would be shiny with grease because Sunday was the day she made grieven, the crunchy remnants of rendered chicken fat. Chicken fat was Hungarian gold, and we had a freezer full of it because chicken, which was always on sale, was our mainstay. Mom always bought several chickens at once. She'd cook one every few days and freeze the rest. But first, she'd collect the fat. She would tear clumps of it away from a chicken's slimy skin, pack it in aluminum foil, and freeze it. Every few weeks, she would defrost the frozen fat and cook it down in a heavy soup pot. As the fat melted, pieces of sizzling skin would float to the top. When they were crispy and golden brown, Mom would dredge them with a slotted spoon, drain them on a paper towel, and sprinkle them with salt and pepper.

"Is it ready yet?" I'd ask.

"Let it cool."

Impatiently, I'd press my nose as close as I could to the plate of warm grieven. As soon as Mom gave the word, I'd starting popping pieces into my mouth, taking occasional bites of the rye bread that she said would soak up excess grease in my stomach. I'd stand there munching while Mom washed dishes and hummed off-key to whatever record was playing, her thoughts drifting so far away that, seeming to forget my presence, she would light a cigarette and sip from the drink that she'd stashed behind the toaster. Despite her humming, I sensed sadness in her, and wondered if she missed Rego Park as much as I did.

✦ ✦ ✦ ✦ ✦

After we left Rego Park, we didn't see much of Mom's aunts and uncles, who had been her closest friends. We saw them at the Passover Seder but not on Sundays for coffee and cake—I guess we'd moved just far enough away to make the trip a hassle. Luckily, Mom found a new best friend, Myrna Berger, a divorced fourth-grade teacher, who lived with her two teenagers directly below us in apartment 4G.

Myrna was tall and skinny. She had inky black hair like Mrs. Green, and wore it short and teased high on top, with spit curls on the sides. Her eyelashes were thick with black mascara. Her lips were bright red, as were her long nails, which were ideal for pulling Virginia Slims out of their box. Myrna and Mom spent hours talking, smoking, and drinking coffee. They both had raspy voices. They both coughed a lot.

Myrna was loud. She practically yelled when she talked, maybe because she was used to competing with a classroom of chatty students. She was also funny.

"Evyyy!" she would moan, rushing into our apartment with one hand on her forehead. "I NEED chocolate!"

Chuckling, Mom would retrieve the giant Hershey's bar from the breakfront drawer.

"Oh, my GAWD, you save me every MONTH," Myrna would say, shoving a hunk of chocolate into her mouth. "Evelyn, I don't know how you do it. I couldn't keep a Hershey's bar in my house for a minute. I'd eat the whole thing and be as big as a BLIMP!"

Mom said she envied Myrna for being able to eat anything she wanted and stay skinny enough to wear tight black stretch pants. I wished Mom could wear those pants, too, with black flats, like Laura Petrie on the *Dick Van Dyke Show*. Anything would have looked better than the housedresses she wore on the weekends. But whenever I suggested she buy a pair of pants, she'd say, "I don't have the figure."

Myrna was Jewish. She had a mezuzah on her front door. She observed all the Jewish holidays, including Shabbat on Friday nights. I loved Friday nights because Myrna would invite Mom and me down for a cold supper of lox, cream cheese, and bagels. We'd gather around her white acrylic dinette table, as her son David and daughter Rachel said the blessings over the candles, wine, and challah. Then we would take our seats in bright orange vinyl chairs that went perfectly with the room's wildly flowered wallpaper, and pass around the bagels as the candles burned.

"Why don't we celebrate Shabbat?" I asked Mom after one Friday night dinner.

She didn't answer.

"David and Rachel both went to Hebrew school," I persisted. "Why can't I go?"

"Hebrew school costs money, sweetie."

"Does celebrating Shabbat cost money? Can we at least do that?"

"We'll see."

We never celebrated Shabbat. We didn't celebrate Rosh Hashanah or Yom Kippur anymore, either. From the time we left Rego Park, the Jewish New Year came and went without any more Hungarian feasts, sugar-dipped challah, or yahrzeit candles. By the time I'd reached third grade, the only nod we gave to being Jewish was attending Aunt Margaret and

Uncle El's yearly Seder. We were living in a mostly Jewish neighborhood, surrounded by menorahs and synagogues and kosher butchers, while our tenuous link to our heritage frayed.

If Judaism had been more central to our lives, then I probably would have felt its disappearance more acutely. But because we had only ever been Jewish a couple of times a year, the loss of our High Holiday rituals and, eventually, our Seder attendance, was no tragedy. Sharing Friday night dinners with Myrna or spending time with Jewish classmates would trigger my desire to be like other Jews. But that desire was short-lived, at least on a conscious level, not only because I cared less about my Jewishness in 1966 than about getting my first pair of go-go boots, but also because I was trying mightily to stay afloat while my mother's emotional plunges deepened.

Anything could precipitate these plunges—her anxiety over money, going to family court to wrestle child support from Milton, or the looming prospect of Steven moving out. Mom complained that Steven was planning to leave just when she needed him the most, while Steven insisted that he was, at twenty-three, not only entitled to his own space but also desperate for it.

"If you loved me, you would stay," Mom would say.

And Steven, incensed at her emotional manipulation, would fire back, "You're right, Mom. If I loved you, I would."

As soon as Steven said those words, their argument halted. I'd hear the front door slam shut and the liquor cabinet click open.

I would have loved to have been able to get away from Mom, too, but at eight years old, I had nowhere to go. Except Myrna's.

"Do we need any milk?" I meekly interrupted one night during one of Mom and Steven's arguments. The tension in the air was impenetrable. "I can go down to the basement for you."

Mom didn't bother checking the refrigerator. She rummaged through her purse and handed me a quarter.

"Come right back," she instructed.

With a cold quart of milk in my arms, I rang Myrna's bell.

"Well! What a nice surprise!" Myrna said when she opened her door. "C'mon in, doll. How about a nice piece of pound cake to go with that milk you're carrying?"

Probably assuming that Mom and Steven knew where I was, she cut me a slab of Sara Lee cake and poured me a glass of milk. We sat quietly. I ate my cake. She smoked. I wanted to tell her about what was going on at home but I couldn't muster the nerve. Myrna was Mom's friend, not mine. She cared about me. But she had Mom's back. I stared at the giant orange flowers on the dinette wall, wishing I could live here, or anywhere else. Then, the doorbell rang.

"Is Andrea here by any chance?" It was Steven. His voice had an edge.

"She sure is. She's having some pound cake. Would you like some?"

"Pound cake? She left half an hour ago for a quart of milk."

A lump of cake sat in my mouth.

"Let's go, Andrea," Steven fumed. "Leave the cake. Now."

"Don't forget your milk, doll." Myrna handed me the quart that she'd put in the refrigerator. "Looks like we're both in trouble. Next time, make sure Mom knows you're here, okay?"

Steven and I rode the elevator in silence. No sooner did I set foot into our apartment than Mom started screaming at me. Her boozy breath scorched my face. It stank.

Mom had plenty of reasons for being miserable, but because I understood none of them, I simply assumed I was the cause. I would apologize at the slightest suspicion that she was upset. I apologized for everything, all the time, even when she denied that anything was wrong. I'd nag her to tell me what

I'd done to trigger her bad mood, which infuriated her and gave me additional reasons to apologize.

"Are you mad at me?" I'd ask.

"No."

"You look mad," I'd press.

"I'm NOT mad."

"What did I do?"

"I'm NOT MAD."

"You sound mad."

"You're MAKING me mad."

"How?"

"You're nudging me."

"How am I nudging?"

"Just stop."

"Why are you yelling at me?"

"Because you're being a NUDGE!"

"I knew you were mad."

"I wasn't mad but I am mad now."

"You're always mad at me."

"STOP!"

"I'm sorry! What did I do? I just want to know—"

"Stop nudging or I'll GIVE you something to be sorry for!"

Mom would never reveal what was upsetting her, nor discourage me from apologizing. It was a pitiful, two-sided game that never got me what I really wanted, which was her love.

If acting remorseful was never the key to Mom's heart, acting sick was a surefire way to snag her affection. The ailment or its severity didn't matter. Just being under the weather was enough to tap into her soft spot. All I had to do was say I didn't feel well and she'd press her dry lips against my forehead to feel for fever and caress my cheeks with the back of her nail-bitten hand.

Although I'd settled nicely into P.S. 196, I continued to suffer terrible anxiety, especially as tension at home increased. New semesters, new teachers, homework I didn't understand, and tests also wrought havoc on my nervous system. I became a first-class hypochondriac. Feigning illness served dual purposes: It earned me a pass from school, and it won me a hearty dose of Mom's sympathy.

"What's wrong with your leg?" she asked one morning as I limped toward the dining room table, dragging my stiffened leg behind me. It was the first week of third grade.

"I don't know," I whimpered, theatrically easing myself onto a chair. "I woke up and it hurt. I don't think I can go to school." In one hand I held half of a toasted English muffin. With the other hand, I massaged the phantom pain in my leg. Mom scrutinized me. Her eyes shifted from my leg to my face back to my leg.

"I'll drive you."

"Mom, I can't even walk!"

That's all it took. The next thing I knew, she was on the phone, scheduling an appointment with our family doctor and fellow Hungarian, Paul Weiss. Mom said that Dr. Weiss—I called him Dr. Paul—was one of her distant cousins, although I could never quite follow the lineage. It didn't matter. Dr. Paul had known Grandma Irene. He knew Roy and Steven. He'd known their father. He knew about Mom's losses and struggles. To be with him was to be with family.

I feared that Dr. Paul didn't believe me most of the time, either. Still, like the hero that I'd made him out to be, he would listen to my complaints.

"I think you will be fine, Andrea," he would say, smiling. "Oy-yoy-yoy, look at you. You're growing up so fast. Try to relax a little bit, eh? Mom loves you."

The bum leg was only one—and the mildest—of several ailments that I concocted to stir Mom's sympathy. Over time, I invented a catalog of diseases, including the "sneezing disease," an affliction that caused me to fake-sneeze repeatedly and for so many days that Mom wrote a hashmark every time I sneezed. The sneezing disease convinced her to take me to the hospital, as did my ongoing complaints of stomach pain, for which I underwent batteries of tests, including X-rays and barium enemas. Each and every one of these procedures, no matter how painful, was worth what it earned in Mom's concern and kindness, not to mention the impetus they provided to stem her drinking. None of it lasted.

✦ ✦ ✦ ✦ ✦

Job cuts at the salon and at Bloomingdale's triggered Mom's first deep dive. She saw electrolysis customers at home but still had too much time on her hands. She'd clean and cook but unless she was working, she didn't dress up. She stopped having her hair dyed regularly, so it faded from yellowy blond to mousy brown. She also started gaining weight, which I couldn't understand, since she hardly ever ate. During a chicken dinner, she'd spend most of the meal sucking marrow out of the bones. On the rare occasion when she took me out for a cheeseburger, she'd have coffee. She should have been emaciated.

However, she was a middle-of-the-night binger. I knew this because the sound of her scrounging through the refrigerator and unwrapping leftovers often awakened me. Once, when she came back to bed, I smelled peanut butter on her breath. The next day, I discovered flecks of peanut butter in the can of Hershey's chocolate syrup and threads of chocolate syrup in the peanut butter jar. A spoon with a smear of both remained in the kitchen sink.

Booze was also putting weight on Mom. Once she lost her job at Bloomingdale's, she began drinking nightly. Sometimes she drank in the late afternoon, sometimes earlier. Scotch was her drink of choice; occasionally, she'd have vodka or gin. It didn't take much to make her sloshy.

"OUCH!" she muttered one afternoon as she weaved toward me and into a chair. Her face, like her gait, was lopsided. Her eyes were half-moons. Her breath was rank.

"What? No kiss?" she slurred as I slithered past her.

Not kissing Mom hello, good-bye, or goodnight was the kind of slight that could easily have tripped her short fuse. Although, when she'd been drinking, everything provoked her. "I'm not your MAID," she'd thunder when I left my clothes on the floor. "You never lift a FINGER around here! Do I have to do EVERYTHING?"

As Mom's drinking increased, our home turned into a field of landmines and I was a foot soldier whose survival depended on spotting and dodging them. At eight years old, I became a skillful scout, looking for a liquor bottle on the kitchen counter, listening for the plunk of ice cubes in a glass. The older I got, the more adept I became at navigating this loaded landscape. I became an expert at reading Mom's face. I monitored her every move and shift in mood. In time, I recognized when it was safe to be near her and when it was risky. Mornings were best because then she drank coffee. But from mid-afternoon on, I took cover, volunteering to run errands or busying myself in my room—anything to avoid her.

I N MRS. STERN'S THIRD-GRADE CLASS, I FINALLY
met the girl in apartment 6C Victor had been telling me
about, Sarah Friedman. Because Sarah lived on the other side
of our building and wasn't in my class, we didn't come across
each other until we ended up with the same teacher. We
became best friends fast.

Sarah and I hung out together a lot, walking to and from
school, doing homework and extra credit projects together, and
listening to records. Every day, we took turns eating lunch at
each other's house. We'd dash home from school and buzz our
mothers from the lobby to see who could make us something
to eat. Since Mom usually drank late in the day, I knew it was
safe to invite Sarah over for lunch. It was after school that I
avoided bringing her home.

I didn't care for the lunches that Sarah's mother made—
bowls full of yogurt and cottage cheese, peanut butter and
jelly, or bologna sandwiches—but I loved being inside Sarah's
apartment. It was larger and more beautifully decorated
than ours, with plush velvet furniture, colorful woven rugs,
and billowy floor-to-ceiling drapes. There were pictures
everywhere. Against one living room wall was an upright piano

with family photos perched all over its high, flat top. More family photos crowded side tables, filled the china cabinet, and hung on the walls. There were pictures of her parents on their wedding day, baby pictures of Sarah and her brother, school portraits, and shots of her family together on vacation.

I rarely saw Sarah's dad because he worked long hours in a bank in the city. He was tall, silver-haired, and very handsome. He didn't talk much, and when he did, he didn't talk to me, which I didn't mind. Being around a dad, even a friend's dad, was completely foreign to me. What's more, my mother's villainization of my father implanted in me a fear of all dads, and for many years to come, of men.

Sarah's mother wasn't much warmer than her dad but she was beautiful. A stay-at-home mom, she always dressed like she had to go someplace important. She wore skirts and blouses, or slacks with matching jackets. A wide velvet headband pulled her frosted blond bob away from her perfectly made-up face. Small pearls dotted her ears.

I found her intimidating. She would stand in the kitchen and watch us eat, commanding us to finish everything on our plates, and scolding us for giggling or acting silly. And she'd constantly remind Sarah to come straight home from school to do homework, practice piano, or go to Hebrew school. "No dawdling, Sarah," she'd say.

"You're so lucky," Sarah told me during lunch at my house one day. My mom was in between customers and had made us buttery grilled-cheese sandwiches.

Me, lucky? Our apartment was not nearly as grand as Sarah's, and I didn't even have my own room. Mom and I shared the master bedroom, where she had set up her electrolysis equipment, with Steven in the second, smaller bedroom. Our only living room furniture consisted of two chairs, two side tables, and the big black breakfront. The movers hadn't been able to fit our sofa into the elevator, so Mom had had to give it away. We had no plush pillows or rugs or drapes to make the room cozy, and our wood floors were bare. So were most of our white walls. Three cracked oil paintings of some random, ugly old men hung in the living room. Wide-slatted venetian blinds covered our windows. There wasn't a family photo anywhere. And there were lots of dirty ashtrays.

"Why do you think I'm lucky?" I asked, licking butter off my fingers.

"Well, you don't go to Hebrew school, do you?"

"No."

"I do. I have to go twice a week, Monday and Thursday. I hate it."

"Why do you have to go?"

"My parents make me. They made my brother go, until he became bar mitzvah. I have to go until I become bat mitzvah. Then I'm done. I can't wait."

"Bat what?"

"Bat mitzvah. Aren't you Jewish?"

"Yeah." I smiled sheepishly.

"My parents said becoming bat mitzvah is part of being Jewish," Sarah said, scraping a blob of melted cheese off her plate. "They said it's important to know you're Jewish and to be proud of it because there aren't many Jews left."

Sarah's parents were from France. Both had lost much of their family in the Holocaust. I told Sarah about my relatives escaping Hungary. I told her about Aunt Vera seeing her son shot. I told her about the Jewish star that Grandma Irene had given me.

"Where is it?" she asked, scanning the apartment.

"My mom keeps it in a velvet box in her sweater drawer."

"Why don't you wear it?"

"I do. On holidays."

"I wear mine all the time." She twirled the delicate gold chain around her finger. "Do you go to synagogue?"

I shook my head.

"Do you keep kosher?"

"Nuh-uh."

"Celebrate Shabbat?"

"No."

"Rosh Hashanah and Yom Kippur?"

"Yup, except we haven't for a while. My mother's been pretty busy."

"You don't have to go to services? Boy, you are lucky!"

I didn't feel lucky. I felt left out.

Sarah and I finished lunch and put our dishes in the kitchen sink. Mom was treating her next customer. The air smelled of rubbing alcohol.

"We have a mezuzah on our door," Sarah commented, noticing our naked doorjamb.

I shut the heavy steel door behind us.

✦ ✦ ✦ ✦ ✦

The more time I spent with Sarah, the more glaring the differences in our lives became. She had two parents who were happily married. I had a single mother who was depressed and drank. Her family belonged to a country club and traveled to France every summer. If I was lucky, Mom would take me to Jones Beach maybe once in August. Sarah got new clothes twice a year. I wore the same jumper or skirt with the same few blouses every week, all year long, or until I outgrew them. Sarah's mother was lean and well dressed. My mother was fat.

Unless she was working, Mom wore a housedress with no shoes. She'd bought a pair of black stretch pants but her thighs rubbed together so hard, they made a washboard sound when she walked, so she gave them away. Her hair was too short for any kind of headband, and without having it set and combed out, it looked like a ragged dust mop. When she didn't dress up, she didn't bother putting on makeup, either. Because money was tight, she stopped buying expensive cosmetics, including skin cream. Instead, she smeared Crisco all over her face. The lard gave her skin an oily shine but she said it was just as good as Lancôme for keeping it soft. "It's my little secret," she'd say.

I coveted Sarah's privilege, a privilege that I was beginning to associate with being Jewish. I longed for my own room and a closet stuffed with new clothes twice a year. I dreamed of taking piano lessons, or going somewhere other than Jones Beach during the summer. Sarah did invite me to her family's country club on Long Island once. We spent the day splashing in the pool and tanning ourselves on thickly cushioned lounge chairs. Sarah wore a white bikini from Paris that showed off her flat stomach. I wore a red, white, and blue two-piece suit from E. J. Korvette whose bottoms came up high enough to cover my belly rolls.

"Mom might want to think about buying you a one-piece, dear," Sarah's mother told me.

My school and my neighborhood were full of kids like Sarah, kids from well-to-do, two-parent families who lived in big beautiful apartments and belonged to country clubs. Although Jewish kids were not the only ones who were privileged, all the ones I met were. I wondered: If all of these Jewish kids have a mom and a dad, and are well-off, then what does that say about me? I didn't want to answer the question. I didn't want to hear myself say that I didn't have the things, however superficial, that it took to be Jewish.

The chasm between our material lives wasn't all that separated Sarah and me. It was the way we were Jewish that made us worlds apart. In Sarah's family, being Jewish was something to honor. It wasn't something they acknowledged just once or twice a year and then forgot about. It was who they were all the time. It shaped their lives. They were proud of their Judaism, not fearful or apologetic.

My pining for a Jewish identity was twofold: a desire to fit in and a desire for tradition to unify my family the way it seemed to unify my Rego Park neighbors who came together at Christmas. I had never felt such unity, not during Passover Seders or the High Holiday meals that Mom and I had once shared. Every Monday and Thursday, I would listen to Sarah complain about having to schlepp to Hebrew school and moan about how jealous she was of me for not having to go. Yet, I was jealous of her. Seeing her rush to synagogue with my other Jewish classmates, even seeing the Catholic kids leave school early on Wednesdays for catechism, made me ache with envy.

It came as a huge relief to learn that I possessed one trait that, according to Sarah, was uniquely Jewish: smarts.

"Jews are smart," Sarah told me one day when we were comparing report cards. "Look at Albert Einstein and Sigmund Freud, two of the smartest men in the world—Jewish. Albert Schweitzer? Jewish. Lawyers, doctors, and dentists? All Jewish. We're born smart."

I figured Sarah was mostly right because I soared in school, although I had to work at it. I studied constantly. When I wasn't doing homework, I was combing the *World Book* for extra credit project ideas. I accepted nothing less from myself than a perfect report card. I was determined to be the top student in every class. And I was. My teachers lauded me. My classmates admired me. Steven rewarded my stellar grades with trips to Parson's toy store and the purchase of anything I wanted that he could afford, which regularly ruled out the Easy-Bake Oven. But the only incentive I needed to work hard was the glowing attention I received for my academic success. Hard work was my refuge. External praise was my balm. Both helped me forget, if only temporarily, about life at home and about all the other ways in which I didn't measure up as a Jew.

✦ ✦ ✦ ✦ ✦

Christmas in 1966, when I was eight, brought the best gift since my Chatty Cathy doll: a round-trip plane ticket just for me to Norfolk, Virginia. Roy was stationed there. Although he was rarely in touch, he had called enough to know that life at home was getting tough.

I hadn't seen Roy since the previous spring, when he'd shown up at the apartment unannounced. He had been at sea, training to become a navy pilot. The idea struck me: What a neat show-and-tell he'd make! No one I knew had a relative in the service, let alone an older brother who flew navy jets. If being the smartest kid in the class wasn't impressive enough, this certainly would be.

"Show-and-tell?" Roy had exclaimed. "You want to bring me in for show-and-tell?" I wasn't sure if he was incredulous or flattered.

"Please! None of my friends have met you, and I know none of them have ever met a real pilot! Could you wear your uniform?"

The next morning, in a rare and remarkable display of love and generosity, Roy donned his navy whites and accompanied me to school. I was so excited, I practically skipped down 110th Street alongside him.

"Wait here," I said, when we got to the door of Mrs. Stern's classroom. With her permission, I waved him in.

The room fell silent. Like the officer he was, Roy stood regally at the front of the room. He spoke slowly, in a voice that was much deeper than I had remembered. He described his life on an aircraft carrier, and the thrill of taking off and landing a jet on the deck of a ship that looked like a postage stamp from so high up in the air. My classmates were awestruck. When Roy finished, a flurry of hands went up, everyone vying for his attention. I sat quietly, glowing.

Now, nearly a year later, Roy was meeting me at the Norfolk airport. He wore blue jeans, a T-shirt, and sneakers. He was not alone.

"Hey-heyyy, kiddo! You made it!" he said, kneeling down to hug me. "This is Cassie," he told me, seeing me eye the pretty blonde next to him. That I would be sharing my brother came as a not-very-pleasant surprise.

"It's so naaahs to meet you," Cassie said, extending her hand. "Ahhh've heard so much about yewww!" Cassie gushed with warmth. Yet, I resented her presence. She was, after all, a source of competition for my brother's attention.

I gave her a limp handshake

I stayed with Roy in his small, sparsely furnished apartment. He worked much of the time that I visited, leaving me alone during the mornings to entertain myself. At lunchtime he'd drop me off at Cassie's house, and then return to his aircraft carrier. For a treat one day, he took me to the officers' dining room for lunch. Later, he gave me a tour of the ship, leading me down winding staircases and through needle-thin passageways to his cramped quarters.

"Why can't I stay with you?" I asked as we pulled into Cassie's driveway.

"Because I have to work."

"Then why can't I wait for you at your apartment?"

"Because I don't want you watching TV all day."

"I won't."

"Yes, you will. Anyway, I don't want you to be alone all day. That wasn't the point of you flying down here."

"I'm used to being alone."

"I know. But you'll have more fun with Cassie. Besides, I think she has a surprise for you."

The reason Cassie was able to take care of me was because she was on vacation from school. High school. She was only seventeen years old. Roy was twenty-four. She said she was planning to become a dental hygienist after she graduated, unless she got married first.

As soon as we walked into her living room, I saw a naked pine tree.

"Y'all gonna help me decorate?" Cassie asked.

"I've got to head back to work. But I'll see you girls later," Roy said.

Not a closet full of Easy-Bake Ovens, not an entire family of Chatty Cathy dolls, not even Paul McCartney himself could have overjoyed me as much as decorating my first Christmas tree. Just sitting amid boxes of decorations—fragile glass ornaments, gold garland, and silver tinsel—was bliss.

Cassie gave me free rein to choose any trimmings I wanted to adorn the tree. While she threaded strings of tiny electric lights through the limbs, I cradled each ornament as if it were a butterfly, searching for the precise spot to hang it.

"Hey, aaah know. Whaaa don't we make us some popcorn? Then we can put it on a string with cranberries and wrap it all around the tree. Wouldn't that be naaahs?"

We sat side by side, eating a few pieces of popcorn for every one we strung. By the time we finished decorating, it was dark outside.

"Should we see how it looks?" Cassie turned off the overhead light and table lamps and plugged in the electric lights. They blinked blue, green, red, and white.

"Purty, ain't it?"

I could not speak. I inhaled the aromas of popcorn and sweet pine, exhaled deeply, and beamed.

From that moment on, I never wanted another Christmas tree made out of the Sunday *Times*. Now that I knew what having a real tree was like, there was no way I could even pretend to enjoy a fake one. Besides, I didn't believe in Santa Claus anymore. And I wouldn't have wanted to have to explain to Sarah or anyone Jewish the presence of a Christmas tree in my house, even if was only made of newspaper.

Cassie and I spent much of the week together. She let me try on all her clothes. She did my hair. She painted my eyes with shadow and mascara. She let me play with Sunny, her Siamese cat.

"I wish I could have a cat," I said.

"Well then, whaaa don't you ask your mama?"

"She won't let me. She hates cats. She says they make a mess."

"Awww, Sunny don't make no mess," she said, scratching the silver, blue-eyed cat as it stretched its body long. "Y'all just have to clean the litter box. Cats pretty much clean theirselves."

On Christmas Eve, Roy took us to Bob's Big Boy and I had my first double-decker cheeseburger. It was nothing like the burgers at Hamburger Train in Queens. A Big Boy had two patties with a slice of bun in between and some Thousand Island dressing–type sauce that dribbled down my chin with every bite. It was heavenly.

Back at Cassie's, I noticed two presents under the tree with my name on them. I picked up each gift, turned it over, and shook it to see if I could tell what was beneath the wrapping.

"What do you think they could be?" Roy teased.

"Well, lookit," Cassie announced, "it's just past midnight. Ahhh think it's a faaahn time for Andrea to open her presents."

I tore the wrapping off one to find a small leather pocketbook with fringes on the shoulder strap. It was from Cassie. The other present was from Roy. It was a pair of little gold balls on posts for pierced ears.

"Just what I wanted!" I yelled, admiring the earrings. "But Mom won't let me have them. She said I'm too young for pierced ears."

"Awww, once she sees how pretty they look on you, she won't be able to say no," Roy said.

"Hey, how 'bout ahhh pierce your ears right now?" Cassie offered.

She gave me a plastic bag filled with ice cubes to numb my earlobes. She wedged a yam behind one ear at a time, pressing the frozen lobe against it. I squeezed Roy's hand and gritted my teeth, trying to ignore the sound of Cassie's sewing needle puncturing my flesh. She swabbed both ears with alcohol and popped in an earring.

"Have a look at yourself," she said, handing me a mirror. The gold balls sparkled like tiny Christmas ornaments.

At La Guardia Airport, Steven and Mom were waiting for me at the arrival gate.

"There she is!" Mom said, waving her hands in the air.

I ran straight into Steven's arms. Mom and I had had a ferocious fight right before I'd left and I wasn't too happy about having to come home. I gave her a perfunctory kiss on the cheek, expecting her breath to smell of liquor. It didn't. But I didn't let my guard down.

"Boy, did we miss you!" she said. Then, her smile vanished. "What in the world do you have in your ears?"

"Earrings. Roy gave them to me for Christmas."

"Oh, did he?"

"Uh-huh, and Cassie pierced my ears!"

"Oh, did she? Well, we'll see—"

"Mom, relax," Steven said. He took my hand. We headed for the car. Mom obligingly dropped the subject of my pierced ears but never really let it go. At every opportunity, she'd frown at my sullied earlobes, which she insisted were unevenly pierced, stopping only after she'd convinced me to let the holes close.

✦ ✦ ✦ ✦ ✦

In late winter, my mother came down with mononucleosis. I had never seen her sick before, not even with a cold. Now, she was completely incapacitated. She didn't eat. She didn't drink. She slept all the time. She dragged herself out of bed only to go to the bathroom. She was highly contagious, so Steven and I weren't permitted near her. They traded rooms. Now he slept in the bed next to me.

Days passed, then weeks, with Mom sequestered in the bedroom. It felt odd. She was home, but she wasn't. Life became strangely calm. There was no fighting or yelling. I didn't have to worry about how she would greet me when I got home from school. For the first time, I thought about inviting Sarah to come over during the late afternoon (although Mom was too worried about passing on her germs, even from the back bedroom). I felt free.

During Mom's illness, Steven took care of me. He packed my lunch every day. When he came home from work, he cooked dinner. On weekends, we grocery-shopped, and he let me pick out a treat, including a bag of popcorn that was practically as tall as I was. He helped me with homework. He took me to the movies. Sometimes, he brought me with him when he visited his friends. We talked. We told jokes. We made each other laugh. He was twenty-three and I was eight, but we were friends.

Mom was quarantined for six weeks. Every now and then, I'd catch myself wondering what life would be like if she died. The notion sent a wave of guilt through me at first. But after a while, I allowed myself to envision life with just Steven and maybe Roy, without all the fighting and screaming and saying sorry for nothing. I still felt guilty. But I didn't stop thinking about it.

By the time the last snows had melted, Mom had recovered, although she was still weak on her feet. One night, after *The Tonight Show* ended, she stood up to go to bed, lost her balance, and came crashing down on the floor, breaking her ankle. Drunkenness hadn't made her fall. She hadn't had any alcohol since before her bout with mono. She hadn't yelled at me since then, either. I was sure that having a cast on her foot would make her angry, especially after having just spent a month and a half in bed. But she laughed about it. "Oy, what a klutz I am!" she told Myrna the next night over lox and bagels.

"Can I draw on your cast?" I ventured, excited about embellishing the white sheath with my name in magic marker bubble letters.

"Of course you can, sweetie."

I couldn't remember the last time Mom had spoken to me so affectionately or that I'd seen her so tranquil. If it took being sick and injured for her to be this nice and not drink, then I never wanted her to be well or able-bodied again. I wondered how long this newfound peace would last.

Though Steven helped me with homework during Mom's illness, she stepped back in once she started feeling better. I didn't typically need homework help, except on Sunday nights, when I routinely flew into a panic about the current events report due the next day, which I had chronically avoided all week long.

The current events report was a dreary weekly chore. Every Wednesday, Mrs. Stern handed out the *Weekly Reader*, where we were supposed to find articles to write about and share with the class. *The Weekly Reader* was, without a doubt, one of the dullest publications on the planet. What's more, I had zero interest in current events. So, without glancing at it, I would stuff the *Reader* into my book bag, only to find it crumpled at the bottom on Sunday night, when, like clockwork, I would remember my untouched assignment.

"Oh, my God, my current events!" I would scream, frantically smoothing the *Reader*'s pages and hunting for an article.

At times like these, it was nearly impossible to drum up sympathy from Steven or Mom.

"You've known about this all week!" Steven would bark. Then he'd plop the Sunday *Times*' "Week in Review" section in front of me. "Here. Start reading."

"I can't use *The New York Times* for current events! It's way too hard!" By now, I would be sobbing and practically hyperventilating. "I'll just use the *Weekly Reader*. I'll find something."

"Absolutely not," Steven would snap. "Tell yourself you can't do something and you'll never be able to do it."

Luckily, Mom would usually start feeling sorry for me and step in.

"Look, Andrea," she said one time, pointing over my shoulder to a Sunday *New York Times* article about leukemia research. I knew that Steven and Roy's father had died from the disease. Mom and I read and discussed the article. I wrote the report.

Knowing that everyone else in my class had most likely relied on the *Weekly Reader* for their reports, I was eager to present mine. I faced the class.

"My current event comes from *The New York Times*," I bragged. I could see that Mrs. Stern was impressed. Everyone was. I read in a loud, clear voice. Then, after I finished, I did something unexpected. I took a quick, deep breath and, shifting my focus from my teacher to my classmates, I blurted, "Mrs. Stern, my father died from leukemia." As soon as the last word escaped from my mouth, I realized that I had told a bald-faced lie. Nervously, I waited for the attention that I craved. I relished seeing Mrs. Stern's face drop and hearing the hush that swallowed the room. Returning to my seat, I shivered and burned, keeping my head down so no one would see me smile.

What had compelled me to tell such a lie? I wanted to impose a different truth onto my life. I didn't want the story of a father who had terrorized my mother and my brothers and did not love me to be my story. I wanted death to be the reason that I didn't have a father at home like my friends, all of whom were Jewish. It was less horrific, less stigmatizing.

The next morning, Mrs. Stern called me over. She circled her arm around my waist and softly asked, "Andrea, your father didn't really die from leukemia, did he?"

I felt my cheeks flush. "No."

"Okay, dear. You can sit down."

Later that afternoon, Mom told me that Mrs. Stern had called.

"Am I in trouble?"

"No, sweetie, of course not." That's all she said. Then she hugged me for a long time. I'd expected her to chastise me for lying. But she was tender, perhaps because she saw how deeply I longed for a father.

✦ ✦ ✦ ✦ ✦

From the time I was very young, I had asked Mom to recount her story about falling in love with Leslie. The more steadily she unraveled, the more I thirsted for a glimpse of the woman she had been when she felt cared for and content, before she had begun drowning her grief and depression in drink. She would skirt my questions. She would change the subject. She would send me outside to chase robins. But I would press her, undeterred by her eyes welling up and her face crumpling as she choked on her words.

"He was a wonderful man," she would say, forcing a smile.

Seeing Mom's grief saddened me. So did my unrealistic belief that I had been a victim of lousy timing, that I had simply arrived too late and missed out on this amazing man being my father, that had he lived long enough to have conceived a third child with my mother, then that child would have been me—the same "me" that she had conceived with Milton Kott. This belief was beyond illogical. Yet, my need for a loving father, and for evidence of my own lovability, was so intense that I ignored its biologic impossibility. Sometimes the need was so deep that I told myself I really was Leslie's child, that he had died before we'd had a chance to meet. The fantasy felt so real and so comforting that I didn't think twice about announcing to my classmates that my father had died of leukemia. Nor did Mom see any need to set me straight. Every time I asked, "If Leslie hadn't gotten sick and died, would he have been my father, too?" she would smile knowingly and say, "He would have loved you very much." It wasn't exactly what I wanted to hear, but it was close enough. More important, she never tired of saying it. No matter how often I prodded her to repeat these words, she did, as if her dead, beloved husband were standing next to her, whispering them into her ear.

MY FATHER MADE ONE MORE APPEARANCE IN my life a couple of years after we moved to Forest Hills. I thought we had left Milton Kott behind forever, along with our old house in Rego Park, and that I would never have to endure another visit with him again. I had even heard Mom say to Myrna, "I'm not too thrilled about him knowing where we live." But Mom still wasn't working much and Steven was practically supporting us. She sued for child support, and as always, Milton asserted his right to see me.

I was watching *Wonderama* when the bell rang. Mom peered through the peephole in the center of the door. The bell rang again.

"Aren't you going to open it?" I asked.

She unlocked the door and pulled it open.

"Hello, Evelyn."

My stomach tightened at the sound of his voice.

"Hello." Mom didn't say his name. She didn't look at him.

"And who do we have here?" he said, brushing past her into the apartment. "Is this the one and only Andrea Kott?"

I figured he was trying to get me to smile. I focused on the television. From the corner of my eye I glimpsed his gray overcoat and matching fedora. He was taller than I'd remembered.

"Aren't you going to give your daddy a proper greeting?"

I felt queasy. "Hi."

"Well, that's some fine greeting for someone who drove all the way from Long Island to spend the day with you!"

The DAY? I thought. He's spending the WHOLE DAY?

Milton plunked down in a chair. He stretched his legs out and rested them on a footstool. I sat in front of the stool, cross-legged on the floor.

"Still watchin' *Wonderama*, eh?"

I didn't answer. I stared at the TV and listened to my heart pound in my ears. Mom sat in the chair next to Milton. She stared at the TV, too. It was like old times.

"How's school?" he asked. "Do you have a lot of friends?"

I ignored him. With one foot, he slowly pushed the footstool into my back.

"Quit it," I said, shoving the stool toward him. I knew I was being fresh. I didn't care. He wasn't wanted and I wanted him to know it. I knew he didn't really want to be there with Mom and me. In the years that had passed since our last visit, he had not contacted me once. Only when Mom sued him for child support did he reappear. Now, he would make her pay for having dragged him back to court. He must have known how terrified we were of him. Bringing that fear back into our lives was the perfect revenge.

"How about we all go for a drive?"

"We don't want to go anywhere," Mom said.

"I wasn't asking you, Evelynnnnn. I was asking Andrea."

"If Andrea goes, I go, and Andrea doesn't want to go."

"Why don't you let Andrea speak for herself, for once?"

"Andrea has spoken to me plenty. She doesn't want to go anywhere with you."

"Thanks for turning her against me."

"Thank yourself."

"Evelyn, I swear—"

"NOT in front of Andrea!"

"Listen, I didn't come here to watch television. I'm entitled to spend time with my daughter. You're making it impossible!"

"Andrea," Mom said with a sigh. "Turn off the TV."

I turned off the TV and returned to my spot on the floor. Mom chewed her nails.

"So, how's the new neighborhood?" Milton asked.

"Okay," I said, flatly. "I miss our old house."

"Yeah, me too. It stinks that your Mom sold it. Heyyy, why don't we visit the old neighborhood? Swing by the house? See who's living there? Grab a bite at Hamburger Train? Like a family."

A family? He's my FAMILY? I thought. I didn't want to take a drive, but I was curious to see my old house. Even more, I wanted to go to Hamburger Train. That's where Mom used to cheer me up after forcing me to wear a pixie haircut or black-and-white saddle shoes. I'd climb onto a counter stool sniffling, but as soon as the toy electric train rambled down the track that ran along the edge of the counter, balancing my cheeseburger and fries on its flatbed car, I'd be smiling.

"Can we, Mom?"

She glared at me.

"Fine," she conceded, looking at Milton for the first time. "You win."

Milton had parked his white Cadillac in front of our building. It was February 1967 and spring felt like a far-off dream. Mountains of grimy snow sat stubbornly on street corners with no promise of melting anytime soon. Black ice covered the sidewalks. Car doors were frozen shut. Windshield wipers were entombed in ice. I slid onto the front seat and sank into the soft leather. Mom sat next to me. Then Milton got in and lit a cigar.

"Can we open the windows?" I whispered.

"Please crack the window," Mom said in Milton's direction.

"It's freezing out there," he protested.

"Just a little bit. The cigar is making Andrea nauseous."

"I've got the heat on."

"You'll still feel the heat. Please."

Milton pressed a button on his door and the passenger window opened an inch. I gulped fresh air.

"Okay? Happy now?"

My stomach wrenched. That's how I responded to fear. It didn't take much: a sharp voice, a steely look. The slightest inkling of danger bore into my gut. We drove in silence. A few minutes into the ride, Milton placed his hand on my left thigh and squeezed. The back of my throat closed. I couldn't breathe. I crossed my left leg over my right and pressed hard into Mom. Milton returned his hand to the steering wheel.

When we got there, the house didn't look like ours anymore. There were no more rose bushes on either side of the red-brick walkway. Slabs of gray slate had replaced the bricks there and on the stoop. The milk box was gone. Billowy drapes instead of venetian blinds hung in the living room window.

"Ring the bell," Milton coaxed. "Go see who lives there now."

"I don't want to."

"What do you mean, you don't want to? What did we come here for anyway?"

"She said she doesn't want to," Mom said.

"Awww, g'won. Tell 'em you grew up here. Say you just wanted to visit your old house. They won't mind. Go on, ring the bell. It won't kill you."

"I don't want to."

Mom wrapped her arm around me.

"Suit yourself."

We drove down the street and over to my old school, P.S. 174. A fancy jungle gym stood where the swings had been.

"Everything changes," Milton said mechanically. "How 'bout that hamburger?"

"I wanna go home."

"Yeah. You would."

I rested my head on Mom's shoulder as we drove back to Forest Hills. Milton pulled up in front of our building. I couldn't get out of the car fast enough. I didn't say good-bye. I didn't wave. I didn't even close the car door. I just turned and walked inside. I knew then and there that I never wanted to see my father again.

✦ ✦ ✦ ✦ ✦

The thaw of spring brought hope. I walked the neighborhood scouting for robins, turning my head skyward and counting the first tiny green buds on the maple trees. I unzipped my jacket and drank in the sweet spring chill. It was impossible not to feel happy.

Another Passover came, and with it, our trek to Brooklyn for Aunt Margaret and Uncle El's Seder. Had it not been for the Seder, and for Sarah's grumbling about how much she missed eating bread, I would have gladly forgotten the holiday.

"I miss pizza!" Sarah moaned as her mother spread peanut butter and jelly on squares of matzo. Even though school was closed for spring break, we still ate lunch at each other's houses. Mostly we ate at Sarah's. Mom, fully recovered from mono, had started drinking again, and I didn't want to risk bringing Sarah home to find my mother smelling like Scotch.

"Life has to be very hard for your mother," Sarah's mom said as she poured two glasses of milk. I almost never talked to Mrs. Friedman. And I never told Sarah about Mom's drinking or about her secret appointments in the city. But she had clearly passed on to her mother what little information about my home life I had shared. "She has to be a mom and a dad, you know. It must be very difficult."

Maybe it was. Maybe that's why Mom was in such a bad mood so much of the time.

Sarah changed the subject. "Oh, my God, you are so lucky," she said, wiping sticky matzo crumbs from the corners of her mouth. "You get to eat Pop-Tarts even though it's Passover, don't you?"

Mrs. Friedman looked at me questioningly but remained silent. I took a slow sip of milk and watched my breath fog up the glass.

"I can't wait until Passover is over!" Sarah said.

"Sarah." Mrs. Friedman shot her an angry look. "Enough."

I couldn't wait for Passover to be over, either, not because I couldn't eat bread but because I didn't want to think about how improperly Jewish I was. For that reason alone, I had come to hate all the Jewish holidays. I had come to hate all school breaks, too, because I had no place to be other than home with Mom.

I did all I could to stay out of her way. I walked through the subway underpass to the other side of Queens Boulevard for an ice-cream cone at Addie Valens bakery. I looked at the pictures Mom kept in the gift box from Lord & Taylor. I watched TV. I tried to catch robins with salt, although I was losing faith in Mom's guarantee that I would ever nail a bird. And I was losing sight of why she had said I should never stop trying.

"Have you gotten close enough to a robin to make it stand still yet?" Victor the doorman teased me one afternoon.

"Not yet, but I will," I said half-heartedly.

"Now, that would be something to see."

I stayed outside until the sun set and the air turned cool. Back upstairs, I found Mom sitting at the dining room table with the newspaper and a cocktail.

"Any luck?" she asked. Her eyes were heavy.

"Do you think Myrna's home?" I asked, desperate for a reason to leave our apartment.

"Myrna's at temple."

"Why are we the only Jewish people who don't go to temple?"

"Because temple costs money!" Mom growled.

"You say that about everything!"

"You want pretty things? You want to go to camp?" Her words came fast, like a spray of pebbles. "How do you think I'm supposed to afford these things? Do you think money grows on trees? Would you like to find me a job?"

"Mom, I was just wondering—"

"You were just wondering, while I've been sitting here worrying my head off about how I'm going to feed you and clothe you and take care of you all by myself with no help from anyone!"

"Mom, I'm sorry, I was just asking, because Sarah—"

"Sarah has a father who supports his family! If you like Sarah's family so much, then why don't you go live with THEM!"

"I wish I could!"

"You're ungrateful, you know that? You're ungrateful and you're spoiled."

"I am not spoiled!"

"Yes, you are. You're spoiled rotten. Now go find something to DO!"

"I did! I chased robins until I ran out of salt."

"Well, go outside and play."

"It's dark."

"Then do something ELSE!"

"There's nothing else to do!"

"You'd better FIND something to do or I'll GIVE you something to do and you won't like it."

Then, without thinking, the words shot out of my mouth, just as they had during my current events report. "You're always yelling at me! And you're always drunk!" I couldn't stop myself. "Maybe if you didn't drink so much you wouldn't always be yelling at me!"

Mom rushed toward me, readying her arm like a pitcher on the mound and letting it go with all her might. The back of her hand smacked one side of my face, then the other.

"I HATE YOU!" I screamed through my tears.

"I HATE YOU, TOO!"

"I'm going to run away so far from here, you'll never find me."

"Good. Go right ahead!"

"I mean it!"

"So do I! I'll help you pack."

My mind raced. Where would I go? How would I live? How badly I wanted to run away and never come home. Boy, would she be sorry then. But I was nine years old. I had nowhere to go. We stood locked in each other's stares.

As soon as I'm old enough, I told myself, I'm leaving. I'm going to move far away. I won't call. I won't visit. I'll never come back. I'll never have to see her again.

✦ ✦ ✦ ✦ ✦

In the fall of 1967, I came up with a new scheme to curb Mom's drinking. Instead of trying to get her to stop, I would propose that she wait until after I'd gone to bed. That way, I wouldn't have to witness the ugliness that came over her when she drank, she wouldn't have to see the disgust in my eyes, and we wouldn't fight.

One night, as she cooked dinner, with a cocktail and a cigarette smoldering nearby, I shored up my courage. My stomach knotted as I anticipated her anger. My heart pounded. I was shaking.

"Mom," I began, my voice faltering. "Do you think you could wait until I go to bed before you have your drink?" She was concentrating on a pot full of chicken paprikash and did not look up. I took a breath and continued, "It's just that when you drink . . . well . . . umm . . . you change."

She rested the wooden spoon against the inside of the pot and glowered at me. I braced myself for the boom of her voice or the back of her hand. She picked up her cigarette and drew deeply on it. Tendrils of smoke unfurled through her nostrils. She swirled the watery remains of her drink, poured it down her throat, and placed the empty glass in the sink.

"Dinner's ready," she said.

For a brief period, Mom did wait until I was in bed to drink. Our fighting subsided. My anxiety eased. I was hopeful yet remained watchful. Then, one late afternoon, when I came home from Sarah's, Mom staggered on her way to greet me at the door.

"Mom," I hazarded, "you said you would wait until I went to bed before you had a drink."

"I haven't been drinking." She was angry. Her words were garbled but her breath didn't smell of liquor.

Risking her fury, I persisted: "Are you sure? You look like you've been drinking, and you promised—"

I'd pushed too far.

"You know WHAT?" Her eyes narrowed. "I don't need YOU telling ME when I can have a DRINK! I have so little in my life, I should be allowed to have a drink whenever I DAMN well PLEASE!"

And with that, she poured a Scotch.

Many years later, I learned that Mom had been taking tranquilizers. Her twice-weekly secret appointments in the city had been with a psychiatrist who wrote her prescriptions for

Librium, which was supposed to calm her nerves and help her sleep. Mom had been taking the Librium at night. She also had substituted it for the pre-dinner cocktail that she had agreed to postpone. In time, she would decide that the two worked better together.

Clearly, I needed a different strategy. I decided to try coffee.

Mom had recently taught me how to brew coffee in her old three-piece aluminum drip pot. Mom loved coffee. Next to Scotch, it was her favorite drink. In fact, she seemed to need it, maybe because she didn't sleep well. Even with Librium and liquor in her, she tossed and turned. Plus, she snored so loud, she'd awaken both of us. But she wouldn't be able to go back to sleep. So, she'd get up, have a cigarette, and eat. By morning, she was passed out. She would sleep through alarm clocks. She wouldn't hear the ringing telephone on her nightstand. To rouse her, I'd have to lean over her and yell, "MOM, it's time to get UP!" I wondered if she taught me to brew coffee because waking up was so torturous.

Somewhere along the line, probably as a result of watching too many television sitcoms, I got it in my head that coffee was the antidote to booze. I had no way of knowing whether this was true. Still, I liked believing that coffee would counteract alcohol in Mom. It gave me a feeling of control. So, I would offer to make her a cup whenever I saw her drinking. Because she loved coffee so much, she never turned down the offer, although she occasionally bristled when I became too insistent, which I often did. Mostly, however, the strategy felt like a win-win: Mom got freshly brewed coffee, and I enjoyed what felt like the power to neutralize her drunkenness.

Ultimately, the surest way to protect myself against Mom when she drank was to stay away from her, which meant staying out of the apartment as much as possible. Though I never again dropped in on Myrna unannounced, I did arrange visits with Myrna's daughter Rachel, who would teach me simple songs on the piano and let me parade around in the brown wig she wore while she was growing her hair long. I also spent as much time as possible at Sarah and other friends' apartments, or just playing outside. Once home, I'd seclude myself in the bedroom and do homework, or look at pictures or all the jewelry Mom no longer wore: anything to stay busy and out of sight.

✦ ✦ ✦ ✦ ✦

Staying away from home was all well and good, until I got a kitten. It was a surprise from Roy. Nearly a year had passed since I'd stayed with him in Norfolk. He had called one day to say he was coming for a visit. He didn't say when. "Tell Mom not to make a fuss. Don't wait up."

Of course, Mom went crazy cleaning and cooking: roast chicken, baked potatoes, salad, and creamed spinach. She looked happier than she had in weeks.

"When is he coming?" I asked, hoping she had inside information about his arrival time.

"I don't know."

"He said not to make a fuss."

"I'm not making a fuss. I'm cooking. Just in case."

Maybe because she was so happy, or because she didn't want to risk being sloshy in front of Roy, she forewent her nightly cocktail. By seven p.m., with no sign of him, Mom and I ate dinner alone. Even though he'd said not to wait up, I was crestfallen. Just as I was about to get into bed, the bell rang. I ran to the door and flung it open. There stood Roy, holding a cardboard pet carrier with round holes in it. From inside the box came a faint mewing.

I didn't know what to do first: hug him or grab the box.

"I know how much you loved Sunny," he began, referring to Cassie's Siamese cat. "Well, she had kittens. I thought you'd like one."

"Oh, my God, I can't believe it! Mom, look! Roy brought me a kitten!"

Roy placed the box on the floor and opened it. He reached inside, gently picked up a tiny whitish-silver ball of fluff, and put it in my arms. The six-week-old, blue-eyed kitten burrowed itself in the crook of my elbow and began to purr. "I love him! I'm going to call him Siam."

Mom stood behind me, her arms folded tightly across her chest. "Thanks a lot," she groused. "And who do you suppose will be taking care of this kitten?"

"I will!"

"Oh, sure you will," she said with a scowl. "I'm telling you something right now, young lady: I am not taking care of this cat. It is your responsibility. You must feed it, change its litter box, and brush it, or else he goes. And I don't want cat hair all over everything."

"Okayokay, IknowIknow, IwillIwill!"

That night, I couldn't sleep. I had Siam on my pillow, purring in my ear. Eventually, he crawled under my quilt and fell asleep on my chest. In the middle of the night, when I got up to go to the bathroom, he followed. I was exhausted and half asleep. Before I had a chance to flush the toilet or lower the lid, Siam leaped onto the seat. Unable to grip its smooth surface with his kitten claws, he slipped and slid before falling into the bowl. Horrified at the sound of him gargling and drowning, I reached in and yanked him out.

"Mom!" I screamed, holding the pee-soaked kitten in my outstretched arms. "Siam fell into the toilet. We have to give him a bath!"

Mom stumbled into the bathroom, her eyes barely open. She dropped a bar of soap into the sink and filled it with warm water. Then, she took the wailing kitty from my hands and tried lowering him into the sudsy water. Howling and flailing, he tried with all his might to squirm out of her grasp. Finally, she single-handedly clamped his front and hind legs, like a chicken she was preparing to stuff. Then she dunked him.

"Meoooowwwwww!"

"You're hurting him!" I said, sobbing.

"I'm not hurting him," Mom snarled, assessing the ragged trail of scratches up and down her arms. "Goddamned cat."

Siam gave me a reason to rush home from school. I couldn't wait to hold him and nuzzle my cheek against his softness or make an aluminum-foil ball for him to bat around our wood floors, like a hockey player pushing a puck down the ice. When he was tired, he'd curl up in his bed—a shoebox lined with towels—and I'd curl up next to him, stroking his velvety ears.

"He has his own motor," Mom said when he purred. She'd sworn she hated cats but I could tell she loved him. Sometimes I'd walk into the apartment to find her reading the paper and holding him on her chest like a baby, his tiny head tucked under her ear. Siam kept Mom company during the day and gave me something to anticipate other than how tanked she might be when I got home.

Our lives hadn't changed in any important way. Mom still barely worked, constantly fretted about money, drank, and didn't sleep. We still fought. But now, amid all our struggles, there was this tiny creature that seemed to be taking as much care of us as we were of him.

✦ ✦ ✦ ✦ ✦

The High Holidays arrived late in September and for the first time since we'd left Rego Park, Mom lit yahrzeit candles on Yom Kippur. I didn't ask why. I'd stopped asking her anything about our being Jewish. I didn't press for an explanation about why she had stopped cooking High Holiday feasts. I didn't nudge her anymore about wanting to go to Hebrew school. I stayed home from school on Rosh Hashanah and Yom Kippur not just because I could, but also because I would have felt too embarrassed about being the only Jewish kid there.

On the second day of Yom Kippur, I spied a coffee cake on the kitchen counter. "Is the cake for us?" I asked hopefully.

"No, it's for Mrs. Lewis next door," Mom said. "Her husband died and she's sitting shiva. I'd like you to bring it over."

I loathed the prospect of walking into this stranger's apartment. First of all, I wouldn't know a soul. Second, I was convinced, despite Mom's assurance otherwise, that dead Mr. Lewis would be laid out in the middle of the room for everyone to see. Where this notion came from, I have no idea. I had never encountered death. I hadn't been to a funeral. I certainly had never been to a wake. I didn't remember my grandmother dying and I didn't know anyone aside from Mom who'd lost a loved one. Yet, the concept of death felt creepy. Now, in anticipation of entering Mrs. Lewis's apartment, my mind reproduced the most haunting image I knew, which must have come from Tarzan movies: a dimly lit cave with half-clad, tattooed, flaming torch–bearing warriors chanting and drumming as they encircled a body, dead or alive—I wasn't sure—that lay flat on a stone slab.

In Rego Park, I had believed in heaven. I had trusted Mom when she said that the twinkling stars in the night sky were the people we loved who had died. Now, the notion of death evoked an eerie and threatening tableau. Perhaps if I had known the littlest bit about Judaism and its approach to death and mourning, I wouldn't have been so terror-struck when I pushed open Mrs. Lewis's door.

Mrs. Lewis's apartment looked nothing like a cave. Still, it felt creepy. It was dim. Heavy, dark-blue drapes blocked out any hint of daylight. A large crystal chandelier gave the dining room a yellow glow. An extra tall candle flickered inside a glass container painted with a Star of David. White sheets shrouded the mirrors in every room, like ghosts.

People milled about, talking in whispers, carrying plates full of bagels and cream cheese, kugel, rugalach, and poppyseed cake. I found my way to the kitchen and put the coffee cake on a counter.

"Don't just drop off the cake and leave," Mom had instructed. "Make sure you say hello."

I found Mrs. Lewis perched on a light-blue velvet sofa, a gold brocade pillow behind her back. She was doll-sized in a black dress and jacket, her short blue-gray hair neatly combed, a diamond Jewish star glittering from around her neck, and a torn piece of fabric pinned to her lapel. All around her were framed photographs of her husband, onstage with a microphone in hand, shaking hands with movie stars, accepting awards. He had been a famous radio comedian.

I was afraid to speak to Mrs. Lewis. What would I say? What if she started crying? "My mom says to give you our condolences," I said feebly.

"Thank you, dahling," Mrs. Lewis said, sandwiching my chubby hand between her cold, wrinkled fingers. "He was such a good man, my Charlie. Did you know him from the radio? Nooo, you couldn't have, he was before your time, but boy, could he make people laugh, I'm telling you." She let go of my hand and glanced at a nearby wedding photo. "Sixty-two years we were married," she said, more to herself than to me. "I knew Charlie Lewis since I was a young girl. Such a crush I had on him. Sixty-two years . . ."

I waited for her to start crying, but she didn't.

"Did you eat?" she asked me, as if suddenly snapping out of a trance. "Please! Eat! There's so much food. What am I going to do with all this food? I eat like a little bird. A *fegeleh*. That's what Charlie used to call me. *Fegeleh*. You like kugel? Take some home, bubelah. Make a plate for Mom."

I headed for the front door, eyeing the smorgasbord on the dining room table. I grabbed a napkin, pondering which treat to wrap for later. Even if the food had appealed to me, I didn't feel Jewish enough to deserve it. I crushed the empty napkin in my fist, shoved it in my pocket, and kept walking.

✦　✦　✦　✦　✦

Mom and Mrs. Lewis were friendly in a next-door-neighbor kind of way. Mom must have mentioned something about needing work because Mrs. Lewis stopped by a few weeks later to tell her about a job. Luckily, Mom hadn't had a drink yet. I pretended to watch TV while I eavesdropped.

"I hope you don't mind," Mrs. Lewis said from the doorway.

"Please come in!" Mom said. "Would you like a cup of coffee?"

"No, thank you, dahling. Listen," she began, waving a small slip of white paper. "I know it's none of my business, but my daughter Sybil manages a country club in New Rochelle. You know New Rochelle? It's in Westchester County. The Riviera Shore Club. Charlie and I used to go there. Nice place. Anyway, Sybil says they need a switchboard operator. Not today. It's off-season. But come summer, when things get busy, oh my God, those phones ring off the hook."

"Thank you very much," Mom said, turning the paper over in her hand like a piece of bruised fruit. Why doesn't she sound more excited? I wondered. "You sure I can't make you a cup of coffee? Tea?"

"No, no, dahling, thank you. I have a pot roast on the stove. Listen, I don't know what this job pays. I know you'd have to commute and that could be hard with the little one here home alone," she said, looking my way. "But she could stay with me until you got home. God knows I could use the company. . . ."

"It's very kind of you."

"Don't thank me yet, bubby. But maybe you want to call her? Here's her number at home. She's divorced. Her daughter's grown. Who knows, maybe the two of you could be friends."

Mrs. Lewis left and I followed Mom into the kitchen. "Are you going to call?"

"Boy, you're nosey." She was boiling water for coffee.

"But are you going to call?"

"We'll see."

✦ ✦ ✦ ✦ ✦

New Rochelle. I never knew it was a real place. I thought it was a made-up TV town, where Rob and Laura Petrie from the *Dick Van Dyke Show* lived. Nor had I heard of Westchester County, until the day Steven told me that we were moving there.

The day had begun with a trip to Parson's toy store to celebrate my most recent report card. Then, Steven took me to Hamburger Train.

"There's something we need to talk about," he began.

"Am I in trouble?"

"No, of course not."

"Is Mom sick?"

"Andrea, relax. Let me talk."

The train was creeping down the track with our cheeseburgers. But my appetite was fading.

"You know how I haven't been home at nights and on the weekends lately?"

"You've been working a lot, right?"

Steven shook his head.

"With friends?"

He shook his head again.

"What, then?" I asked.

"I've been painting an apartment for you and Mom."

"An apartment? Where?"

"In Eastchester."

"Why?"

"Mom's been having a hard time. She isn't working much and money's tight. Forest Hills is a very expensive place to live. Our rent is going up."

"Mrs. Lewis told her about a job . . ."

"Mom needs a place that she'll be able to afford when I move out."

"You're moving out?"

"Not yet. But I will be soon, and Mom needs to be able to pay the rent."

I stared at my cheeseburger and fries, feeling my stomach chew on itself. "But, Steven, I finally like my school. I have friends. I don't want to be the new kid again!"

"It's not gonna work, cookie. We can't afford to live there."

Steven didn't pull punches. He presented the truth, no matter how difficult it was. He'd hand me the facts of a situation and expect me to carry them. It wasn't callous. I knew how much he loved me. He believed in me. "You can handle it," he'd say when he saw doubt in my face or my mouth quiver. "You're capable." Steven didn't sugarcoat things the way Mom did. There was never any "maybe" or "someday" in our conversations—no false hopes or promises. With Steven, I always knew where I stood. I loved that. And I loved his faith in my sturdiness, although it felt like a lot to live up to at times. I never told Steven about catching robins with salt. I couldn't bear to hear him say it was childish or, worse, impossible.

"When are we moving?"

"Next month," he said, eating my untouched fries.

"Next month? But I'm only halfway through fourth grade!"

"We can't pay the rent anymooooore!" He was losing patience. "I have an idea: Let's go see the apartment right now. I have the keys."

We drove along Queens Boulevard, over the Whitestone Bridge, and onto the Hutchinson River Parkway. I pressed my face against the window as we passed Orchard Beach and City Island, leaving Queens behind. Naked trees lined the snow-caked banks of the narrow parkway, their branches framing the sky. I read the road signs aloud: "Pelham, Mount Vernon, New Rochelle, Scarsdale, Eastchester." The neighborhoods looked so different from Forest Hills. There were no apartment buildings or streets crammed with double-parked cars. Some streets didn't even have sidewalks. There were only private homes, with wide driveways, spacious garages, and yards in front and back.

"Here we are," Steven announced as he parked in front of a tall, beige, stucco two-story house. "We have the whole bottom floor."

On my way inside, I noticed the house next door. On its lawn stood a statue of a forlorn-looking woman draped from head to toe in what seemed to be a sheet. In its driveway was a car with a string of beads hanging from its rearview mirror, suspending a crucifix. I remembered the simple gold crucifix that Joey Imbrolio's mother used to wear. But it was nothing like this one, with a half-clad man bleeding from his hands and feet attached to it.

The apartment reminded me of how much I had missed living in a house. Every room had two big windows and sunshine streamed in from all sides, casting an orange tint on the rust-colored shag carpeting. Rounded archways separated the kitchen from the dining room, the dining room from the living room, and the living room from the den that faced a rose garden. There were two bedrooms.

"This is my room," Steven said from inside the smaller of the two rooms.

"That's yours and Mom's," he added, pointing down a short hallway. "So, whaddya think?"

"It's really nice!" I said, surprised by my own excitement. "But my friends . . ."

"You'll keep your friends, cookie. And you'll make new ones. You're going to be fine."

Suddenly, Mom, Steven, and I were very busy. Steven worked all day, grabbed dinner at a diner, and went straight to Eastchester to finish painting the apartment. On his way home, he picked up empty boxes at the supermarket. Mom and I spent evenings wrapping dishes and glasses in newspaper and arranging them in boxes in layers, separated by thick bath towels. Every day, our apartment got emptier. Mom wrapped pictures in pillowcases. She dusted all the books and records before packing them away.

"Get busy, you," she said, handing me a damp cloth. She said it smiling, like we were a team.

She seemed happier. She said she was sad to be leaving Myrna and to have to pull me away from the school and friends I had come to love. But she said things would be better now. We would have more space. I would have a yard to play in again. We wouldn't be so financially strapped. And eventually, I'd have my own room after Steven moved out. Plus, there was the job that Mrs. Lewis had mentioned. Mom said she would contact Mrs. Lewis's daughter once we got settled.

"I think we should go out to dinner and celebrate," she said one afternoon, after we'd finished packing.

"What are we celebrating?" I asked, shocked by her good mood.

"We're celebrating our move to a better place. We're celebrating the future."

We went to Wu's, my favorite restaurant. Our table had a white tablecloth and a little candle inside a glass cup. Mom ordered me a very pink Shirley Temple with a maraschino cherry that anchored a miniature umbrella. She ordered a Scotch and soda for herself.

"Order whatever you want, sweetie," she said between sips.

"What are you gonna have?" I asked when my wonton soup arrived.

"Oh, I'll just pick from yours," she said, turning boozy.

✦   ✦   ✦   ✦   ✦

The day before we moved, Myrna invited us down for a farewell lox-and-bagel dinner. She and Mom cried when it was time to say goodnight. Everyone hugged and kissed and promised to stay in touch.

"Oh gawd," Myrna said. "Now I'm going to have to keep my own chocolate in the house! Who's going to stop me from eating it and turning into a blimp?" She cupped my face in her hands. "Be good for Mom, doll. I know it's hard to understand, but she's doing this for you."

I didn't see how taking me away from my friends and putting me in another new school was good for me. Then I thought about having my own room, and I smiled.

The movers came early the next morning. Sarah and I stood out front, holding hands. We promised to call each other and visit. She said she'd invite me to her bat mitzvah. Before we got into the car, Victor the doorman came out to say good-bye. "Good luck to you, kiddo. Maybe in your new neighborhood, the robins will stand still for you."

PART THREE:

EASTCHESTER, 1967

THE SMELL OF FRESH PAINT MADE ME THINK OF starting over, with everything clean and new. With money not so tight, Mom would be happier. She might even get a new job. Maybe she'd stop drinking.

Our new neighborhood was much quieter than Forest Hills, where honking horns and sirens had continually rattled the air. In Eastchester, we occupied the bottom half of an old house that sat at the edge of a quiet cul-de-sac. The mid-December day we moved in, I roamed our horseshoe-shaped street. It had no sidewalks, so I skimmed the edge of people's lawns to avoid cars, although there weren't many. I read the names on mailboxes: Delgado, Carlucci, Domenici, D'Alessandro. Figures of the Madonna or Jesus adorned almost every door or lawn and Christmas decorations, every house. The neighborhood was a kaleidoscope of colored lights. In Forest Hills, I had feared sticking out for not being Jewish enough. Here, I feared sticking out for being Jewish at all.

"There are no Jewish people on this street," I announced as I walked into the kitchen where Mom was unpacking dishes. Frank Sinatra's voice boomed "Some Enchanted Evening" while she hummed along, singing every other word. A gin and tonic sat on the counter, next to the radio.

It was almost three p.m. Greenvale School, where I would be attending fourth grade, would let out soon. Mom hadn't enrolled me right away. She gave me a day to settle in. I looked out the kitchen window to see how many kids would get off at the corner school bus stop and walk past our house. I prayed that I wasn't the only soon-to-be-ten-year-old in the neighborhood.

"We're the only Jewish people on the whole block," I repeated, as Mom pondered the cabinets above the refrigerator for storing pots and pans.

"Don't worry," she said. "I'm sure there'll be plenty of Jewish children at school. It's an excellent school. That's why we moved here."

One advantage of being new to our neighborhood was that nobody knew we were Jewish. I seized the opportunity: "Now can we have a Christmas tree?" I asked.

"Andrea, please don't start. I've had a long day." She opened the freezer, pulled out an ice tray, smacked it on the edge of the sink to loosen a few cubes, and dropped them into a glass. They crackled and split as Mom freshened her drink.

"We could get a small tree and put it in the corner of the living room, away from the window, where nobody would see it."

"And when Jewish friends come over? How will you explain the tree?"

Mom didn't realize that explaining the tree to Jewish friends would be less odious than having to explain why I was not attending Hebrew school or preparing to become bat mitzvah. I would rather have concocted a story about not being fully Jewish and permitted, therefore, to have a Christmas tree, than divulge why I had an absent father, moved so often, and was poor. A tree would have justified my emerging identity as a non-Jew, and freed me from feeling like an imposter.

That winter was full of blizzards and snow days. I hadn't made many friends yet, but I was content to play alone in the snow. After having lived in an apartment for the past three years, I was thrilled to have a yard again and, even better, to have unfettered access to the mountain of snow that the village plow dumped at the end of our driveway. I'd spend hours crafting the mountain into a fort, complete with a doorway and window, smoothing its snowy walls as if I were planing wood.

I'd return home only to pee, or to have Mom wrap my cold, sopping mittens in plastic sandwich bags in a useless attempt to prevent them from absorbing any more icy water. She'd pull my hat over my ears and retie my scarf to cover the bottom half of my face, leaving a narrow slit for my eyes. Then I'd climb back inside my fort and play "house" until the streetlights came on, losing all track of time. Being in the fort gave me the same feeling that I'd experienced as a very young child, dreaming about being trapped in the belly of a giant wave, where I could curl myself into a ball and breathe.

It was impossible, of course: to breathe underwater and survive the crushing weight of the sea. That's why I loved the dream so much. It was one place where no one and nothing—not Mom, not Milton, not the emotional brutality at home—could reach me. I felt the same way in my snow fort: bundled up tight, my chin tucked into my scarf, my mittened hands pulled up into my sleeves, feeling sheltered from all the sadness and rage that filled my house, oblivious to the ice and cold.

Only when Mom called me in for dinner and I entered the steamy kitchen, where the radiator hissed and the aroma of roast chicken filled the air, would I realize how frozen I'd become. I'd stand shivering, too sodden and frigid to undress myself, as chunks of melting ice dropped from my hat to the floor.

"Thank God for the pom-pom on your hat!" Mom would exclaim as she peeled off my jacket, scarf, snow pants, sweater, polo shirt, undershirt, socks, tights, and underpants. "As long as that pom-pom moved, I knew you were alive!"

She'd hold my hand as I dipped one foot then the other into a lukewarm bath, my frozen skin burning as it thawed. As I sunk lower into the water, goosebumps would erupt all over my arms and legs and my teeth would chatter.

"I'll be right back," she'd announce, as I shivered uncontrollably.

She'd returned with a small glass of light-brown liquid. "Here, drink this. It'll warm you right up."

"What is it?"

"A little bourbon. Take a sip. It won't hurt you."

I loathed the idea of drinking the stuff that made my mother so revolting. Even more, I hated that she'd recommended it. But I was too cold to argue. I swallowed the tiniest drop, which burned my mouth and throat. I despised the taste. But I welcomed the warmth that spread into my chest and belly. I was suddenly very tired. Closing my eyes, I slid down into the water and rested my head against the porcelain tub. Mom hung up my dripping clothes. She put my drenched boots next to the heater. Then, she helped me out of the water and wrapped me in a thick towel like a crêpe. She smelled of onions. And bourbon. How I hated that smell.

✦　✦　✦　✦　✦

Steven's announcement the following summer that he was moving out shouldn't have come as a surprise, but it did. I had put the thought of his leaving out of my mind.

"Roy and I are going to live together," he told Mom and me one night at dinner. After five years of service, Roy had received an honorable discharge from the navy. It was 1968.

Opposed to the Vietnam War, he had filed for conscientious-objector status. Now he and Steven would share a two-bedroom apartment in the Bronx.

Inheriting Steven's bedroom eased the sting of seeing him go. I was ten years old and for the first time in my life, I would have my own room. Steven left behind his desk, his bookshelves, and his turntable. He bought me a coconut-scented candle that made the whole room smell like a Mounds bar. He also bought me the original Broadway soundtrack recording of Hair.

About six months after we moved to Eastchester, Mom called Sybil Lewis, the daughter of Mrs. Lewis, our elderly neighbor in Forest Hills. Sybil was the chief financial officer for the Riviera Shore Club, one of several beach clubs that sat on a strip of Davenport Avenue in New Rochelle, overlooking Long Island Sound. The Riviera had tennis courts, a pool, and private cabanas. It wasn't an especially fancy place, although even after Mom started earning money we could never have afforded to belong there.

Sybil put in a good word for Mom with the beach club's manager, who hired her to be the new switchboard operator. Mom sat in a closet-sized cubicle, facing a wall of wires and plugs. When a call came in, she'd plug a wire into a socket with a flashing light and speak into the tiny microphone of her headset. "Hello, Riviera Shore Club, how may I help you? One moment, please. I'll connect you."

The big perk of Mom's job was that I could use the club during the summer. We'd arrive just before nine a.m. and I would run down to the pool deck and claim a chaise longue. Then I'd grease myself up with Ban de Soleil and wait for the sun to fry me. Later, I'd swim. Sometimes I found kids to play with. Other times I played by myself, pretending to be Jacques Cousteau underwater and doing handstands.

Mom wouldn't bring me to work with her every day. She said she didn't want to abuse her boss's generosity, especially since he was already letting me eat at the snack bar for free. Besides, she wanted me to be doing more than lying in the sun all day long and frolicking in the pool. "You should be making friends."

I had been quite content whiling away my summer days at the beach club. Then Sybil told Mom about a sleepaway camp that Westchester County subsidized so that low-income kids could attend. Most of the children at Camp Spruce came from financially stressed families, which I did not know. And, now that Mom was working, she could afford to send me to camp. In fact, she signed me up—not for one week or two, but for eight. My heart pitched into my throat when she told me.

"Why do I have to go for so long?" I asked as we drove to the army-navy store for a sleeping bag. "Why can't I go for a couple of weeks and spend the rest of the summer with you at the club?"

"I can't bring you to the club every day, sweetie," she said, putting coins in the parking meter. "Besides, you'd get bored."

"No, I wouldn't." I was skipping to keep up with her as she headed into the store.

"Yes, you would, and I have to work. I don't want to have to worry about you." She walked toward a bin filled with packets of blank nametags.

"But, Mom—"

"These are iron-on nametags. I want the sew-on kind—"

"Mom!"

"You're going to love camp, Andrea," she said reflexively as she rifled through the bin. "I promise."

We selected a sleeping bag whose soft flannel lining had pictures of wild ducks, along with a mess kit, canteen, flashlight, knapsack, rain slicker, bug spray, and a big black steamer trunk.

"Eight weeks is sooo long."

"It's going to fly by, you'll see. You won't even want to come home."

Given the stress of life at home, I should have been thrilled at the thought of being away for two months. But the familiar, even when it's despicable, is less terrifying than the unknown.

✦   ✦   ✦   ✦   ✦

Camp Spruce was located in North Salem, just ninety minutes north of Eastchester. It wasn't the kind of camp that Sarah Friedman or my new Jewish friends attended. It didn't have tennis lessons or horseback riding or sailing. Mom couldn't afford such fancy camps. Still, Camp Spruce was beautiful, with acres and acres of hilly spruce and pinewoods, walking trails, cabins, tents, and a huge lake with a dock.

Mom and Steven drove me up to camp and pulled into the dropoff zone where parents were unloading trunks and duffel bags. Counselors held up signs with the names of their units. Campers assembled in groups.

"TERRACE CAMPERS HERE!" a pretty teenage girl with a brown ponytail screamed.

"We'll see you on visiting day," Steven said as he and Mom got back into the car.

I hoisted my knapsack onto my back, grabbed my sleeping bag, and followed the girl, my counselor, down a winding gravel road to my cabin. A truck had already deposited my trunk. I chose a corner bunk and quickly made my bed, unzipping my sleeping bag and smoothing it over my blankets so the wild ducks would show. Then I sat on top cross-legged and watched my bunkmates unpack. Starting that night, and for the next two weeks, I cried.

It seems strange to me now, the intensity with which I longed for home, a locus of tumult and deprivation. But being friendless in yet another foreign place made me ache for what I knew, even if that was a mother who continually rejected, emotionally abused, and terrified me.

I cried on hikes. I cried in arts and crafts. I cried at campfires. I cried through meals and during our weekly trip to the camp candy store. I cried at bedtime and when I woke up in the morning. The only time I didn't cry was during swimming. Being in the water had always soothed me, and by the time I was ten, I was a proficient swimmer. I was so advanced that instead of taking lessons, the instructor suggested I swim laps alongside a fifty-yard-long rope that extended from the dock to a buoy. Twice a day, every day, I swam. The rhythm of my arms pushing and pulling the cool lake water temporarily distracted me. When swimming ended, my tears returned.

Toward the end of my second week, I remained inconsolable. My counselor, at a loss for solutions, brought me to the two camp directors. Estelle, the head director, was a tall, lanky woman with a deep, velvety voice who wrapped her spindly fingers around my hands when she talked to me. Estelle was kind yet serious, a thoughtful listener who spoke slowly. Reenee (pronounced REE-knee), the codirector, was a squat woman with a gap-toothed smile and thick glasses that slid down her nose. Reenee spoke quickly. She was loud and ebullient, not somber like Estelle. She also wasn't as patient. She would listen for a few minutes, and then, slapping both palms on her thick thighs, would announce in her resonant voice that a glorious day was passing us by. Like a sizable portion of the camp population, both women were African-American.

"Would you like to call your mama, Andrea? Do you think that would help?" Estelle asked as she stroked my hands. "You can call her if you want, baby. But truthfully, I'd like to see you overcome this homesickness on your own. I think you can."

Reenee piped in. "Most kids have trouble for the first two weeks, then one day they wake up, and they realize they're having fun."

"We hear you're quite a swimmer," Estelle said. "I bet kids look up to you." Her words surprised me and I began to smile.

"You're a strong girl, Andrea. There's kids who come to this camp who need someone to look up to. You could be that kid."

Reenee continued, "You know what I think? I think you're gonna beat this ole homesickness. I bet you could even help other kids beat theirs." Then she invited me to Sunday church services.

"But I'm Jewish," I explained, apologetically.

"Do you like to sing?" Reenee asked.

"Uh-huh."

"Then come sing."

Church was makeshift. It took place in the mess hall every Sunday morning after breakfast. Estelle and Reenee, both Baptists, led the service. Estelle played the piano and Reenee belted out hymns, while everyone stood and sang along, clapping and stomping their feet. I had expected to feel uncomfortable in church, as one of the few white faces and possibly the only Jew in the crowd. But the music drew me in. Singing connected me to everyone in the room and filled me with a joy that I had never known. For the first time in my life, I didn't feel out of place. I clapped along, trying to catch the words and melodies, and eventually joined in, singing at the top of my lungs.

After services ended, Estelle escorted a little girl to my table. Her eyes were wet and she was sniffling. She cleaved to Estelle's side and stared at the floor.

"Andrea, this is Shauna," Estelle said. "Shauna's in the unit below yours. This is her first time away from home and she's feeling sad. I thought you might be able to tell her how you overcame your homesickness."

Shauna sat down next to me. She was smaller than I was, and a couple of years younger.

"I cried for almost two weeks straight," I said, surprised by the strength that suddenly fueled me.

Shauna's eyes grew wide. "Two whole weeks?"

"Yup. The only time I didn't cry was during swimming."

Shauna laughed. I gave her the M&Ms that I had planned to eat after lunch. As she ate the candy, I told her what Estelle and Renee had told me: that she wasn't alone, she was strong, and that she had it in her to overcome her homesickness. Soon, we were both smiling.

The kitchen staff began setting the tables for lunch. Before we left, Shauna hugged me. From her seat at the piano, Estelle gave me a wink. Every Sunday for the rest of that summer and for the next two summers that I spent at camp, I went to church.

✦   ✦   ✦   ✦   ✦

After that first summer, being away from home wasn't difficult. Camp offered relief not only from Mom but also from my self-consciousness at not being Jewish enough. At camp, I had a mixture of friends. A couple were Jewish. Most weren't. Some were black. No one came from wealthy neighborhoods or homes. We never talked about anyone's wardrobe or family vacations. We never discussed religion or who did or didn't go to Hebrew school. We all lived in dusty bunks and wore the same camp T-shirt and were too busy hiking and swimming and scheming to get to the boys' camp on the other side of the lake to care about anything else.

Eastchester was different. All of my friends there, most of whom were Jewish, came from well-to-do families, like Sarah Friedman from Forest Hills. They lived in magnificent homes with two parents, took music lessons, went on family vacations, had expansive wardrobes, and attended Hebrew school. I was the only Jewish girl among them who didn't go to Hebrew school and wasn't becoming bat mitzvah.

Once again, I was in the awkward position of having to explain why I didn't attend Hebrew school. This often happened during Shabbat dinners at friends' homes. I would watch their parents light the candles and say the blessings over challah and wine. Then, I'd wait for the questions: When is your bat mitzvah? You don't go to Hebrew school? You don't belong to a synagogue? I never knew how to answer. I would just stare at the napkin that I was shredding in my lap. Ultimately, I'd say something about Mom not wanting me to go. That's when they would ask about my father.

"I don't have a father."

"Everyone has a father, Andrea," Ariel Schwartzman's father retorted during one Friday night meal. "Do you know where yours is?"

"Ummm, he's not around."

"Oh, so your parents are divorced?"

"Not exactly."

"But your Mom is all alone?"

"Uh-huh."

"And what does she do?"

The questions kept coming until Ariel asked her dad to stop. Eventually, he did, but the looks that he and Ariel's mom traded didn't. I couldn't tell if they felt sorry for me or simply disapproved of my Jewishness, or lack of it. At those moments, my thoughts would drift to Sunday church services at camp, one of the few places where I never felt like I was under a magnifying glass.

In Forest Hills, I had hoped that being smart would be enough to make me feel truly Jewish; that it would compensate for my not having a dad at home or material wealth; that it would bridge the gap between other Jewish kids and me. In Eastchester, despite my continued academic success, I felt the gap widen, especially on Friday nights. That is when I realized my good brains would never change the fact that I lived in a shattered household with a single parent who drowned her depression in liquor. In my friends' homes, Friday night dinner welcomed the beginning of the Jewish Sabbath. In mine, it was like any other, with the clink of ice in my mother's cocktail breaking the silence.

My second summer at camp ended when the Woodstock Festival began on August 15, 1969. As my bunkmates and I waited for our parents to pick us up, we crowded around the TV in Reenee and Estelle's cabin to watch Jimi Hendrix croak "Freedom, freedommm . . ."

Suddenly, Reenee yelled, "Everyone outside! Your parents are here!"

We lined up to hug her, Estelle, and each other. Through tearful farewells, we promised to write. Already, I couldn't wait to come back next summer and the summer after that, when I'd be a teenager and a counselor-in-training. So what if I wasn't going to be a bat mitzvah?

MOM AND STEVEN HAD PROMISED THAT moving to Eastchester would make our lives easier. And, once Mom started working, things did improve for a while. In many ways, she seemed happier. She started buying herself new clothes. She bought me new clothes, too. By the time I reached the sixth grade, girls no longer had to wear skirts or dresses to school every day; on Fridays, we could wear pants. Mom treated me to the pair I had been pining for—bell-bottomed blue jeans with vertical bleached-in stripes. She also bought me a poncho, a brown suede shoulder bag with fringed tassels, and my first pair of penny loafers. Best of all, she quit forcing me to wear a pixie haircut. This was huge, especially in 1969, when it seemed like every girl wore her hair long and straight with a center part. If I couldn't be Jewish like my friends, at least I didn't have to look like I came from another planet.

Sybil had told Mom about a man who was a whiz at cutting curly hair. He worked out of his Victorian house in Mamaroneck. It wasn't far from Eastchester, but Mom had never driven there before, and driving someplace new always made her nervous, even when she had directions. So, I was especially touched that she was willing to take me.

The curly-haircutting whiz opened the door. He wore skintight bell-bottomed jeans and a tie-dye T-shirt. He had bare feet, a clean-shaven face, and a long ponytail. He shook Mom's hand, but I felt certain that he was beaming his smile directly at me. He led us up two flights of stairs to his salon, a spacious but sparsely furnished room with an American flag tacked over a ceiling light, giving it a red glow. The Guess Who's "American Woman" pulsed from two speakers near Mom, who was good-naturedly trying to get comfortable on a large floor pillow.

"American woman, stay away from me . . ."

The room vibrated as the man combed his fingers through my curls. Looking at me in the mirror, he asked what kind of style I wanted. What kind of style do I want? It was the first time anyone had ever asked me how I wanted to have my hair cut. It was also the first time that I recognized feeling drawn to a man differently than I was to my brothers. Goosebumps rose on my skin as he snipped my hair into long layers, stopping occasionally to assess his work.

"You're no good for me, I'm no good for you . . ."

I couldn't wait to show my friends.

Giving me choices about the way I looked was Mom's way of trying to make me happy. What I wanted most, however, was for her to stop drinking. The frequency and quantity of her alcohol consumption had fluctuated over the years, and I had expected our move to Eastchester and her new job to quell her need to drink. They didn't. In fact, her drinking spiked soon after we moved.

"My job is very stressful, okay?" she snarled once when I asked why she couldn't just have a cup of coffee when she got home from work. "I don't want a cup of coffee. A little Scotch helps me unwind." Some nights, she poured a drink before taking off her coat. By the time dinner was ready, she'd be on her second cocktail.

"Haven't you already had one?" I'd ask timidly.

"STOP watching me like a HAWK!"

I persisted. "Do you think maybe you could try again to wait until I go to bed before you drink?"

"I work HARD all DAY. I'm ALLOWED to have a drink when I get HOME!"

It was all I could do to get through a meal with her sitting next to me, thoroughly pickled and sucking on chicken bones.

No one who knew Mom or had ever met her would have suspected her dependence on alcohol. She got up every morning, dressed nicely, went to work, and came home every night to cook and care for me. She was professional, gracious, and responsible. Even though she'd put on weight over the years, she groomed herself well. She washed her hair every day (she couldn't afford the beauty parlor anymore). She wore makeup. When she was sober, there were no outward signs that she and liquor had a toxic relationship. Her face wasn't permanently flushed. Her eyes didn't have the yellow cast that suggests liver damage. Mom wasn't a stereotypical alcoholic. Not drinking didn't give her the shakes. Nevertheless, in her body, liquor was poison. Any amount was too much.

Alcohol did more than relax my mother. It stripped away the inner controls that kept her anguish and fury in check. It turned her Dr. Jekyll into Mr. Hyde. She'd take tiny sips, savoring them like water in the desert. But after those first few sips, any speck of pleasantness in her melted, like the ice in her drink. She became raw and reactive, a live wire stripped of its rubber casing. She grew surly and mean, and it took little more than a wayward glance to incite her.

I'd try not to stare, but I could not hide my disappointment at seeing her beautiful face sag like soft clay. It was impossible to conceal my revulsion as her words jostled like marbles around her thickened tongue. "Whaat?" I'd say sarcastically, cocking my head and squinting my eyes, not because I couldn't decipher her words but because treating her like a buffoon was my fiercest weapon. I simply would not swallow my contempt for her, this woman who called me every afternoon from work to say hello but who, once home, turned into a sorrowful and sloppy drunk.

As I had done in Forest Hills, I tried to minimize my contact with Mom. Camp saved me during the summer. And on weekend nights, I babysat our landlords' two young boys. Even though I was just in the apartment upstairs, the physical distance from Mom helped me breathe. I stashed my meager earnings in an empty, blue-velvet jewelry box, dipping in for an occasional candy bar or some cheap trinket from Woolworth's. I liked having my own money. It made me feel independent, as if I needed Mom just a little bit less.

Finding activities to keep me out of the house during the winter was harder. Heavy snowfalls and icy roads could trap Mom and me inside for a day or two, which could be unbearable when she started drinking, sometimes as early as lunchtime.

Friends' homes were my favorite escapes. I accepted every invitation for lunch or dinner, or even better, to sleep over on weekends, but I rarely reciprocated. I was too ashamed of our apartment and of Mom. Sleepovers were ideal because they afforded me the longest respite, although I was more comfortable at some friends' homes than others'.

Take Ariel Schwartzman. She was a good friend but I always felt uneasy at her house, even when her parents weren't grilling me over the state of my parents' marriage or my Jewish upbringing. Ariel's father manufactured lace. He must have done well, because Ariel was always getting new clothes, and her mother, who did not work, always seemed to be redecorating their house. This meant replacing every stick of furniture, every rug and lamp, with something new.

She converted Ariel's room—with Ariel's enthusiastic approval—from a pink and white dollhouse with a canopy bed into a lavender boudoir, with a sleek white daybed, deep purple carpeting, and a mood lamp. Every conspicuous display of excess made me feel that much more deprived. Seeing Ariel's parents' room, which she insisted on showing off, made me feel worse. On the lavender wall above their king-size bed was a blown-up photo of their faces pressed cheek-to-cheek, their toothy smiles stretched wide, as if I needed reminding that I lacked not only two happily married parents but a happy parent of any kind.

The one home where I felt the most comfortable was Celeste Marchese's. Celeste was my closest friend. She was Catholic. Both sets of her grandparents came from Italy. Her mother was a teacher. Her father was a lawyer. Celeste lived in the same neighborhood as Ariel, although nothing about their split-level ranch house screamed wealth. Aside from the baby grand piano in their living room where Celeste took lessons, the rest of the house was modest. The furniture was worn, the kitchen was small and cluttered, and the beige wall-to-wall carpeting was dingy. Plus, everything smelled a little like the family's old black Labrador, Tallulah. Celeste's and her sister's bedrooms barely fit their twin beds, desks, and dressers. Her brother, the oldest of the three, had the largest bedroom, the finished attic with a queen-size sofa bed and a big color TV. When he slept at friends' houses, Celeste and I would commandeer his room.

Sleepovers at Celeste's started with dinner. We'd eat pizza with her family. Then, we'd make popcorn, get into our pajamas, watch *The Brady Bunch*, and talk until we couldn't keep our eyes open. Celeste and I were each other's closest confidantes. We gossiped, but mostly we talked about our insecurities.

I couldn't believe Celeste had any reason to feel insecure. She was beautiful, tall, and willowy, with large brown eyes and perfectly smooth olive skin. Her lips were full. Her thick, wavy dark hair reached the middle of her back. On my best days I was cute. My shag haircut did nothing to hide the fact that I was short and chubby and getting chubbier all the time.

Celeste was also really smart. She was an ace at math, spoke Italian, and played the piano and the flute.

"You're smarter," she said on the phone one night.

"No, you are."

"Nuh-uh. You got the highest score on the science test."

"You always do better in math."

"You're better in French."

And so it went. We were each other's fiercest champions. The only thing that I wouldn't share was the state of my home life. It's not that I thought Celeste would judge or reject me. It was her parents I worried about. They were nice people, but they were curious. I hurriedly answered Mr. Marchese's questions about my mother and father, so I could brag about my brothers.

"They're so much older than you," he said.

"They're from my mother's first marriage."

"So they're your half-brothers."

"No. They're my real brothers."

"No, dear. They're your half-brothers."

It was an honest observation, something I should have known. Yet, neither Mom nor anyone I knew had ever described Roy and Steven as my half-brothers. It might not have bothered me so much, had the rest of my family life not been so broken. But this new piece of information hit me hard. Something about the term *half-brother* sounded so disqualifying. It was as if our relationship was fake. Now, along with my Jewishness, there was something else about me that felt phony.

Luckily, I spent most of my time at Celeste's house in the attic bedroom, talking about far more important things, like our budding sexuality and boys.

"Did you know that Ariel wears a bra?" I said as we pulled out the sofa bed.

"Yeah, Larry Gold snapped her strap during social studies!"

"Oh, God, I hate Larry Gold."

"Beth Adelman wears a bra, too."

"Yeah, but it's a training bra. She begged her mother to buy it for her. It makes her look flatter than she already is."

"I know, but she thinks she's cool anyway."

"Ariel thinks she's cool, too, and she doesn't wear a training bra! She wears cups!"

"I know. And she needs them!"

In truth, Celeste and I envied Ariel for her big boobs and for being the first among us to experience the mystery of menstruation. She wasn't particularly pretty. She wore braces. She wore glasses. But she had the most developed body of any girl we knew. Instead of hiding it, she flaunted it in tight turtlenecks and clingy sweater dresses. We watched her in awe, couching our jealousy in feigned repulsion, coveting her confidence.

The one thing Ariel didn't have was a boyfriend. None of our friends did. We did, however, have serious crushes. My crush was on Michael Shapiro. Celeste's was on Michael's cousin Ethan. Michael and Ethan were Jewish, but we didn't care about that one way or another. Boys were boys. All we cared about at twelve years old was whether the boys we liked, liked us back. Such obsessing provided delicious distraction from the rest of my life. It also made me feel like I was no different from any other preteen girl. It seemed to erase the gulf between my Jewish girlfriends and me.

In the morning after a sleepover at Celeste's, and with very little sleep, we would eat a pancake breakfast and then walk to Woolworth's to play with the costume jewelry and makeup samples. At lunchtime, I'd call Mom to ask her to pick me up by four. I always called hours ahead of time, hoping to reach her before she started drinking and fell asleep—her weekend habit. She always showed up at least an hour late, as she did one stormy Saturday. It was dusk. The air inside the car was thick with her boozy breath and cigarette smoke.

"Mom, I called you hours ago."

"I fell asleep."

"It's so embarrassing. Celeste's dad kept asking me if I needed a ride home!"

"I FELL ASLEEP! Close the window. It's raining."

"The smoke makes me nauseous."

I didn't add that her fermented breath made me want to puke. She didn't respond anyway. I could tell by the way she poked her tongue into her cheek and squinted that she was aggravated. She dragged on her cigarette. The smoke curled out through her nostrils.

"How was it?" she asked.

"How was what?"

"Your time?"

"Fine." I didn't want to talk to her. I couldn't stand to hear her slur. It was dark and foggy and raining hard. We were two blocks from home when suddenly, we were driving on the sidewalk, heading straight for a "No Parking" sign.

"MOM!"

She slammed her foot on the brake, heaving both of us forward.

"Oh, my God, Mom!

"I didn't seeee it. Isss foggy."

"I'm getting out!" I grabbed my sleeping bag and backpack. "I'm walking."

"You can't walk, issss pouring."

I stayed in the car. I didn't want to walk in the freezing rain. We inched along. My teeth clenched. I searched for obstacles in the road. We pulled into our driveway. With the car still running, I flung open my door, charged into the house, and headed straight for the liquor cabinet. I grabbed the first bottle that my fingers touched, ran into the bathroom, lifted the toilet lid, and poured the Scotch into the bowl. Before Mom reached the kitchen, I flushed the toilet and replaced the half-empty bottle. Then, I returned to the bathroom, shut the door, and ran water in the sink to muffle the sound of my pouring Clorox into the bowl and scrubbing.

Spilling out Mom's booze was sweet revenge, my secret weapon. I never emptied any one bottle completely. I didn't want her to catch on. I'd spill a little Scotch, a little gin, and a little vodka every few days, so that she would run out of everything at once. If I calculated correctly, then there might be one day during the week when she'd have nothing to drink. I felt righteous as the liquor splashed into the water and triumphant as the disinfectant masked its smell. Every bottle I drained empowered me. Every empty bottle bought me time.

✦ ✦ ✦ ✦ ✦

Although Mom's drinking had escalated after we moved to Eastchester, I tried throwing my own slumber party. I invited Ariel and Celeste. I asked them to come after dinner so I had time to wash all the dishes and straighten up the house. Around midnight, the three of us squeezed into my full-size bed. We couldn't sleep, not because the bed was too small but because we couldn't wait to raid the refrigerator. We tossed and talked until two A.M. Then, we got out of bed and tiptoed toward the kitchen. When we switched on the dining-room light, we found the table set with tuna salad, egg salad, chopped liver, lox and whitefish, bagels and cream cheese, plates, and silverware. The thrill of raiding the refrigerator was in its illicitness. Mom, in her attempt to be generous, had crushed our fun.

"You ruined it!" I complained the next morning after my friends had gone home. "We were supposed to raid the refrigerator, not have a smorgasbord!"

An outburst like this could have made Mom feel unappreciated and resentful. But it seemed to befuddle her. Like the archetypal Jewish mother, she had always equated food with love. Feeding people was her way of making them happy. So, what was so wrong with having surprised my friends and me with a middle-of-the-night feast?

"I'm so sorry," she said, her brow furrowed. "I thought I was doing something nice."

My friends loved my mother, despite the bumbled refrigerator raid. "You have the nicest mother in the world!" Ariel and Celeste said a few days later. Of course, they had only ever seen Mom in good form.

At her best, my mother was the antithesis of other parents. She didn't treat my friends like strangers or guests. She showered them with sweetness, greeting them at our front door with her infectious smile, a bear hug, and the question, "Are you hungry?" Mom didn't interrogate my friends about what their parents did for a living. She never pressured them to explain themselves. She invited them to talk about whatever was on their mind. Then, fixing her eyes on theirs, she listened. She was so attentive and compassionate that my friends sometimes did share problems they were having at school or with a sibling. When they finished talking but before an awkward silence fell, Mom would say, "Okay, girls, skedaddle." A few minutes later, she'd reappear with a plate of apples, peeled and quartered.

Mom's acts of generosity were spontaneous. She'd come home with small presents—pom-poms for my ice skates or the pink and orange psychedelic knit bedspread that I'd wanted for my room. Even when money started getting tight, she'd manage an occasional splurge—a blue suede belt with fringed ends or fishnet tights.

"We can't afford these!" I'd say, secretly hoping she would dissuade me, which she usually did.

"Don't you worry about it," she'd say. "I put a little money away."

I cherished these times, not for the gifts but for the way they made my mother seem so capable and in control, and gave me a chance to be a kid.

Most of all, I treasured Mom's empathy. So many of my friends' mothers had begun to scrutinize their developing figures and insist that they watch their weight. Mom took a completely different approach. She neither hassled nor ridiculed me for getting fat, probably because she'd struggled with weight her whole life. Instead, she discreetly invited me to join her on Saturday mornings at the nearby Elaine Powers exercise studio. When she saw how self-conscious I was about stuffing my pudgy body into a leotard, she revealed her own discomfort. "C'mon, we'll help each other," she coaxed. And we did, laughing uncontrollably as we leaned against the vibrating belt machines that jiggled our hips and butts so violently, they made our teeth chatter.

"I can feel the fat MELTING off!" Mom proclaimed, her voice vibrating with the machine.

Still, once a week, she took me to Jan's restaurant for a hot fudge sundae. "Everyone needs a treat now and then," she'd say. "We all need something to look forward to."

Mom could tell with one look when I needed a treat or when something was troubling me. Sometimes she would call from work just because she'd had a hunch that I was down. "Mothers know these things," she used to say. She wasn't confident about much, but she swore to the accuracy of her intuition. She was so sure of her emotional radar that she claimed with complete certainty to know that our cat was depressed, and that the remedy, although he was partially declawed, was to force him to climb trees. She would place him on a low-hanging branch where he would cling, terrified, until the landlord had to rescue him.

Mom never stopped trying to convert Siam into a tree-climber. Nor did she seem to recognize that the need for him to climb was hers alone. She had a similar blind spot when it came to feeding people. "Is that all you're having?" she'd ask when visitors insisted they were full. "You ate NOTHING!" If I suggested to her that she was being pushy, she'd look wounded and say, "I meant well."

On the surface, her good intentions seemed heartfelt. And yet, there was an element of selfishness, even narcissism, in them. Mom refused to accept that anyone—even the cat—could decline what she had to offer, whether it was seconds of matzo ball soup or a lift up a tree. Indeed, trying to turn her down was useless. The more people demurred, even the more the cat howled, the more stubbornly she would foist her good intentions. No one seemed to have a bigger heart or a greater gift for taking care of people. But deep down, the person Mom was really taking care of was herself.

THE RYE PLAYLAND AMUSEMENT PARK WAS A favorite winter escape. Playland had an ice rink that was open to the public when professional hockey teams weren't using it. The town of Eastchester provided the round-trip transportation for free with a yellow bus that picked us up in front of our school at ten a.m. on Saturday mornings and brought us back at the end of the day. My friends and I would skate for hours. While the Zamboni cleaned the ice, we'd rush to the snack counter for warm, soft pretzels and hot chocolate piled high with Reddi-wip®. Once restored, we'd slip and slide on the freshly slicked ice and skate until just minutes before four p.m., when the bus driver would threaten to leave with or without us.

On the ice, as in my snow fort, I was a million miles away from the tumult and sadness at home. Gliding to the music, I concentrated on my blades rounding the corners of the rink. Around and around I'd go, singing to the music. Occasionally, I'd venture into the elite circle of orange cones to practice twirling. Pretending to be Peggy Fleming, I'd whip my leg around and fold my arms across my chest to build momentum for a spin that never materialized.

Saturdays couldn't come soon enough. I'd get up early, eat a bowl of cereal, pack a lunch, and walk to school at nine-fifteen to catch the bus. Mom would leave money on the dining-room table for admission, skate rental, and hot chocolate. Because she slept late on weekends, I wouldn't have to see her until I got home at five-thirty.

One Saturday morning, she was up first. As I came out of my bedroom, I saw her in the dining room. She was facing the window, standing next to the open liquor cabinet. In her hand, she held a bottle of something clear and slowly raised it to her mouth, tilting her head all the way back. Silently, I swiveled and tiptoed back to my room. I waited to hear the cabinet click shut. I feared that Mom had sensed my presence and would come barging into my room. But she went back to bed. I grabbed my skating money and ran to catch the bus.

With the change from my hot chocolate, I called Steven from a pay phone at the rink.

"Mom was drinking this morning, right out of the bottle," I told him, cupping my mouth so no one would hear me. "It wasn't even ten o'clock."

"I'll take care of it," he said.

I had never felt so deathly afraid of confronting my mother. I would have ridden the bus all night to avoid going home. Did Steven call her? If he didn't, then she might be really drunk by now. If he did, then she was going to be furious. Either way, I would lose.

The sky was starlit by the time we arrived back at school. I walked the short distance home. The kitchen was empty. The spiral cord from the wall phone stretched around the wall into the dining room where Mom sat with the receiver pressed against her ear, her head hung low. She was crying. From the handset, I heard Steven yelling. Through her sobs, Mom said, "I know, I know. I'm sorry."

I ran a bath, expecting her to hunt me down. She didn't. She started cooking dinner. We ate in silence, never discussing what I had witnessed or my call to Steven. There was no cocktail by her side. I never saw her drink early in the morning again.

From then on, Steven called me every Saturday morning.

"Whatcha up to?"

"Nothing."

"Let's do something. How about Chinatown? Or the Bronx Zoo?"

Every weekend, we went someplace new. We explored the streets of Greenwich Village. We climbed up to the Statue of Liberty's crown. We trolled the Museum of Natural History. During the warmer weather, we rode the carousel in Central Park and rowed a rented boat on the lake. We rode round-trip on the Staten Island Ferry, sitting on the back deck, watching the waves of New York Harbor and talking, never leaving the boat.

Every day after school, I'd call Steven at the periodicals publishing house in Mamaroneck where he worked shipping medical journals to give him updates on how things were at home. They were not good. Mom was having trouble getting out of bed in the morning. Some weekends, she didn't wake up until noon or later. Previously a stickler for cleanliness, especially in the kitchen, she had stopped washing the dishes daily. More than once I'd sloshed into a flooded kitchen where sudsy water from a sink full of soaking pots and pans had overflowed because she'd left the faucet dripping. To prevent friends from seeing the grubby conditions I lived in, I stopped inviting them over.

But everyone invited me to their bar or bat mitzvah. The invitations started arriving near the end of sixth grade. All the ceremonies were scheduled for the next school year, after the High Holidays. Venues, menus, hairdos, and outfits were all my friends talked about. They didn't include me in their conversations. There was no reason. I should have felt relieved. After all, I didn't have to pretend or explain myself anymore. But I felt alienated and angry. It was embarrassing enough to be a low-income Jew with a mother who drank too much. But that Mom had thoroughly stopped recognizing the High Holidays or acknowledging any aspect of our Judaism felt unfair. Couldn't she have continued to light the yahrzeit candles, at least? Did she have to let every inch of our Judaism die? Didn't she realize what she was depriving me of? My friends were about to achieve a major milestone, one that would sanctify their connection to a birthright to which I felt I had no claim.

Luckily, my friend Celeste and I had other things on our mind, like the approach of seventh grade, which was considered junior high. Eastchester Junior High was connected to Eastchester High School, two sides of one monolithic red-brick building with many floors and wings. I had never seen the inside of the school. I had also never had to take a bus to school before. Everything was going to be different.

"It's so big and confusing," Celeste said of the school. "There are four floors and an east and a west wing. Plus, we're going to have remember locker combinations."

"What if we get lost?"

"I know."

"We're gonna look dumb, not knowing where we're going. Kids will laugh at us."

We weren't worried about just any kids. We were worried about the greasers. Greasers were the tough kids—girls, in our case—who dressed in black leather jackets and picked fights with anyone who wasn't in their crowd or cool: girls like Celeste and me. Greenvale, our elementary school, hadn't had greasers. But the junior high and high school drew kids from schools throughout Eastchester, which had a few rough neighborhoods. I'd never had any contact with toughs, and I didn't know the first thing about defending myself. My home life had enfeebled me. I was a coward and a crybaby.

When it came to teaching me about dealing with confrontation, Mom hadn't been the best role model. Whenever she got off the phone with my father, who almost never called, she trembled and wept. The same thing happened when either of my brothers yelled at her. Afterward, she drank.

"Just say you're sorry," she had advised way back when I was in first grade with tyrannical Mrs. Green. Now, she was suggesting I apologize in response to my seventh-grade math teacher's tirades.

"But he screams at me just for not understanding the math!"

"Just say you're sorry."

This was Mom's stock advice: Apologize first and ask questions later—or better yet, not at all.

✦ ✦ ✦ ✦ ✦

The summer of 1970 ended with a jolt. I came home from camp to a tower of dirty dishes in the kitchen sink, papers stacked on every counter, and ashtrays overflowing in every room. In Mom's bedroom, a shattered window and shards of broken glass blanketing the floor caught my eye first. Next, I saw a charred basketball-size hole at the foot of her mattress.

"Mom, what happened?"

"Oh, the boys next door were playing football and their ball crashed through the window. The landlord is going to fix it."

"No, I mean your mattress. What happened to your mattress?"

"Ohhh. That. I had a little fire."

"A little fire? What do you mean a little fire?"

"I fell asleep. With a cigarette."

The mattress coils stood tall like steel trees. She must have been obliterated to have slept while the fire destroyed her bed.

"Mom! You could have burned the whole house down! Didn't you smell the smoke?"

"I guess not."

"Mom! You could have died!"

"But I DIDN'T, okay?"

It made no sense. Mom had seemed fine on both visiting days at camp that summer. She had brought southern fried chicken for a picnic. I had written her about the raccoon that devoured the chicken in the middle of the night, and she had written back, saying she wished she could mail me more. Instead, she had sent a giant care package from Schrafft's with chocolate-covered English toffee, marshmallows rolled in toasted coconut, and Tootsie Pops. It had to have been expensive. Surely, she must have been working. She hadn't indicated otherwise. Little did I know that while I was having the best summer of my life an hour and a half away, our apartment was turning into a dump with my mother inside, sinking, sinking.

"We gotta get you outta there," Steven said when I called to tell him about the fire. I'd been home from camp for only a day and he was already making a rescue attempt. I knew that any rescue Steven could manage wouldn't be permanent, though, at least not as permanent as I would have liked. I knew that the best he could do was to get me out of the house and away from Mom on weekend afternoons.

Sometimes we went to his apartment in the Bronx. Even though he and Roy had rented the place together, Roy was never there because he spent all his time with his girlfriend in Greenwich Village. Steven had started dating someone, too, a woman named Dierdre whom he'd met in a nighttime English class that he was taking for his master's degree.

Dierdre was a magazine editor and short-story writer. At thirty-two, she was five years older than Steven. She was tall and lean. Her thick brown hair, with its center part, tickled her collarbone. She had blue eyes, pale skin, and a thin, wide mouth. She didn't wear makeup or tweeze her bushy brown eyebrows. Her round, oversized glasses gave her owl eyes.

"Isn't she beautiful?" Steven would ask adoringly. "I love how she looks like a Cheshire cat when she smiles."

I could tell by the knowing looks they exchanged, the passion they shared for literature and music, the playfulness in their intellectual banter, and the affection in their humor that they were crazy about each other.

"She's the smartest woman I've ever met," Steven told me.

What they didn't share was a love of God. Dierdre was Irish-American and Catholic. At one point when she was younger, she thought she wanted to be a nun. After college, she entered the novitiate.

"I didn't stay long, maybe a year," she told me years later, when I was in college. "I missed men too much."

After living in the convent, Dierdre quit practicing Catholicism formally, although she still went to Midnight Mass on Christmas Eve. She also remained in the church choir so she could sing Handel's *Messiah*.

"I still pray," she said. "I've never not believed in God."

Steven was academic and atheist. Yet, he seemed to admire Dierdre's deep spirituality. "Isn't it wonderful?" he'd say about her relationship with God. Was he envious? Hadn't he once had a relationship with God? As a youngster, he had studied to become a bar mitzvah because Grandma had insisted, although he never completed the ritual. Still, I wondered what he had done with all that he learned or if he had ever even cared about being Jewish. I thought he had. I thought that's why he wore the Moses pendant. But he had insisted that his love for Grandma Irene was his only reason for wearing it. I thought it had represented more: his link to Judaism and God. I wished it had been a link that we could share. But he no longer wore it. The link he seemed to care about most was to Dierdre.

On the few nights of the week that Steven wasn't at Dierdre's apartment, he was at his place in the Bronx. I loved hanging out in Steven's apartment, except for seeing the cockroaches scurry in all directions when he turned on the light. The living room was big and empty. Steven had no furniture other than beds. It didn't matter. His friends would come over with their guitars and we'd sing Bob Dylan and Joan Baez and Neil Young songs, sitting on the bare wood floor next to two jumbo plastic trashcans where they brewed beer. The day always ended too soon.

Mom would have dinner ready when Steven dropped me off, and sometimes she'd convince him to stay. The meals were tense and usually interrupted when Steven ordered me out of the room so he and Mom could talk. Within minutes, they'd be yelling at each other. Mom would be sobbing.

"You can't do this to Andrea! You're not being fair to her," Steven would say.

"Fair? How can you tell me what's fair? Has my life been fair?"

"I'm not worried about you, Mom! I'm worried about Andrea. She's twelve years old!"

"What am I supposed to DO?"

"I don't know. You might start by doing the laundry. Just figure it out!"

"I'm going to kill myself!"

"Fine. Just don't do it in front of Andrea."

After Steven left, I'd come out of my room to find Mom sitting at the table, our half-eaten dinner grown cold.

"Thanks a LOT," she'd say.

"What did I do?"

"You know what you did."

I'd clear the table and clean up the kitchen while Mom poured herself another drink. Then I'd make a beeline for bed.

"Okaaayyy," she'd tell me. "BE that way."

"What way?"

"You know what way."

If I didn't kiss Mom goodnight, she wouldn't speak to me in the morning, or sometimes for days. In fact, if I didn't thank her repeatedly for every little thing she bought or did for me, I'd get the silent treatment. If I dared to get angry or talk back to her, I'd risk the back of her hand across my face or any other place she could reach.

"You're spoiled rotten, you know that?" she growled one night during a particularly ferocious fight. She was leaning against the door to my room, trying to block my entry. The wall seemed to be holding her up. "You miserable thing. You're a rotten, miserable child. You ruined my life."

I wouldn't give her the satisfaction of seeing me cry. Instead, I'd envision the next bottle of booze that I planned to dump into the toilet. Then I'd push past her and shut the bedroom door.

By the next morning, with coffee instead of Scotch coursing through her veins, Mom would be a different person. Yet, she never apologized. "Parents don't apologize to their children," she used to say. She proclaimed it as if it were a law, just the way she had proclaimed that salt on a robin's tail would make it stand still. Except this proclamation had nothing to do with hope.

Mom wasn't big on forgiveness. Once she got angry, she stayed angry. Her anger lasted for days. She wouldn't speak to me. She wouldn't look at me. I would follow her from room to room, grabbing her sleeve, saying sorry repeatedly, and crying.

"You're always sorry," she'd scoff.

"But I am. I really am."

"I'm sorry too . . ." she'd snarl, sarcastically. "For you."

My pleas stoked her anger. No matter how heartfelt my apology was, she wouldn't accept it—not immediately, anyway. She'd merely consider it, the way she considered fruit before purchasing, turning it over in her hand slowly, looking for bruises.

I was almost a teenager, but still her rejection unnerved me. I was certain she hated me. I felt desperate for her to take me back into her heart. I couldn't eat. I couldn't sleep. I couldn't function in school. The more frantic I became, the more enraged she grew: "Stop crying or I'll give you something to cry about." Every bout of her anger felt like a siege. And during every siege, I'd resolve that she had stopped loving me, and that it was my fault. As the days passed, my desolation would grow. Resolved to earn back her affection, I would clean the house, brew fresh pots of coffee, and volunteer to run errands.

"Do you need anything at the store?"

"I could use cigarettes," she'd say, handing me a five-dollar bill. "Benson & Hedges 100s. In the blue and white package. Get a carton."

Of course, I had a plan. I would buy her something with the change. I would win her love. Roaming the aisles, I'd choose anything I could afford for a dollar.

"I got you a present," I said, handing her a brown bag containing a clear plastic makeup case. "You can exchange it if you want. I kept the receipt."

She opened the bag and pulled out the case. "Very nice," she said, dryly.

For weeks, the case sat on a dining room chair. Months later, I found it in one of her drawers, unused.

✦　✦　✦　✦　✦

By the time I started junior high in the fall of 1970, Mom was spending more and more time in bed. She began calling in sick to work. On weekends, she didn't emerge until lunchtime or later. I figured she was ill. I started taking care of the apartment. I'd spend Sunday mornings cleaning. I'd do the dishes. Sometimes I'd start dinner. I became good at roasting a chicken. I stopped hounding her about the dirty laundry and washed out my underwear in the bathroom sink without complaining.

Instead of replacing the burned-out mattress, Mom slept on the adjoining one. It was a ghostly sight, a king-size headboard anchoring two connected twin beds, one made up with sheets and a comforter and the other, burnt and bare. She didn't throw out the gutted mattress. She didn't even cover the hole. She just left it there, like an exposed and rotting corpse.

✦   ✦   ✦   ✦   ✦

On Labor Day weekend, Steven took me camping in Montreal. He packed his forest-green VW Bug with a Boy Scout pup tent, two sleeping bags, a Coleman stove, a cooler full of hot dogs and buns, and his cheap guitar. He picked me up early Saturday morning and we drove all day, talking, laughing and hunting for songs on the radio, and singing "Hey Jude."

"Hungry?"

Steven had just finished pitching our tent. He had reserved a space with a picnic table at a public campground. He took out the hot dogs and buns. It was the only food he'd brought and all we ate for the next three days. We spent the weekend talking, telling jokes, singing Beatles songs, and doing homework. Steven was on scholarship at Hunter. He had to keep his grades up.

"I've applied to graduate school at Washington University," he told me on Sunday morning, as we rolled up the sleeping bags.

"But you're already in graduate school."

"They offered me a teaching fellowship. I can get my Ph.D. for free."

"Where's Washington University?"

"St. Louis. Missouri."

"Missouri? Steven, it's so far away."

"I'm not in yet. Besides, it won't be forever."

✦   ✦   ✦   ✦   ✦

My relationship with Steven had many layers. On the Coney Island roller coaster, he was my brother. Listening to the *1812 Overture*, he was my mentor. Scolding me for back-talking Mom, he was my parent, and whisking me away from her, he was my savior. When he shared off-color jokes ("A man walked into a bar . . ." was the way some of his phone calls began), he was my friend and more: He made me feel like an equal, like the fifteen years between us didn't matter. Steven made me laugh, think, and work harder than anyone else did. He could be irreverent. He could be biting and intimidating. Sometimes he made me cry. Yet, I looked up to him like no one else. And I loved him more than anyone in the world. Once, I had idolized Roy, but it was Steven who saved me as life at home disintegrated.

I DISCOVERED THAT MOM HAD LOST HER JOB AT the Riviera Shore Club on a late autumn afternoon, when I came home from school and found her in her nightgown. She had just gotten out of bed.

"Did you call in sick again today?"

"No."

"Then why are you in your nightgown?"

"I'm getting up."

"Just now? Didn't you go to work today?"

"No."

"Why not?"

"They let me go."

"You mean you're fired?"

"I'm let go."

"Why?"

She didn't answer.

"Mom," I began, then hesitated. "Michael Shapiro's bar mitzvah is next Friday night. Ariel Schwartzman's bat mitzvah is the Friday after that. . . ." The list was long. "I need something to wear."

"We'll get you something to wear," she said, lighting a cigarette.

"I need shoes, too."

"You'll get shoes."

"I have to buy presents."

"You will."

"How? If you're not working ..."

She dragged hard on her cigarette, and blew a mouthful of gray smoke into the air.

"Don't worry, sweetie. Everything will be fine."

Later that week, while I did homework at the dining-room table, Mom walked in. She was dressed up.

"Did you get a job?" I asked, excited.

"No."

"Why are you all dressed up?"

"I had an appointment at Social Services."

"What's Social Services?"

"The Department of Social Services. We're going to be getting a little help."

"What kind of help?"

"Fnancial help."

"You mean welfare?"

"And food stamps." Her eyes welled up. "It's temporary, sweetie. Just until I get back on my feet."

I felt mortified, even though Mom was the only other person in the room. I would rather have died than anyone find out just how low our lives had sunk.

We found me a dress at E. J. Korvette, a lime-green and white gingham maxi with short puffy sleeves. I twirled around and around in the dressing room, admiring myself in the mirror.

"You better really love it," Mom cautioned, "because it's the only dress you're getting."

I wore that dress and a pair of white patent-leather Mary Janes to every single bar and bat mitzvah I attended.

On the Friday of my first bar mitzvah, I sat in the dining room all dressed up, waiting for Mom to drive me to the synagogue. It wasn't like her to be late and I had no idea where she was. I was starting to worry when I heard her fumbling with her keys. I opened the door and saw her hugging a heavy cardboard box crammed with canned food.

"Gimme a hand," she panted, heaving the box onto the kitchen table. I stared at the cans of corned beef hash, okra, succotash, spam. They were dusty and dented.

"This looks like the stuff our class just donated to the Thanksgiving food drive."

"It could be," Mom said.

"What do you mean? Where'd you get it?"

"Social Services."

"Mom! My friends donated these."

"Children from all over the county donated these cans. This is all temporary, I promise. Now, let's look at you. How pretty you look! We better get you to the synagogue!"

✦ ✦ ✦ ✦ ✦

At twelve years old, I had never been inside a synagogue. I had imagined that it would resemble a church, even though the only church I'd ever attended had been the makeshift one in my camp mess hall, and the only other ones that I'd ever seen had been in the movies. But instead of being a dimly lit space with stained-glass windows and dark wooden pews, the synagogue looked like a school auditorium, with a stage, rows of upholstered bucket seats, and enormous windows through which the last rays of autumn light streamed.

From the back where I sat with my friends, I watched Michael Shapiro hunch over the unfurled Torah scroll. I had never heard the word Torah or seen a Torah scroll. I had never met a rabbi or a cantor. And I had never heard anyone—other than my uncle El—chant Hebrew. I recognized the "brucha" from Shabbat dinners, but all the other prayers were gibberish to my ears. After three summers with Reenee and Estelle, I knew more Baptist hymns than Hebrew songs.

Because every bar or bat mitzvah was conducted entirely in Hebrew, I felt lost and bored. Michael sped through his parshah and haftarah. Listening to him captivated me as much as hearing my uncle drone from the Haggadah at Passover. From time to time, Michael would lose his place, and the rabbi would point to a spot on the scroll and whisper for him to slow down. Then Michael would look up at his parents, take a deep breath, and start reading again. I'd never seen anyone work so hard. No wonder my friends said I was lucky for not having to go to Hebrew school.

As I had done during family Seders, I spaced out. Now, instead of distracting myself with a visual tour of Aunt Margaret's beauty parlor, I envisioned the box of cans that Mom had brought home. As I looked around at my friends, I couldn't help but wonder, whose soup did we get? Whose tuna fish? Our teacher had emphasized that the Thanksgiving drive wasn't meant for getting rid of the old, unappealing food in the back of our pantries. But I knew we had inherited other people's castoffs. After all, who would choose to keep succotash or cocktail wieners? And who would part with a can of SpaghettiOs if there wasn't something wrong with it? Of course, some of those cans could have come from our cupboards, since I had also donated to the food drive, although I never would have surrendered SpaghettiOs.

Toward the end of the service, Michael's parents joined him on the bima. Together, they lit the Shabbat candles and sang blessings over wine and challah. Then, the rabbi placed his hands on Michael's head and gave him a special blessing. His parents hugged him and cried. When I get home, I told myself, I'm shoving those cans to the back of the cabinet where Mom won't see them. I'm never eating that food. Ever.

Throughout seventh grade, I spent half of every weekend at a bar or bat mitzvah, and at every one I felt more and more alienated and ashamed. I didn't know what had sent my mother into a tailspin. I didn't understand the chokehold of depression that had incapacitated her. I didn't care. All that mattered to me then was that she had lost her job, pitched us into poverty, and would be sloshed by the time I got home. The chasm between my Jewish friends and me yawned. Calling myself Jewish felt like a bigger lie than ever.

✦ ✦ ✦ ✦ ✦

Social Services was pushing Mom to take my father back to court. They said she shouldn't be getting public assistance because she technically had a husband who should have been paying child support and alimony. Mom couldn't afford a lawyer. Her caseworker contacted Milton.

I was nine the last time I'd seen Milton. In the three years that had passed, I had matured. Still, the thought of seeing him made me feel like a small, helpless child. Once again, Mom and I geared up for his visits. Week after week, we watched Sunday morning television and waited. He never came.

One Sunday morning in the winter of 1971, a man in an unfamiliar car pulled up. "Go see who that is," Mom directed, her voice jittery. I started drawing the venetian blinds. "Don't stand right in front of the window!" she whispered, as if the driver could hear us through the glass windows of our apartment and his car. "He'll see you!" Her eyes darted from the window to the phone to the door. "Crawl. On your hands and knees. Get right under the window. Then peek." The stranger drove away. Milton never showed up. And he never sent us any money. But Social Services did. Every month, Mom received a check that was supposed to cover our rent and living expenses: utilities, transportation, clothes—and entertainment. If there was enough money left over, we sometimes went out for a hamburger.

The monthly welfare check did not cover food. For that, Social Services distributed food stamps. Food stamps reminded me of Monopoly money. They came in booklets of one-, five, ten-, and twenty-dollar bills, and were bundled and stuffed into an envelope that Mom had to claim in person every month at the Social Services office. She tried to be matter-of-fact about using food stamps, but she always looked mortified. It simply wasn't easy to use food stamps nonchalantly. For one thing, Mom couldn't carry them around like regular money because the booklets were too thick for her wallet. For another thing, she had to keep the coupons intact until she was ready to use them. Because she never knew how many stamps she'd need on a given shopping trip, she toted the fat envelope with all the booklets around in her pocketbook.

It was impossible to use a food stamp surreptitiously. If the crinkling sound of the envelope's clear plastic window didn't draw attention, then the time it took Mom to find the right food stamp did. Torturously, she'd thumb through each booklet, hunting for the denominations she needed. The checkout line would grow as she painstakingly tore out each coupon along its perforated line. She had to sign each one before presenting it to the cashier, who would then scrutinize each signature with the one on her driver's license and compare her face with her photo ID. The longer it took Mom to pay, the more people would check their watches, tap their feet, drum their fingertips on the handles of their shopping carts, rifle through magazines, and exhale in audible irritation. Their impatience only flustered Mom more, which further hamstrung her ability to locate the stamps she needed and drew out the entire, excruciating ordeal even more.

The worst part was seeing Mom come up short. This almost always happened at the end of the month, when the food stamps started running out. Then, she'd have to comb through our tightly packed grocery bags, in front of annoyed yet pitying onlookers, and cherry-pick the foods we could do without. The cashier, aggravated by the lengthening queue of exasperated shoppers, would then pore over Mom's receipt and locate the items to subtract. All the while, I would stare at the floor, lest anyone I knew, especially from a recent bar or bat mitzvah, saw my face.

Mom was a genius at stretching a food stamp. Her ability to be culinarily creative on such a limited budget amazed me. Our staple was chicken, which she rarely prepared the same way twice. She either roasted, broiled, or fricasseed it, or turned it into paprikash, cacciatore, Shake 'N Bake, cutlets, or Parmesan. She could turn every part of a chicken into a delectable dish. Chicken necks and stomachs? She fricasseed them in oniony gravy and ladled them over rice. Chicken stomachs, also known as gizzards, were one of the most economical meals Mom made. She didn't buy them separately. She'd excavate them from every chicken she bought. She'd plunge her hand deep inside a bird's cold, squishy cavity and rummage for its intestines as if they were prizes in a box of Cracker Jack. Methodically, she'd wrap these innards in foil packets, label, and freeze them. My friends' freezers were full of ice cream and TV dinners. Ours was stuffed with chicken guts. When the freezer was full, she would defrost everything and create a mouth-watering Hungarian stew.

Chicken livers received separate attention. Mom saved and froze those, too. When she had enough, she'd sauté them in onions and chicken fat, and grind them in an old-fashioned food mill with hard-boiled eggs and a little more chicken fat, for chopped liver sandwiches.

Mom was a wizard with more than fowl. She could transform any cheap or unlikely piece of meat into a sumptuous meal. Calves' livers? She fried them alongside crispy, caramelized onions and paired them with her fluffy and buttery mashed potatoes. Beef hearts? I would have balked at the thought of eating those had I not tasted them, stewed until they were so tender that they fell apart, piled onto a heap of steaming egg noodles. Chicken backs and wings, turkey butts and necks, cow's tongue, and very occasionally, a thick, marbled slab of chuck steak that was more fat and bone than meat: I learned to love it all, until the leftovers showed up in my lunch. "What is that?" friends at the cafeteria table would ask. No matter how blasé my reply, there was no way to say, "Tongue sandwich" without making everyone gag.

Food stamps came with strict rules. Mom couldn't buy cigarettes or liquor with them. However, she devised a way to skirt this obstacle. When she had spent most of a food stamp, she'd receive real money as change. She'd save up the cash, and when she had enough, she'd buy cigarettes and a bottle of the cheapest vodka or Scotch she could find.

How had we come to this? What had happened to the elegant woman I'd watched with such admiration as she splashed on toilet water and slipped into high heels? Why couldn't this bright, skilled electrologist who had worked on Fifth Avenue and run her own business keep a job? When had she stopped pressing a salt shaker into my hand and sending me on robin hunts? How had she, who had once prayed over yahrzeit candles and believed that dipping challah in sugar would sweeten the New Year, become a welfare mom?

"Why don't you unpack your electrolysis table?" I asked one day. Mom was chopping onions. A slice of Wonder Bread, pressed between her lips, covered her chin like a surgical mask.

"The bread absorbs the onion vapors, so they won't burn my eyes," she explained.

She tossed the onions into a pool of bubbling chicken fat in a large pot on the stove. She added slabs of slimy beef heart and links of rubbery chicken gizzards, and covered the concoction with broth and paprika.

"It would fit in your bedroom," I persisted. "You could start seeing customers again. We could get off welfare." She removed the bread from her mouth and blamed the onions for making her cry.

I felt helpless in the face of her sadness.

"Would you ever consider dating?" I asked one afternoon in early spring as we unpacked groceries.

"Ohhh, I don't know. Maybe," she said half-heartedly as she arranged tomatoes in a bowl to ripen.

"Would you ever get married again?"

"If I met the right man, maybe."

I feared that the right man didn't exist for Mom. When I looked at her, I didn't see an open heart. I saw an open wound.

✦ ✦ ✦ ✦ ✦

Mom had few friends. She and Myrna, our neighbor in Forest Hills, had lost touch. During our first summer in Eastchester, Mom had tried reaching out to the next-door neighbor. It was a sweltering Saturday afternoon and she had seen the woman and her teenage daughter tanning in their backyard. Without saying anything, Mom made two ice-cream sundaes, complete with Hershey's syrup, Reddi-wip, sprinkles, and a maraschino cherry for each.

"Here," she said, handing me two bowls. "Bring these over to our neighbors."

"Mom, it's boiling outside. They're gonna melt."

"Just bring them over. Go."

"But, Mom, you don't even know them yet! Do they even know your name?"

"No. But this is a nice way of introducing myself."

"How do you know they even want ice-cream sundaes?"

"Who doesn't want ice cream on a hot day?"

I carried the sundaes out to the women. Their faces, hidden behind silver reflectors, glistened with baby oil. From their transistor radio, Herb Alpert and the Tijuana Brass crooned, "You say this guy, this guy's in love with you . . ."

"Ummm, excuse me," I stammered, holding the now-soupy sundaes. "These are from my mom."

The women bolted upright, looked at each other, then at the sundaes, and then at each other again.

"Oh, how nice," the mother said, handing one of the melted desserts to her daughter. "Please tell your mother thank you."

From Mom's bedroom window, I watched them finish the sundaes, shove the empty bowls under their chaise longues, and reposition their reflectors. The next day, I found the cleaned dishes outside our apartment door. There was no note.

Over the years, Mom attempted other friendships. When she had first started working at the beach club, she and Sybil became friends. Sybil was divorced and had a college-age daughter, Julie, and an Alaskan Malamute puppy. We often went to Sybil's house in New Rochelle for lunch. While she and Mom visited, Julie and I would walk the dog. Sybil gave me the clothes that Julie had outgrown. She gave us their old piano (even though Mom couldn't come up with money for lessons). It was Sybil who had told Mom about the free bus that took kids to Playland for Saturday morning ice-skating. She and Mom seemed close. But Sybil was also Mom's senior at work. She'd warned her that coming in late and continually calling in sick would jeopardize her job. And it did. Mom got fired, and their friendship ended.

For a while, also before she lost her job, Mom was friends with Grace, a divorced mother of two who worked at the beach club as well. Like Mom, Grace had an ex-husband who'd skipped out on paying child support. She and her twin girls lived with their two cats in a cramped fourth-floor walk-up in the Bronx. Because her daughters were my age, I didn't mind schlepping with Mom to the Bronx so she and Grace could visit. It also didn't hurt that Grace, who was Greek Orthodox, served freshly baked butter cookies and baklava. Yet, Mom never seemed quite as excited about spending time with Grace as she had with her old friend Myrna or even with Sybil. With Grace, Mom talked. With Myrna and Sybil, she kibitzed. In Grace's kitchen, Mom listened politely. In Myrna's and Sybil's, she elbowed her way into conversations, waving her arms and jabbing her fingers into the air. With Grace, Mom seemed reserved. With Myrna and Sybil, she seemed hamish.

Mom's oldest and dearest friend was Zelda. Like Mom, Zelda was a nonreligious Jew with Hungarian parents. They had met as twelve-year-olds growing up in Brooklyn and for a long time had been inseparable. Our families were so close that my brothers and I regarded Zelda and her husband, Bill, as our aunt and uncle and their kids as our cousins. Because they lived far out on Long Island, Mom and I didn't see them often. When we did drive out to their house, either from our apartment in Forest Hills or, later, from Eastchester, we'd spend the night. Visiting Zelda and Bill gave Mom and me a much-needed break from our lives. They took care of us. They cooked. They listened. They made us laugh. Best of all, they didn't drink. As long as we were there, Mom was sober.

No matter how infrequently Mom and Zelda saw each other, they were like an old married couple. They told the same stories, laughed at the same jokes, talked with the same inflections, and finished each other's sentences. They could've been the same person, except that Zelda lived contentedly in her family's embrace, while my mother fell asleep drunk most nights in front of the TV, her snores drowning out the signal that hummed when all the stations signed off.

In the spring of 1971, when I was halfway through seventh grade, Mom's brother Doug started calling from San Diego. He'd moved there with his family seven years earlier, right after Mom had sold the house in Rego Park. Then, his wife divorced him. She got their two kids. He got Pepe, their standard French poodle.

Doug was campaigning for us to move to San Diego. He said life was easier there and less expensive than New York. "Why would you want to spend another winter freezing in New York when you could be here, walking on the beach?" he asked. He wanted us to live near him. He said it would be good for Mom, especially since she still wasn't speaking to Aunt Lila.

Because he forgot about the three-hour time difference, Doug often called in the middle of the night. The phone, which sat on Mom's night table, woke up both of us. I had begun sleepwalking and crawling into bed next to her. I had also begun to wet my bed and would slip under her sheets when mine were soaked in urine. The sleepwalking was sort of funny, but the bedwetting was humiliating. Looking back, I think both problems arose from my deep need to have Mom care for me as if I were an infant. But she wanted no part of it.

Her single, unburned mattress could not accommodate both of us. Irked at being awakened, she would tug me out of her bed and walk me back to mine.

Now half-asleep, I heard her say, "Doug, it's three o'clock in the morning." She did little talking after that. She scrounged in the dark for a cigarette and then struck a match. I smelled the smoke.

"I don't know what to do, Doug," she said. "I just don't know what to do." They stayed on the phone until the sky turned light and the birds started chirping.

✦ ✦ ✦ ✦ ✦

Throughout the spring Doug called, presenting different reasons why our lives would be better in San Diego. He was used to canvassing. He made his living as a door-to-door salesman, trying to persuade homeowners to buy fake-stone siding. Convincing Mom to move to California was just another sales pitch.

"Have you given it any more thought, Evy?"

"I'm thinking about it, Doug."

"I'm doing well. Business is good. I can take care of you and Andrea. Just until you get back on your feet."

"It's not so easy, Doug. Andrea is very happy here. She's finally settled in. She likes her school. She has friends."

"The schools are great out here. Andrea will make new friends. Plus, she'll be twenty minutes away from the beach. And you'll find work. There are plenty of jobs out here. What else are you going to do, live on welfare for the rest of your life?"

"I'm thinking, Doug. Really. I'm thinking."

The thought of moving to California was beginning to excite me. I loved the snow. But I loved the ocean more. Plus, I couldn't resist the fantasy of living among palm trees and movie stars.

"Are we going to move, Mom?" I asked one early morning after she'd gotten off the phone with Doug.

"I don't know. Maybe."

"It would be so cool to live near the beach! And to see movie stars!"

"We'll see."

✦   ✦   ✦   ✦   ✦

Dreams of California preoccupied me that spring. As Mom deteriorated, spending swaths of time in bed, drinking and sleeping away the days, I took solace in the thought of leaving behind what our life had become. I wasn't thinking about how sad it would be to say good-bye to Celeste or how scary to start a new school again. I simply wanted an escape.

This is what I was thinking about one afternoon in March, shortly after my thirteenth birthday. I was headed to the drugstore to buy Mom cigarettes when something hard struck the middle of my back. I turned and saw half a dozen greaser girls in black leather jackets appear from behind the last filthy mound of snow in the shopping center parking lot.

"Hey, FAT girl!" they yelled, lobbing me with chunks of sooty ice.

I ran into Woolworth's, and hid in the pay-phone booth at the back of the store. When I finally stepped back outside, they had gone.

The next day at school, I came upon them, congregated in the stairwell, pretending to flick their unlit cigarettes. They looked identical in their black mini-skirts, fishnet stockings, boots, and cropped leather jackets, their eyes edged in heavy black liner and barely visible behind their bangs.

"You won't be so lucky next time," the ringleader jeered as I tried to walk past. Around her neck glimmered a silver chain bearing a small cross.

I had always regarded religious symbols as signs of closeness to God, and closeness to God as a commitment to being decent. How could this girl be so wicked and be close to God? It felt as contradictory as having a jobless, alcoholic, welfare mom and being Jewish. Of course, appearances revealed nothing about the depth of anyone's faith or spiritual goals. But I had yet to learn that important truth. The cross slipped beneath the greaser's leather jacket.

"What are you staring at?" she asked, smirking.

I averted my eyes and hurried away.

✦   ✦   ✦   ✦   ✦

In the summer of 1971, everyone in our family moved away. Mom's aunts and uncles—Margaret, El, Vera, and Yawshee—all went to Florida. Roy moved to Los Angeles to take a job in the financial industry. We hadn't seen much of him since he'd left the navy and finished college. By then, I was long accustomed to his absence from my life. But it was losing Steven that broke my heart. He married Dierdre.

I should have been happy for him. He was twenty-eight years old and had spent half his life yoked to Mom, who had increasingly leaned on him for financial help. Before we left Forest Hills, he'd spent weeks preparing our apartment in Eastchester, spackling and painting until late every evening, getting up early the next day for his job shipping medical periodicals, and then returning to Eastchester to paint some more. Now, he was finally free. And he was leaving me behind.

The wedding took place in North Salem, New York, not far from Camp Spruce, on the back lawn of the family estate of Dierdre's best college friend. It was June 12, 1971, the same day that Tricia Nixon married Edward Cox on national television. The president's daughter looked like a porcelain doll, petite and blond in a white lace gown and veil. My soon-to-be sister-in-law wore a light brown, calf-length dress with purple paisley print that matched the purple irises in her arms and the purple ribbon around her straw-colored, wide-brimmed hat. The hat and her big round glasses took up half her face. She looked blissful as she walked toward Steven, who wore brown slacks, a white shirt, cream blazer, and red tie. I wore the stupid green and white gingham maxi dress and white patent-leather Mary Janes that I'd worn to every bar and bat mitzvah that year. Roy wore a dark suit. I don't remember what Mom wore. I didn't see her for most of the wedding. I stayed with Roy, watching the ceremony from a balcony on the side of the house where we could best see over the crowd of guests. There's a photo of us that someone took—Roy with a camera in his hand and me, chewing on a fingernail and crying.

The ceremony took only a few minutes. A portly, distracted-looking justice of the peace muttered some words. He did not mention God. I shouldn't have been surprised. Neither Steven nor Dierdre had wanted a religious wedding. Mom didn't seem to care, although she had cautioned Steven that marrying a non-Jew could cause complications if he and Dierdre ever decided to have children. My brother and his bride exchanged rings and a short kiss. They beamed, as did the crowd of friends who encircled them and then closed in, making them disappear.

A few weeks later, Steven and Dierdre moved to St. Louis.

"What am I going to do without you?" I said, not even attempting to squelch my sobs.

"You'll do fine. Keep busy. Work hard in school. Stay out of Mom's hair. And remember, I'm just a phone call away."

I had a sinking feeling he'd be farther away than that.

✦ ✦ ✦ ✦ ✦

The end of seventh grade brought some relief—no more bar or bat mitzvahs. I was still dumping liquor down the toilet, and

Mom was still buying more. I couldn't wait to get back to camp. This summer, I'd be a junior counselor. I'd see Reenee and Estelle, counsel more homesick campers, and sing in church on Sunday mornings.

"Sweetie, I'm afraid you won't be able to go to camp this summer," Mom said when I told her that I'd outgrown my camp clothes.

"Why not?"

"We're moving."

"Moving? Again? Where?"

"California."

✦　✦　✦　✦　✦

"You're moving to California?" Celeste shrieked, as we cleaned out our lockers.

"Who's moving to California?" Ariel Schwartzman asked.

"Andrea's moving to California?" The news echoed through the hallway.

"Oh, my God, California? You're so lucky!" Leslie Gold said. "That's where all the movie stars live!"

"You can go to Disneyland all the time!"

"They have palm trees with coconuts!"

"And beaches!"

"You can tan all year long because it never rains there!"

My friends crowded around me. "When are you leaving? Where are you going to live? Do you know the name of your new school? Can you surf? Are you going to learn? We have to have a going-away party!"

For as long as I had known them, I had wanted their houses and clothes, their two-parent families, their piano lessons and summer vacations, their synagogue memberships, and even their Hebrew homework. I had wanted their lives. Now, they wanted something I had. I would never have believed that anyone could want my life. As I anticipated once again leaving good friends for an unknown place, this time clear across the country, I wasn't sure why anyone would.

✦ ✦ ✦ ✦ ✦

Tall brown fiberboard barrels filled our dining room that summer. There was much that we couldn't take with us to San Diego because we'd be living with Doug until Mom started working and could afford our own place. Storage was expensive, so she had to be selective about what to bring. She chose the china and silver, linens, our only two living-room chairs, a couple of shade-less table lamps, the breakfront, and her bedroom furniture. She put the filthy lampshades in the garbage. She finally trashed her charred mattress, as well as the good ones. "We'll buy brand-new beds in California!" It had been a long time since she'd sounded so hopeful.

Four years had passed since we'd moved to Eastchester. I had a circle of close friends. I had Celeste. I had a new junior high that I loved, greasers aside. Yet, here I was again, helping Mom wrap dishes in sheets of *The New York Times* and nesting each bundle inside a barrel, in between towels and layers of straw. Books, records, and pictures went inside giant cardboard boxes. Mom gave away everything else.

"Can I look at pictures one more time before we pack them up?" I asked.

"Quickly," she said. "I want to close up the box."

I brought her wedding album to my room. We hadn't packed the records yet, so I put on After the Gold Rush. Steven had bought me the album for my thirteenth birthday. Thanks to him, I had a pretty good record collection with *Songs of Leonard Cohen*; Joni Mitchell's *Song to a Seagull*; Crosby, Stills, Nash, and Young's *Déjà Vu*; and Johnny Cash's *At Folsom Prison*.

"I was lying in a burned-out basement, with the full moon in my eyes," Neil Young sang as I flipped through pictures from Mom's wedding to Milton.

I stopped at the first photograph of them together and removed it from its clear plastic sheath. With the tip of my finger, I drew an imaginary line between them. We are moving to California, Milton Kott. We are moving far away from you. Mom won't have to be afraid anymore. And I'll never have to see your ugly face again, or listen to your stupid jokes, or spend another Sunday morning waiting for you to show up. Our life is going to be so much better.

I grabbed a pair of scissors and snipped along the invisible line, severing my parents and watching my father fall to the floor. Page by page, I excised him. Then, I slipped each butchered picture back into its sleeve and returned the album to the box for Mom to pack.

PART FOUR:

SAN DIEGO, 1971

THE AMERICAN AIRLINES 747 WAS MASSIVE.
A column of seats, three abreast, ran down either side of
the cabin. Down the center ran a column of four seats with an
aisle on each side. Just beyond the nose of the plane, a spiral
staircase coiled up through the ceiling to a second-floor lounge.

"Can we go upstairs?" I asked Mom, thrilled to be on a
double-decker airplane.

"Let's find our seats first."

We didn't have to look far. We were assigned to the roomy
section at the front of the plane that was curtained off from the
rest of the cabin. Six pairs of extra-wide, reclining seats flanked
both sides of a wide aisle, where passengers were reading
newspapers and sipping champagne. I'd only ever sat in coach,
and we would have sat there now, had Mom bought our tickets.
But Uncle Doug had paid for us to fly first-class.

"As long as you gals are moving all the way across the
country, you might as well do it in style," he'd said. I felt like
royalty.

Mom was weepy. Zelda had assured her that moving to
California would give her the fresh start she needed, even

though they'd both spent a good part of our last barbecue crying.

"Aren't you excited?" I'd prodded during our final weeks in Eastchester, trying to inject Mom with the excitement I was feeling about the new life I'd envisioned on a beach, among movie stars. But once I'd started saying good-bye to my friends, my elation began to fizzle. Would I ever find someone like Celeste? We had vowed to remain best friends. But now I would be the new kid in school all over again. The enormity of our move was hitting me.

Saying good-bye to Steven was the worst part. Even if Mom and I weren't moving to California, we'd be losing Steven, who was moving to St. Louis with Dierdre. The last time we had dinner together, Mom kept dabbing her eyes with a napkin. I couldn't eat.

"I miss you already," I said to Steven, surrendering to tears.

"I miss you, too, cookie. But we'll talk on the phone."

"It won't be the same."

"It's all we got, kiddo."

Mom had explained that we'd be living with Doug until she got back on her feet. Then we'd get a place of our own.

"Who'll buy food?"

"Doug."

"Who'll buy me clothes for school?"

"Don't worry, sweetie, you'll have new clothes," Mom had assured me. "Doug will take care of us."

Strapped into my window seat, I worried about Siam. The vet had given us medicine to make him sleep and Mom had bought a cat carrier. But we couldn't bring it into the cabin.

"Where are they taking him?" I'd asked at Kennedy Airport when we checked our bags.

"They're putting him below, with the luggage."

"With the luggage? No one can hear him cry down there! What if he needs me?"

"He's going to be fine, sweetie. He'll sleep the whole way."

I cringed at the thought of my cat being stowed for six or more hours in the belly of the jet. Being on a tree limb had made him hysterical. How would he survive the roar of engines and the smell of fumes? Siam and our suitcases were all that we had checked. In a week, a moving van would deliver to storage our few pieces of furniture and our brown barrels.

Once we were airborne, the stewardesses began collecting champagne glasses and serving lunch. A smiling woman who looked like a fashion model handed me a plate with a thick slab of filet mignon and a steaming baked potato with sour cream. I'd never even heard of filet mignon, having only ever eaten chicken, fricasseed organ meats, and fat-streaked chuck steak. I stared at my lunch like it was gold, savoring every succulent bite and licking my plate clean. I loved our new life so far.

✦　✦　✦　✦　✦

Doug met us at the airport. "Heyyy, you're here!" he said, giving Mom a hug. I couldn't remember ever having met my uncle. Like Mom and me, he was short and stocky. The buttons of his white shirt strained just above his belt buckle. The belt must have been there for decoration because it didn't seem to be holding up his tan slacks. They were much too tight to fall down. His eyes looked small and beady against his round fleshy face, which grew a second chin when he smiled. He combed his thin gray hair from one side of his balding head to the other. He wore light-brown, woven leather loafers with tassels that flopped like fish out of water when he walked, and a gold pinkie ring with a diamond chip the size of a sesame seed. He gave me a squeeze. I smelled like aftershave for the rest of the day.

Mom and I slid onto the front seat of Doug's gold Lincoln Continental. I sat by the door, with the cat carrier between my feet. Siam was splayed out in a drug-laced stupor. On the backseat were several big black books containing samples of the fake-stone siding that Doug peddled for a living. Strewn around the books were at least a dozen empty Fudgsicle boxes. Curled up in a corner of the seat was Pepe the poodle.

"I'm really not supposed to be driving," Doug said, raising his pants leg to reveal the cast on his left foot. "Good thing this car has cruise control."

The air-conditioned Lincoln smelled of new leather and old dog. As we pulled away from the airport, I started looking for movie stars. All I saw were navy ships in the bay and an airstrip with steel-gray military airplanes.

"Where are the movie stars?" I asked. "Where's the Walk of Fame?"

"There are no movie stars here, doll," Doug said as he shifted his leaden left foot. "You're thinking of Hollywood. About two hours north of here, in L.A. This is San Diego. Navy town. Lots of sailors. Great beaches."

"What about the palm trees?" I persisted, disappointed at the stubby palms that looked like upside-down pineapples. "Why don't they have coconuts?"

"Florida palms have coconuts, honey. San Diego palms are just short and fat."

I put my head on Mom's shoulder.

"You gals hungry?"

"Actually, we just ate, Doug," Mom said. "They served a lovely lunch on the plane. We're stuffed."

"We had steak!" I piped in.

"Well, I'm taking you gals out anyway."

"Doug, we're really not—"

"Evyyy, I'm taking you and Andrea out to lunch!"

We drove along Mission Bay to a seafood restaurant that looked out onto the water. A floor-to-ceiling fish tank separated the waiting area from the dining room. Starched white cloths covered the tables. Although it was only one in the afternoon, the restaurant was dim. Flickering tealights on the tables gave the room a gentle glow. Doug asked the maître d for a window table so we could see the bay. I suddenly felt very tired. We'd gotten up early and had been traveling all day.

"Hey, I bet you gals have never had abalone. It's a San Diego delicacy. Andrea, go look at the abalone in the fish tank."

"Doug," Mom began, "this is so sweet of you, but—"

"Oh, you have to try the seafood omelet. Evy, I'm telling you, it's got shrimp and crabmeat . . ."

"Doug, we really—"

"Just TRY it!" he barked.

My stomach rolled over. Does he always yell like this?

Doug ordered seafood omelets for Mom and me, and fried abalone for himself. Then he began explaining how he had broken his foot.

"I'm talking to a customer . . . well, a prospect," he said, slathering butter on a breadstick and putting half of it into his mouth. "I've got this guy sold on a nice pale pink stone and I'm closing in on the deal." He tore off a heel of sourdough bread while he munched on the breadstick. "I'm telling him how classy his house is gonna look with this new stone siding. I don't wanna lose eye contact with him, see, because once you lose eye contact, you lose the deal. So, I'm backing away from his house and I'm keeping my eyes on him and boom! I fall right off the damn curb." He shoved the bread into his mouth. "You'd think the guy would've warned me. And I didn't even make the sale."

The food arrived. I gagged at the smell of seafood and eggs. I took a few bites, then put my head on Mom's lap and closed my eyes. I overheard Doug telling her how hard it had been to work with the cast on his foot.

"I'm a little behind this month," he said. I heard him suck his teeth in between sentences.

"What do you mean, 'behind'?"

"I mean, I still owe last month's alimony and child support. Plus, I have to make up a payment on the Lincoln. It's leased. Then there's the apartment. And the rented furniture . . ."

"Doug, I had no idea. You said—"

"I know what I said, Evy. And all of it was true, until I broke my damn foot."

"So, what should we do?"

"You'll do exactly what we said you were gonna do. You and Andrea will live with me until you get back on your feet. It'll be fine. I'm still working. Money's just gonna be a little tight, that's all."

The waitress packed our uneaten omelets in Styrofoam containers. Back in the car, Doug fed Pepe a couple of breadsticks that he'd sneaked into his pocket. Siam slept. Mission Bay disappeared as we headed toward the freeway. The Lincoln felt like a plane before takeoff, picking up speed until it was flying at eighty miles per hour, skating over bumps in the road as the red-roofed houses, green scrub grass, blue sky, and dumpy palm trees became a passing blur.

Fifteen minutes later we were in La Mesa, a small town about twenty miles north of Tijuana, Mexico. La Mesa was a largely blue-collar, working-class town with small ranch houses, a Jack in the Box and a Taco Bell, an abundance of active and retired navy personnel, and of long-blond-haired, shirtless surfers in baggy swim trunks who darted around in two-seater Datsun pickups with their boards strapped on top. There was not a single synagogue.

"La Jolla has a nice synagogue," Doug noted about the wealthy beach enclave. "Pricey as hell there, though."

I felt no need to live anywhere near a synagogue. I'd actually felt relieved to learn that the closest Jewish community was twenty minutes away.

Doug turned into a sprawling complex of terra-cotta garden apartments with cement patios and landscaped cacti.

"There's a pool," he announced.

"There IS?" I screeched. "Mom, can I swim right now?"

"Hold on, hold on! Let's get out of the car first!" she said.

As soon as we entered Doug's dreary apartment, my heart sank. It had low plaster ceilings and brownish indoor-outdoor carpeting. The tables and chairs reminded me of the furniture I'd seen in the waiting room of the garage where Mom had once had the Falcon fixed.

"The apartment came furnished," Doug apologized.

A few slivers of natural light peeked in through the sliding-glass door that led to the patio and through the bedroom windows, all of which were covered by white, pleated polyester drapes. Doug claimed the room with the queen-size bed. Mom and I got the room with the twin beds.

I dug out my bathing suit. "Now can I go to the pool?"

The pool was my piece of heaven. For hours every day that summer, I swam, tanned, and wrote letters to friends in New York. Mom would lie on a chaise longue, smoking or sleeping.

With neither car nor cash, we had little to do. The apartment complex wasn't near any stores. The only way we could go grocery shopping during the week while Doug worked was to take the bus—if he gave us money—and lug home what we could. As a result, the refrigerator wasn't fully stocked most of the time. At least there was no booze in the house. Doug didn't drink and Mom wouldn't ask him to buy her Scotch. Only when he took us to dinner would she have a cocktail. It was the only good thing about living with him.

The last time I remembered Mom not drinking for any significant stretch of time was during her bout with mono when I was seven. Now, at thirteen, I was seeing her sober for the first time in years. She didn't seem to struggle without booze; in fact, she seemed less morose and reactive. I prayed it would last.

✦   ✦   ✦   ✦   ✦

Doug was a night owl. He started working late in the morning, got home late, and stayed up late. He thought nothing of going food shopping at eleven p.m. or later.

"C'mon, Evy, I'll run us down to Safeway so we can pick up a few things."

"It's nearly midnight, Doug."

"So? They're open twenty-four hours."

Food shopping had always topped my list of least-liked activities, but with Doug it became abhorrent. Without fail, he would get hungry in the store. He'd cruise the aisles, tossing back fistfuls of Planter's peanuts or demolishing a box of Fudgsicles before checking out.

"Did you pay for those yet?" I'd ask, trying to mask my embarrassment with incredulity.

"Don't worry," he'd say with a full mouth, ignoring my snarkiness. "I'll pay at the counter."

Doug had two favorite restaurants: an all-you-can-eat Swedish smorgasbord where he filled his plate three times, and a Chinese restaurant where he'd met a waitress named Wendy whom he occasionally dated. Dating overstated it. He'd sit in the restaurant until closing and wait for Wendy to finish working. Then they'd go out.

"You gotta meet this gal, Evy," I heard him tell Mom one morning after he'd returned home. "She's something else."

The most difficult part of going out to dinner with Doug was waiting for him to get home. He'd call at six p.m., say that he was on his way, and then not arrive before nine. By then, I'd stuffed myself on crackers and jelly.

"Doug, we've been waiting . . ." Mom said one night.

"I've been working, Evelyn," he said, hobbling across the living room, his cast making a dull thud on the carpet. "I'm trying to drum up business. I've got to make more money if I'm going to support you and Andrea. So, whaddya gals feel like eating?"

"Doug, it's after ten. Why don't I just scramble some eggs or make some tuna fish?"

"Evelyn, I've been busting my ass all day, looking forward to a nice meal. Let's go out. You can have a drink."

"We're tired, Doug. It's too late for us."

"Let's do Chinese. C'mon, Evy. A cocktail would do you good."

The restaurant was open but nearly empty. Doug ordered a Shirley Temple for me and a Scotch on the rocks for Mom. A petite Chinese woman in a short black skirt and white blouse with a plunging neckline delivered our drinks. She wore her long black hair loose and brushed back, away from her face. Cerulean blue shadow covered her eyelids.

"Heyyy, Wendeeee," Doug crooned, his eyes moving from her face to her cleavage back to her face. "This is my sister Evelyn and my niece, Andrea. They just moved here from New York. I'm showing them the town."

"Nice to meet you," Wendy said demurely, smiling.

"Sooo, you busy later?" Doug asked. I averted my eyes. I knew I was someplace I didn't belong.

Sometime after eleven, our food came. Mom rested her chin in her palm, struggling to stay awake. Doug talked and ate. "Evelyn, you gotta try some of this moo goo gai pan." It was the last thing I heard before falling asleep in her lap.

Doug spent his days driving around San Diego. He'd pick a neighborhood, park the Lincoln, and walk from house to house, hauling a couple of big black books full of stone siding samples and ringing doorbells. He'd bring Pepe with him to keep people interested. He'd say, "Hey, I bet you've never seen a talking dog!" People were so curious that even if they didn't want the siding, they'd let Doug stay so they could hear the poodle talk. The dog didn't actually talk, of course. But somehow Doug managed to coax out of him these heartbreaking guttural sounds. "Pepe, say 'Happy birthday,'" Doug would command, and Pepe would open and close his mouth to produce four low, rhythmic groans, arr-rarr-RARR-rarr. "Pepe, say 'I love you.'" And Pepe would flap his jaws and say, arr-RARR-rarr. As a finale, Doug would balance a piece of American cheese on Pepe's nose. "Leeeave it, leeeave it," he'd instruct, while the poodle trembled and drooled. "Wait, wait, wait, aaand GO!" Then Pepe would fling the cheese off his nose like a circus seal and snap it up mid-air. People loved this act, but most of the time they didn't buy any siding.

Doug complained that business was slow. "It hasn't been easy canvassing with this goddamned cast on my foot for the past two months," he'd gripe. Sometimes he'd quit work early, sit in his Lincoln with Pepe, and eat an entire box of Fudgsicles, to satisfy his insatiable craving for chocolate. Because he was hypoglycemic, the sugar would knock him out, and he'd sleep in his car until dinnertime. Then he'd wake up, drive to a new neighborhood, and ring more doorbells until it got too late to bother anyone. It seemed like a terrible way to make a living and made it nearly impossible for him to take care of himself, let alone my mother and me.

The thrill of moving to California, of waking up to warm sunshine every day, and having a pool outside my door quickly waned. With no car or money, Mom and I had nowhere to hang out but the pool, or the apartment, where we were stuck together. I started missing my friends, and Mom, who could not numb herself with alcohol whenever she wanted, started smoking more, which elicited angry lectures from Doug, an ex-smoker and self-anointed expert on the evils of tobacco.

My mother dancing with her husband, Leslie Neuwirth, around 1940

My mother, around age twenty

My mother and Leslie with my brothers Steven (left), around age five, and Roy, around age six and a half

Mom and Grandma Irene in 1956, on the day Mom married Milton Kott

Mom in Miami, early 1950s

Mom, Roy, and me at five months, in August 1958

*Grandma Irene
and me in Miami,
sometime around
1960*

*Roy, Mom, Steven,
and me in Rego Park,
Queens, 1963*

*Saying good-bye to Roy,
with Steven, in 1963*

*My brother Roy in
his early twenties
aboard a U.S. Navy
aircraft carrier*

*Steven and me,
around 1964*

*Roy, Mom,
Steven, and
me in 1963*

Roy and me in Norfolk, Virginia, 1966—with my first real Christmas tree

Mom visiting me at Camp Spruce, around 1968.

Steven and me at Camp Spruce.

Mom, shortly after we moved to La Mesa in San Diego, early 1970s

Mom and me at the pool in La Mesa

Me at around age fourteen

Me, age sixteen, after winning first place in impromptu speaking at my first speech tournament

Me, around age seventeen, in San Diego

Me, age eighteen, in La Mesa

BRANDEIS UNIVERSITY FOOD SERVICES

3 Meals Per Day

Andrea Kott

STUDENTS SIGNATURE

VOID IF MARRED OR DEFACED.

Present to checker for meal service
Coupons are not transferable and mus
remain in the book until removed b
the checker.

Student must have coupon book a
each meal. Coupons are valid only o

STUDENTS N

*My meal
ticket book
from Brandeis
University,
1976*

*Steven in St. Louis,
early 1970s*

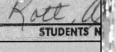

THE
JERSEY
JOURNAL

Name
ANDREA KOTT

Signature
Andrea Kott

*My first press ID,
1987*

My press ID for the Stamford Advocate, 1988

Mom and me in 1990 in New Rochelle, New York

Mom in Florida, 1990

Steven and me in New York City in 1992

Roy (left) and Steven with me on my wedding day, October 3, 1993

Erik and me on Cape Cod around 1997

*Our family—Sophie,
me, Erik, and Ben—
Brooklyn, New York,
2019*

My new, exciting life was turning tedious and tense. I felt trapped. I couldn't wait for school to start.

In September 1971, I began eighth grade at Parkway Junior High. The school was a constellation of single-level, multicolored glass and steel buildings that were connected by concrete walkways. Lockers were outside, beneath an overhang that shielded us from rain. The quad, a sheltered pavilion with lunch tables and benches, was outside, too. Palm trees and flowering cacti dotted the campus. Parkway made Eastchester Junior High look like a red-brick fortress.

Although I'd changed schools several times over the years, walking into a new classroom and locating a seat in a crowd of unfamiliar faces hadn't gotten any easier. It was especially difficult being the only chubby, curly-brown-haired thirteen-year-old in a class of slender, blond, blue-eyed peers. At least no one had to know that I was Jewish.

Rosh Hashanah and Yom Kippur were approaching but I had no interest in celebrating either. Seven years had passed since Mom and I had celebrated the High Holidays and the rituals we'd once observed were no longer part of our life. What's more, the High Holidays were no longer the signposts of fall that they had been in New York. In La Mesa, fall blew in with scorching Santa Ana winds. There was no crisp autumn air or jumping into piles of crunchy leaves, just blistering heat that turned the outdoors into an oven and sparked wildfires that peppered the sky with ash. There were also no challah, yahrzeit candles, or other High Holiday items in our new local supermarket, which felt like a good omen, an affirmation of my decision to bury my Jewishness. In La Mesa, fall would come and go unnoticed, and I'd blend in. No Jews, no pressure

To my surprise, the kids at school welcomed me warmly and, by the end of my first week, a group of girls had taken me into their circle. They'd known each other all their lives, having grown up in the same neighborhood of small ranch houses, wooden rail fences, and American flags, in close-knit families with dads who'd served in the navy and now worked construction or fixed cars, and moms who made Halloween costumes and cupcakes. No one knew about bat mitzvahs or greasers in black leather jackets. No one took tennis lessons or had ever been to sleepaway camp. During school breaks, families packed their campers and headed to the desert.

Being from New York made me a curiosity.

"So, what are you?" a smiley, big-toothed girl named Cindy asked. I feigned bafflement at her question. "You know, what religion are you?"

"Jewish." Why did she need to know? I felt cornered, busted.

"You're Jewish?" I was the only Jewish kid in the school and the only Jew some of them had ever met. "What's that like, being Jewish?" Cindy hammered away. She was a San Diego native, but for some reason spoke with a Southern drawl. "Don't y'all have to eat that funny flat bread? And y'all can't have cheeseburgers, right?" I explained that I wasn't Kosher or observant in any way. Nevertheless, she and everyone else who invited me to their home introduced me as "Andrea from New York who's Jewish!"

"I was born Jewish," I'd add quickly. "But I'm really nothing."

My new friends weren't churchgoers or religious, so I didn't understand why many of them wore gold or silver crucifixes. I also didn't understand the slight discomfort I felt whenever I spied these symbols around their necks. I felt no such discomfort when they invited me to their Christmas-tree-decorating and Secret Santa parties. I resumed my campaign for a Christmas tree but Mom would not relent, although she encouraged me to go caroling and participate in gift exchanges, which I did, happily. After a while, my Jewishness stopped being a novelty. It didn't matter to anyone, including me. At least that's what I told myself.

✦ ✦ ✦ ✦ ✦

We'd been living with Doug for less than six months when he and Mom began fighting. Mom would get angry with him for coming home late after promising to take us to dinner. He would get angry with her for depending on him so heavily, even though he had encouraged her to postpone job hunting until she felt emotionally stronger, and promised to support us.

"You could cook dinner here, you know," he snapped one night. I was in bed, trying to sleep after a meal of tuna fish and Saltines.

"By Wednesday there's very little food in this house, Doug."

"So, go shopping, Evelyn! I give you money, don't I? What's the big deal?"

"It's difficult to carry groceries on the BUS."

"Jesus, Evy. Do I have to do everything for you? Isn't my life hard enough? Have you even begun to think about getting a job and your own place?"

"You said to take my time! You said you would help me get back on my feet!"

"I can't help you forever, kiddo. Besides, Andrea's in school now. You gals get up early. You eat early. I get up late. I eat late. It's not working out."

"I don't have a job, Doug. I don't have a car."

"It's been six months, Evy. It's time you started looking. By the way, California has excellent social services. Better than New York."

"You mean welfare?"

"Just until you find work."

"What about your promise? You said when we moved out here—"

"I know what I said! That was before I broke my foot and couldn't work and got into a hole trying to support the three of us, on top of the alimony I have to pay."

I heard Mom open the sliding-glass door to the patio.

"I'll tell you one thing," Doug called to her from the living room. "Being on welfare might force you to finally quit smoking. I don't know how you've afforded those cancer sticks all these years."

The sliding door opened and closed again. "In the morning, I'll drive you down to Social Services."

"Thanks a lot, Doug. Thanks a damn lot."

The honeymoon was over. Mom and I needed a place of our own.

✦ ✦ ✦ ✦ ✦

A few months into the school year, a friend told me about a one-bedroom apartment for rent in her complex. The next day, Doug drove us over to meet the apartment manager, Mrs. Larson.

"It's just one bedroom," she told Mom.

"I understand."

"One bedroom for the two of you."

"Yes, I know."

"It's small," Mrs. Larson continued. "But it has a lovely garden out front. And your daughter will be able to walk to school. Or ride a bike. And there's a pool."

The tiny garden apartment was one of five in a two-story beige stucco building. Our unit was on the lower level. It shared a wall with the apartment next door where two college students lived. I could hear them talking and laughing. The ceiling had exposed beams, the walls were white, and the carpet a muddy brown.

"How much?" Mom asked.

"One twenty-five a month," Mrs. Larson said. "You pay for heat and electric. I pay for water. I live across the street. You can walk the rent over. Slip it under my door."

"When can we move in?"
"Whenever you want."
We moved in the next day.

✦ ✦ ✦ ✦ ✦

The few pieces of furniture that we had brought from Eastchester filled the space fast. Mom wouldn't hang pictures because she was afraid of damaging the walls and losing her deposit. The living room looked barren. We didn't even have a coffee table. I salvaged a plank of black wood and four cinder blocks from a grassy lot behind the building and brought them inside after scraping off layers of caked dirt and spiderwebs. I placed two blocks on the floor at either end of our living room window. I laid the plank of wood on top and covered it with one of Mom's lace runners. At one end of the table, I put one of our shadeless lamps and at the other I put a half-dead African violet that I'd found on clearance at the supermarket.

Making the bedroom habitable wouldn't be as easy. We had no beds—or money to buy any: Mom had junked the mattress she'd burned, as well as our other ones, certain that once she found work, she'd be able to buy new ones. Plus, the bedroom was damp and chilly, and had no source of heat. Although San Diego's winters were nothing like New York's, our first winter there was exceptionally raw and our chintzy apartment wasn't suited for cold weather. Mom would crank up the wall heater in the living room but the heat didn't reach the bedroom. So, we slept next to the heater on the living-room floor. Every night we constructed a bedroll, layering several blankets on top of our thickest down quilt to cushion the carpet-covered concrete. We'd unzip my sleeping bag to use as a comforter, turning its duck print downward so the flannel would warm our skin. Then, we'd strategically position our pillows so that our heads pointed toward the window and our feet toward the heater. Once we'd settled in, Siam would nestle and purr in the hollow between us. The cross-country move hadn't fazed him. As long as he had someplace to snuggle and didn't have to climb a tree, he was content.

✦ ✦ ✦ ✦ ✦

Of the many secrets about my life, the hardest to stomach was that I bedded down every night on the living-room floor next to my mother. We'd hit bottom. Seeing Mom drink vodka out of a bottle first thing in the morning four years earlier in Eastchester had horrified me, as had finding the incinerated hole in her mattress and accepting cans from the school Thanksgiving food drive. Sinking lower had seemed unimaginable. But we had. We were lowlifes. White trash.

Once we'd rolled up the quilt and blankets, hid them in the bedroom, and shut the door, our apartment looked almost normal, aside from the wood-and-cinder-block coffee table and naked lamps. None of my friends knew about the decrepitude in which Mom and I lived. I avoided inviting them over.

Sleeping on the floor was awful. Even as an agile fourteen-year-old, I woke up achy and stiff. The hardest part was falling asleep. The living room adjoined the kitchen, so if either Mom or I was reading, the other wouldn't be able to doze off. We had to go to bed at the same time, which we did, unless Doug dropped by unannounced, which he did frequently.

"Mom, turn out the lights! Doug just pulled up."

"I can't do that."

"Why? It's eleven o'clock! I have to get up early for school."

"He sees our lights on. He knows we're up."

"So turn them off! Quick! Just do it now!"

"Andrea, I can't DO that!"

"Why does he always show up just as we're about to go to bed? I can't sleep while he's here!"

"He won't stay long."

With that, Mom would throw on a robe, unlock the door, and boil water for coffee.

"Hey, gals," Doug would say, striding in with a solitary knock. "Oh, heyyy, you're about to go to sleep. I'm leaving." But he wouldn't leave. Instead, he'd plop down on a kitchen chair.

I never understood why Mom tolerated these late-night visits and insisted on preparing food when she knew I had to get up in the morning. Perhaps being older than Doug made her feel protective toward him. Or perhaps she felt indebted to him for having taken care of us, such as he had. I loathed my uncle. I couldn't stand his stupid jokes or the way he forced his poor dog to produce those awful sounds. I detested the lascivious way he looked at women he found attractive. I resented his attempts to parent me, especially when Mom and I fought.

"You have a fresh mouth, you know that?" he told me one Sunday on our way to the supermarket. "If you were my kid, I'd smack you."

"Well, I'm not."

"You'd better watch it because I still just might."

That did it. I never forgave Doug for threatening me. I didn't feel sorry for him. I refused to even try to get along with him.

Bedtime was when I hated Doug most. He'd sit inches from where I was trying to sleep. I'd fold my pillow like a slice of Wonder Bread over my head, but I still heard every crunch, slurp, and swallow. I'd toss and turn, and heave huge theatrical sighs, demonstrating how he was keeping me up. He'd suck his teeth. I'd seethe.

"How about a little more coffee, Doug?" Mom would ask, swallowing a yawn.

"Maybe just a splash, then I'm going."

By one in the morning, Doug would finally leave. Mom would turn out the lights and collapse beside me.

Mom and I slept on the floor for about four months. Then, one day, her uncle Yawshee's brother Alex and his wife, Edith, called from Florida to say that they were coming to California. They wanted to take us out to dinner. They wanted to see where we lived.

"Evy, where are your beds?" Edith asked when she arrived, peeking into the bedroom.

"We don't have any."

"What do you mean, you don't have any? Where do you and Andrea sleep?"

"On the floor."

"On the floor? Evy! Oh, my God! Why didn't you call us? Why didn't you tell us you and Andrea needed help?"

Mom smiled weakly. She had tears in her eyes. Alex took us to Sears, where he and Edith bought two mattresses and box springs. They paid to have them delivered the next day.

I slept more deeply that first night on the brand-new mattress than I had in months. Going to bed at night felt like a luxury, a far cry from the rest of my life.

✦ ✦ ✦ ✦ ✦

The welfare check and food stamps came monthly. By now, Mom was a pro. She'd pay the rent and bills, stock up on chicken and organ meats, and use the change to buy cigarettes and booze. Every week, she'd take a bus to Social Services to report her job-hunting progress. With her limited skills, Mom qualified only for low-level file clerk positions. I don't remember how diligently she looked for work. But I do remember how anxious she'd get at the end of the week, when she had to present Social Services with documentation of every job inquiry she'd made, every business she'd called, every person she'd spoken with; and how defeated she looked when she brought home our monthly supply of government-issued food supplements: flour, lard, canned chicken, and a rectangular box of Velveeta-like cheese. The cheese was good for omelets and macaroni casseroles. But I found maggots in the flour and the chicken looked and smelled worse than Siam's cat food, so Mom stopped bringing them home.

Social Services assigned us a caseworker who'd visit us randomly to see how we were managing. Mom said the caseworker just wanted to snoop around to see if we owned anything valuable that we could sell for cash. Before every visit, Mom and I would stash the sterling silver in the linen closet. She'd also clean out all the ashtrays and hide the Scotch, because if Social Services knew that Mom could afford cigarettes and liquor, they might reduce our allotment.

Mom kept assuring me that we wouldn't be on welfare forever. She promised that she would find a job and that our life in California would be happy. But Mom had trouble finding work. Social Services pushed her to register with the Kelly Girl temp agency. Kelly Girl sent Mom out to a few offices that needed a receptionist. But they couldn't give her secretarial assignments because she didn't know how to type or take dictation. Social Services enrolled Mom in a job-training program. Several days a week, while I was at school, she would take the bus to the local community college to attend typing, stenography, and bookkeeping classes. Every evening, she would study the hieroglyphic-looking squiggles in her stenography textbook.

"Test me," she'd say, handing me the book. "Read this letter out loud so I can practice taking dictation."

I'd dictate the letter and time her. If she made a mistake, she'd have me dictate the letter again. Then she'd see how fast she could transcribe the letter back into longhand. She worked tirelessly.

"Why don't you do electrolysis again?" I asked one night as she put away her books. "You could set up all your equipment in the bedroom."

"I don't have a license to practice in California."

"So get one."

"I'd have to learn all new state regulations. Then I'd have to go to Sacramento to take a licensing test and a board exam."

"So?"

"If I don't pass, I'd have to go all the way back to Sacramento and retake the tests."

"But you would pass and then you could work for yourself again!"

"And who would stay with you while I went back and forth? The state makes it so difficult—"

"Mom, if you got your license, we could get off welfare!"

"It's just too DAMNED DIFFICULT!"

Mom lit a cigarette and poured a Scotch. I raised the subject a few more times after that, hoping to change her mind. Eventually, I gave up.

Mom's intransigence infuriated me. I couldn't persuade her that resurrecting her electrolysis practice was the obvious way to get us off public assistance. More important, I couldn't persuade her to take care of herself. She was fifty-two years old and substantially heavier than she'd been in Eastchester. She was only five foot two, and the extra pounds had extended her belly and thickened her thighs, straining the zippers on her dresses and skirts. Aside from walking the quarter-mile to and from the supermarket, she did no exercise. "Carrying heavy grocery bags is hard work!" she'd protest. She'd try to lose weight by starving herself all day and then binge on peanut butter and chocolate syrup at night. She also refused to quit smoking.

"Mom, smoking is so bad for you," I offered one night while she was reading the paper.

"Mmm-hmmm."

"You cough a lot. You should stop."

"Mmm-hmmm."

"At least cut down."

"Mmm-hmmm."

"Will you try?"

"Andrea, stop nudging me. It's all I have."

Most maddening was Mom's indecisiveness. The smallest decisions seemed to overwhelm her. Should she order scrambled eggs or an English muffin in a diner? She seemed incapable of trusting her own decisions, worried that if she made the wrong one, no matter how small, the results would be catastrophic. After staring at a menu for fifteen minutes or more, she wouldn't order a thing to eat.

"I'll just have coffee," she'd apologize to some irritated server who'd waited patiently with pad and pencil in hand. Even trying to choose cheap lampshades at Woolworth's immobilized Mom.

It would be years before I'd recognize Mom's indecisiveness as the remnant of my father's bullying. The prospect of making a mistake terrified her so much that she couldn't even settle on a couple of two-dollar lampshades or commit to taking a state licensing exam. Her impotence enraged me because it was trapping us both.

What I didn't appreciate was Mom's grit. I didn't give her credit for enduring the exhausting bus rides to Social Services every month and the humiliation of hauling home a heavy box of government surplus food. I didn't value the nerve it took for her to attend community college with kids half her age. "These kids can type circles around me," she bemoaned one night as she rubbed her aching fingers. "They do everything so fast." I didn't consider the pride she had to swallow to accept the only job Social Services could find for her—babysitting. "It's all right," she said as she headed out the door one afternoon. "It's money." She had to report what little income she earned, which Social Services then deducted from our monthly check. "Sons of bitches. I'm damned if I do and damned if I don't."

I tried to help by working part-time as a file clerk in the high school maintenance office. I gave Mom the fifty dollars I earned each month, secretly hoping that she'd insist I keep some for myself. She accepted it gladly. She never reported the extra cash. The money bought us some freedom. Being on welfare and having no car had tethered us to our apartment. We had no cash for any recreation. So, we stayed home and drove each other crazy. With my earnings, we could at least take a weekend trip to Fashion Valley.

Fashion Valley was San Diego's most exclusive shopping center. It was probably unusual for a mother and daughter on public assistance to spend a day browsing posh, potpourri-scented designer boutiques. But the elegant, lavishly landscaped outdoor mall with its piped-in classical music gave us a much-needed change of scenery. We'd catch a ten a.m. bus on Saturday morning, arrive at eleven-thirty, window-shop for an hour, grab a snack (coffee for Mom), and window-shop some more. Although we didn't have money to spend, Mom would furtively follow me into every store to see if I fell in love with anything.

"Why don't you try it on?" she said, seeing me admire a striped, V-neck T-shirt on a clearance rack.

"I'm just looking."

"Try it!"

"We can't afford this."

"It's on clearance. We can manage. Try it."

"But, Mom, you're the one who needs clothes."

"I need to lose weight first. Go ahead, try it." The T-shirt fit perfectly.

"I don't need it."

"You love it, right?"

"Yeah," I said, torn between the desire for something new and the sacrifice I knew it entailed.

"Good, as long as you love it. Wear it in good health."

I never knew how Mom managed to scrimp together the twenty dollars for that shirt. I did know that it was her way of trying to make me happy and instill some semblance of normalcy into our lives. But it exacted a price. We caught the last bus out of Fashion Valley and arrived home tired but content at seven-thirty p.m. As soon as we walked into the apartment, Mom headed for the liquor cabinet. My heart sank.

"Do you have to drink right now?" I said in a futile attempt to prevent our day from corroding.

"I just took you shopping! Don't I deserve a little something?"

"I didn't want the shirt! I told you that!"

"But I wanted you to HAVE it!"

"And now you're throwing it back in my face!"

"You're ungrateful, you know that? You're ungrateful and you're spoiled rotten."

And so, our lovely day withered into a volley of screaming insults and Mom's threats to "take off my head," which she occasionally did. The next day, while she was out, I hid her booze in my wooden toy chest, hoping to trick her into believing that she'd polished it off. But as soon as she saved enough change from cashed food stamps, she replaced it without saying a word.

When Social Services learned that Mom and Milton were still legally married, and that he had never paid alimony or child support, they went after him. They also assigned Mom an attorney who helped her file for divorce. Milton never sent us money. But the divorce seemed to bring Mom some relief, although unexpected phone calls and unfamiliar cars out front still frightened her. We were three thousand miles away from my father, but it wasn't enough to make my mother feel safe.

Mom found a job toward the end of my freshman year of high school. The University of California–San Diego hired her to be an administrative assistant in its financial-aid office. Social Services wasted no time booting us off welfare, although Mom didn't earn enough to afford a car and would now have to spend four hours a day commuting to and from La Jolla. She'd wake up at five a.m., shower, dress, gulp coffee, and rush to the shopping center, where she caught the six o'clock bus, went to work, and returned twelve hours later. I'd have dinner started by the time she walked in at 6:20. By 6:25, she'd be sipping Scotch.

It was good to see Mom working again, to be nudged out of sleep by the smells of perfume and cigarette smoke, and to lie there half-awake and watch her in the predawn dark, smoothing on pantyhose, slipping into high heels and then her dress.

"What are you doing up, monkey?" she'd ask, after catching my glance in the mirror. Sitting on the edge of the bed, she'd caress my face and coax my eyelids closed. "It's too early," she'd whisper. "Go back to sleep." I'd drift off to the sound of the front door locking, and awaken a couple of hours later to the lingering aromas of coffee and toast.

Life improved. We inherited an old Chevy sedan from Roy and his new love, a dancer named Elena, whom he'd met shortly after moving to Los Angeles. Now Mom could drive to work, and we could go places on the weekend. She seemed happier. Her drinking continued to be a steady source of anxiety for me, but it was contained at least. Besides, I was learning to compartmentalize, putting it out of my mind when I was at school. I'd made new friends and, after a few months of crash dieting, had transformed myself into a svelte, bikini-wearing fifteen-year-old. For the first time ever, I wasn't embarrassed about how I looked. Boys were beginning to notice me. Mom said I was too young to date but I enjoyed the attention. I was growing up. More important, I was separating myself from Mom.

✦ ✦ ✦ ✦ ✦

Of all the people I'd said good-bye to when we moved to La Mesa, I missed Steven the most. We'd speak on the phone every few months, usually on Sundays when the rates were low and Mom was home. Even though we had a phone in the kitchen and the bedroom, the walls in our apartment were so thin that I couldn't tell him about the troubles Mom and I were having without her overhearing. We spent most of our conversation talking about his teaching English at Washington University and working on his dissertation. When I alluded to things being bad at home, he chirped, "Just think, in a few years you'll be outta there."

Roy maintained his distance. We rarely spoke on the phone. He and Elena had married, and occasionally invited me to L.A., but while there I spent most of my time with Elena, to whom I'd grown close. When Roy and I were together, he'd sidestep my attempts to talk about how miserable Mom was. Years later, he would explain that although he and Steven hadn't experienced Mom's alcoholism as youngsters, they had shouldered the weight of her anxiety and depression. They had also feared her temper. Now, neither of them could manage to have a conversation with her that didn't turn explosive. Neither could abide her continued suffering and complaining. They had removed themselves as much as possible from her orbit. Each of my brothers had saved his own life. It was up to me to save my own.

✦   ✦   ✦   ✦   ✦

In December 1973, my biggest wish came true: Mom agreed to let me have a Christmas tree. Perhaps I had finally convinced her that every single house and apartment in our neighborhood had Christmas decorations, and that not having a tree would single us out. Or perhaps she finally stopped caring about what anyone thought. I was euphoric.

A couple of weeks before Christmas, we dragged home a five-foot-tall pine tree from a lot around the corner and hoisted it into a metal stand in the living room. Gingerly, I opened two boxes of tree trimmings. I hung some ornaments and draped a few strands of silver tinsel, occasionally stepping back to assess my work, careful not to leave any naked limbs. When I'd finished, I inhaled the piney air and beheld my shimmering tree as Siam batted ornaments on low-hanging branches. Despite her vow never to own a Christmas tree or a cat, Mom seemed to love them both. As for the newspaper tree that I'd had as a child, it was a distant memory, along with Grandma Irene's brass menorah, which was now on the top shelf of the breakfront where no one could see it.

From then on, Christmas became the high point of our year. I'd start counting down the days until its arrival, as soon as Thanksgiving ended. Even though Mom was working, money was still tight. Yet, she always managed to surprise me with something. With my babysitting earnings, I would buy her a small bottle of Arpège. We'd put our wrapped gifts underneath the tree, bookmark the *TV Guide* for Christmas specials, and bake Tollhouse cookies to serve when my friends and I returned from caroling.

On Christmas Eve, Mom and her new friend Louise from next door would drink margaritas. Mom would get boozy but not mean, probably because she wasn't drinking alone. At midnight, we'd all hug and wish each other merry Christmas. I didn't know what we were wishing for; indeed, I didn't have a true understanding of what Christmas was about, any more than I'd had of the Jewish holidays. But that didn't matter. After so many years of feeling like a pretend Jew, I just wanted to fit in. Celebrating Christmas made it easy.

New Year's brought another opportunity to belong. Ten years earlier, Mom and I had welcomed the Jewish New Year with sugar-sweetened challah and yahrzeit candles. Now, whatever value I had once derived from these now vaguely remembered traditions paled against the joy of clinking glasses filled with Cold Duck and watching TV to see the crystal ball drop in Times Square.

✦ ✦ ✦ ✦ ✦

When the holidays ended, the rains came. It rained so much during our first winter in the apartment that the groundwater, having thoroughly saturated the sandy soil, soaked through our unit's flimsy foundation and seeped into the carpeting beneath our bed. I discovered this many months later when, while looking for a pair of shoes, I found mushrooms growing straight up out of the floor.

Spring brought relief. It also brought the next big holiday, Easter. I knew that Easter was supposed to be joyous but what struck me about it was its solemnity. On Easter, La Mesa shut down. The streets grew empty and still. Everyone, including my friends whose families were not religious, dressed up and went to church.

But I couldn't adopt Easter as I had Christmas, even though Mom permitted me to exchange candy-filled baskets with my friends, helped me dye eggs, and bought me a hollow milk-chocolate bunny. Easter felt sacred in a way that I didn't grasp, the same way Yom Kippur had. In fact, the quietness of Easter stirred old memories of our Yom Kippur observance, abbreviated though it was, in Rego Park, when Mom had lit candles and prayed, the routines of life came to a halt, and in the surrounding silence, we turned inward. Easter also reminded me of the way I'd felt—and still did feel—about Yom Kippur, like an outsider who didn't understand the meaning of the tradition. That's one reason why I hated Easter.

Another reason was that it coincided with spring break, which was the time when Mom and I had our worst fights. During every spring break, all my friends went away with their families, while I stayed home with Mom, who also had the week off. Without the structure of work, my mother brooded and drank. I'd do my best to stay out of the house. I'd ride my bike or troll around the shopping center. But eventually, I had to come home, and when I did, I'd find her blurry-eyed and unsteady on her feet day after day. My visible disgust fired Mom's anger. Every day ended in a brawl. From then on, that's what I associated with Easter.

✦ ✦ ✦ ✦ ✦

Mom had just one good year at her job.

"They want me out," she said one night, refreshing a drink that was still half-full.

"Are they firing you?"

"No, they can't fire me without three write-ups and they don't have cause. But they can make my life miserable."

Mom had received a promotion since starting as an administrative assistant in the financial-aid office at the University of California–San Diego. The university had paid for her to take a course to become a certified bookkeeper and now she was a senior administrative assistant or "admin II." Her favorite part of the job was helping students with their financial-aid applications. At fifty-five, Mom was still youthful and attractive, although heavy. Her immediate supervisor, Tina, was twenty years her junior.

"She wants somebody younger to do my job," Mom said of her boss. "Younger and faster."

Mom refused to quit. Instead, she worked harder, putting in ten- and twelve-hour days. She ate her lunch at her desk: a wedge of iceberg lettuce, an apple, and a cup of black coffee. The only time she took a break was to go to the ladies' room or refill her coffee cup.

"I can't do anything right," she said, in tears one night. "The harder I try, the more Tina criticizes me. She never takes her eyes off me. I can't think straight anymore." Tina gave Mom poor performance reviews, along with an expanding list of skills that she had to improve. Rather than evaluate her yearly, she assessed Mom's work every few months. The pressure was unrelenting.

Toward the end of her second year at the university, Mom filed a grievance with the union. She claimed harassment and age discrimination. The union assured Mom that her job was secure. Nevertheless, the grievance proceedings escalated tensions with Tina. Mom tried confiding in her coworkers who also were her carpool companions but received little support. Tina was their boss, too. Mom began driving herself to work.

I'd repeatedly ask Mom why she wouldn't quit and look for a new job, or at the very least go to the employee assistance office and see a counselor to help with the stress. But her answers were always the same: She was too old for a new job, and anything she'd say to a counselor might get out.

✦ ✦ ✦ ✦ ✦

Little by little, Mom unraveled. She couldn't sleep. She ate compulsively. To stop herself from eating, she chain-smoked. Besides her friend Louise, Mom had no one nearby to talk to. She couldn't lean on Doug. He was always leaning on her or lecturing her about her weight, her smoking, or both. "Those cigarettes are gonna kill you, Evy," he'd say. Mom started drinking more. She resumed taking tranquilizers.

School was still my refuge. I was a straight-A student and an aspiring writer. But what really saved me was my involvement with the speech team. I'd joined the team during my sophomore year and discovered that I had a natural ability to think on my feet. In two minutes, I could craft a persuasive five-minute talk about civil rights, the Vietnam War, the women's movement, or economic inequality. Competitive speaking raised my consciousness in a way that classroom learning never had, and speaking about social justice issues electrified me. As an impromptu and extemporaneous speaker, I had to be prepared to expound on any topic with only a few minutes of preparation. To stay well informed, I'd read stacks of news magazines every week. I'd practice after school until dinnertime and ride my head-lit bicycle home in the dark.

On most weekends during the seven-month tournament season, I traveled with the team to contests all over the state. At the end of my first year of competition, Mom had to mount shelves to hold all my trophies. I was the California state champion in impromptu speaking in 1974 and second in the state the next year. In 1976, I took first in the national qualifying tournament in extemporaneous speaking. I'd always been shy and struggled with low self-confidence. Public speaking pulled me out of myself. To my surprise, I had an affinity for speaking in front of an audience. My self-esteem soared. Now when I looked in the mirror, I didn't see a welfare kid, the daughter of an alcoholic, or a disenfranchised Jew. I saw a winner.

Speech was my life and my teammates, my closest friends. We spent all our time together, going ice-skating, listening to music, and meeting for dinner and late-night coffees. We were a heady bunch. We had long, existential discussions about the meaning of life and changing the world. We talked about our plans for college and beyond. The more deeply I immersed myself in these relationships, the more I distanced myself from home and the more difficult being there became.

"How was your day?" I'd ask as soon as I walked into the kitchen, filled with loathing at the sight of Mom's cocktail.

"Lousy."

"Why don't you quit already?"

"I wouldn't give them the satisfaction."

To me, quitting would have been a muscular demonstration against maltreatment, an act of personal pride. But to Mom, quitting seemed to signal not strength but cowardice. Regardless of how dismal her job made her, she refused to resign. Not quitting, however pathetic, was her greatest opportunity for protest and, ultimately, power. If only I'd realized this at the time.

My eyes fixed on the half-empty bottle of Scotch on the counter.

"Stop watching me like a HAWK! You're always WATCHING me! You and Tina!"

I couldn't understand why Mom's boss wanted to get rid of someone who worked so hard. "She said I ask too many questions," Mom scoffed. "She said I need too much direction."

This saddened but didn't surprise me. Mom's timidity and anxiety had to have impeded her job performance. I knew firsthand how wishy-washy she could be, afraid of making mistakes and therefore incapable of making decisions. I knew how infuriating her tentativeness was, and I could imagine it making her more of a burden than an asset. I worried about her losing her job and us landing back on welfare.

The prospect sickened me. Being on welfare had been the most humiliating experience of my life. It had made me feel like a loser, cheap and dirty, fit for the gutter. Mom's insistence that we hide it from family and friends had made me feel even worse. It also spoke volumes about her own mortification, which had to have chiseled at her already eroded self-esteem and, in turn, her ability to do her job. But these insights were years away.

"YOU try working for someone who hates you!" Mom told me.

At that moment, I should have made myself scarce, gone into the bedroom, anything to have avoided a confrontation. But I was too angry and I wanted her to know it. I meant for her to know what a disappointment she was, and that every time she drank, she failed me. The pressure and loneliness that were crushing her were irrelevant. I wouldn't be empathetic. As a parent, she wasn't doing her job. I was determined to punish her for it, even if it meant putting myself in the line of fire.

"YOU try raising three children without anyone to help you. Try being alone for the rest of your life."

"I didn't ask to be born, Mom."

"Oh, spare me."

"Well, I didn't. And I'm never having children. I would never have a child to save a rotten marriage."

My words were bullets. Before the last one shot out, Mom charged toward me. I darted into the bathroom but before I could shut the door, she was on the other side, forcing it open. Trapped inside, I lowered myself onto the closed toilet lid. She towered over me, her eyes narrow and fierce. She clamped my arm with her right hand, raised her left, and brought it down hard against one side of my face and then the other.

"How DARE you!" she screamed, slapping wildly at my arms and shoulders. "You ROTTEN, MISERABLE THING!" She continued hitting my hips and legs. "I should take your HEAD off!" Her shouts rang in my ears. "I have sacrificed EVERYTHING for you! And YOU . . . you have ruined my LIFE!" Slap. Slap. Slap.

Finally, she stopped. I sprang up and bolted. I grabbed my house key and tore out of the apartment, sprinting down the parkway toward the nearest gas station. I didn't have enough change to call Steven from a pay phone, so I called my speech coach, a twenty-eight-year-old English teacher named Donna Michaels who had become my mentor and my friend.

"My mother and I just had an awful fight," I cried into the phone. "Can you come get me?"

It was close to eleven p.m. when Donna arrived. She could have been fired for taking me in but she did anyway. I stayed with her for the next week, going to school every day and sneaking home once to pick up clean clothes.

"You should call your Mom," Donna said one night. "She's got to be frantic, wondering where you are."

"I don't care. I hope she has a heart attack and dies."

"You should call her, Andrea. You should call someone. You can't stay with me forever."

I called Steven. Mom had already spoken with him.

"Call her now," he said, sounding angrier than I'd ever heard him. He'd moved far away from Mom but she was still leaning on him. "She's worried sick."

"She hates me."

"She doesn't hate you."

"Well, I hate her."

"Call her and tell her where you are."

"I don't want to talk to her."

"If you don't call her, I will."

I called. The next day after school, I went home.

"I could have that woman fired," Mom said as soon as she got home from work.

"She saved me."

"Oh, I'll bet. And just what do you think I do every DAY?"

"Lately, you drink a lot," I said, baiting her, anticipating a smack, looking for another reason to run away.

"You'd better stop while you're ahead—"

"Or else what?"

She walked toward me. "I'm warning you . . ."

"Go ahead. Hit me. I dare you," I said, not budging.

"Don't push me. . . ." She got closer.

"Hit me. Go ahead. Do it."

"You are going to be so sorry . . ."

"I can always leave."

"And I can have that woman arrested."

"I have other places to go."

"Oh, really?"

I grabbed my driver's license and her car keys and headed toward the door.

"Leave the keys," she commanded. I dropped them on the floor and opened the door. "Where are you going?"

"Out."

I didn't run away. And Mom never hit me again. But from that moment on, we circled each other like two big-horned rams, our heads bowed and our eyes raised, watching to see who would jab first, each of us knowing what the other was capable of.

✦　✦　✦　✦　✦

Shortly after my seventeenth birthday, Mrs. Larson the apartment manager informed Mom that the two-bedroom place next door had become vacant. The rent would be one hundred dollars a month more than the one hundred twenty-five our one-bedroom cost. Scraping up the extra money would be tough, despite the small raise that had accompanied Mom's promotion. She was also still worried about losing her job. But with the constant tension between us always threatening to erupt, we had to stop sharing a room and a bed. She took the apartment.

For the first time since Eastchester, I had my own bedroom. I had a telephone, my record player, and a queen-size bed that I'd inherited from Roy and Elena, who drove it down from L.A. on one of their infrequent visits. Now I could shut the door and shut out Mom. I could write, listen to music, and most important, hang out with my boyfriend, Dean.

Dean had joined the speech team during my senior year. He was a sophomore but looked older. He was tall and muscular, with silky strawberry-blond hair and robin's egg–blue eyes. He was my first love. I was not his. I coached him in speech. He coached me in everything else.

I was a late bloomer. Most of my girlfriends had boyfriends by the end of freshman year (my closest friend and speech teammate, a girl of immense courage, came out in the ninth grade), and pretty much everyone was drinking or smoking pot. Because of Mom's dependence on alcohol and tranquilizers, booze and drugs terrified me, and my libido didn't start stirring until the end of sophomore year, when I developed crushes on a couple of boys on the team, both of whom were dating girls on the team. Two years later, I met Dean and strategically offered to help him prepare for an upcoming tournament. I don't know what shocked me more, my unbridled lust for him or his for me. I do know that nothing in my life up to that point had prepared me for the exhilaration I felt with him. Our tender romance, for the few months that it lasted, gave me a sense, for the first time, of my desirability. That this young stud wanted me was the best antidote to Mom's abuse. In his arms, I was no longer an overweight loser (I'd starved myself into thinness years earlier) or the welfare kid who had ruined my mother's life. I was lovable. And even more important, I was hot.

That I was able to have such a positive first sexual experience seems miraculous to me now, considering my growing anxiety and depression, not to mention the fear of men that Mom had instilled in me. "Be careful," she'd cautioned. "Boys get very excited and you can find yourself in a situation. . . ." That was the closest she ever got to talking to me about sex. But her dire warnings were no match for my raging teenage hormones. Because her idea of contraception was forbidding me to be at home alone with Dean, we spent afternoons at his house, listening to Jethro Tull and making out.

The more time I spent with Dean, the colder Mom became. She didn't even pretend to be happy for me. Perhaps she was jealous of Dean for having become the center of my universe. Perhaps she was jealous of me for discovering what she had lost long ago.

✦ ✦ ✦ ✦ ✦

Senior year was a whirlwind. I was working two jobs (selling children's shoes at a Stride Rite store and cashiering at Jack in the Box), scouting for a cheap stereo, completing college applications, and qualifying for the national speech tournament in Colorado Springs. When time permitted, I'd grab a friend or two and head for La Jolla Shores, driving barefoot in a bikini with all the windows down, listening to the Eagles at full blast. Life felt bright and full of possibility.

Of the schools that I applied to, Brandeis University was the most unlikely one for me to attend. Had I known anything about it, it would have been my last choice.

"They're supposed to be very generous with financial aid," Mom had said with authority.

"What about the English department?"

"I'm sure they have an excellent English department. It's a very fine school."

I didn't go to the library to read about Brandeis. I didn't request a catalog. I didn't research Waltham, the down-on-its-luck Massachusetts town where the school was located. I didn't even ask Steven, who was in the process of getting his doctorate. What I cared about more than the caliber of the school's English department was its location across the country, far away from home. In late November 1975, a few weeks before decorating our Christmas tree, I mailed my college applications, including one to Brandeis.

In spring 1976, the acceptance letter arrived. I squinted at the blue and white stationery.

"Why is there Hebrew on the letterhead?" I asked Mom. "Is Brandeis a Jewish school?"

"It used to be."

"And now?"

"I'm not sure."

I could have attended San Francisco State, which was known for its creative writing program. But San Francisco was too close to La Mesa. Waltham was about as far away as I could get without actually leaving the country. Besides, Brandeis offered me a nearly full ride.

A few weeks later, I received a thick welcome packet containing information about housing and meal plans, kosher dining, and Jewish campus life. Everything bore the school's blue and white Hebrew logo. I was nervous.

"Mom, everything in this envelope has Hebrew on it."

"It's just their tradition, don't worry. Brandeis is an excellent school. By the way, a Mr. Sheckman called from the school. He wants to pay us a visit."

"But I'm already accepted."

"He's from financial aid. He wants to meet you in person."

"Does he have to come here? Can't we meet him at Denny's?"

"He wants to see where we live."

Mr. Sheckman was pudgy and flushed. The stiff collar of his blue suit dug into his fleshy neck. Mom served fruit salad. As we ate, Mr. Sheckman's eyes darted from the clipboard in his lap to the piles of mail on the kitchen counter to the chairs with the ill-fitting Indian bedspreads to the lace-covered plank of wood on cinder blocks. Every now and then he jotted something down.

"So, Andrea, tell me, why do you want to go to Brandeis?"

I put down my fork. What do I say? Because Mom said a low-income Jew would probably get a lot of financial aid? Because I want to be as far away from my mother as possible?

"I want to be a writer and I heard Brandeis has a good English department."

"That it does. All the departments are superb. Are you interested in Jewish studies?"

"Uhhmm..."

"I understand you were a state speech champion?"

"In 1974. I was second in the state for 1975. I was supposed to go to nationals last month but I got mono."

"Oh, that's terrible! But you're a straight-A student and you're in the National Honor Society. You will thrive at Brandeis." Mr. Sheckman slid his clipboard under his armpit, where a large circle of sweat that had soaked through his white shirt. He shook Mom's hand, then mine. "Thank you for the fruit salad. I expect you will be getting some good news soon."

The letter announcing my financial-aid award came a week later. What money the school didn't give me outright I'd earn through work-study. Mom was thrilled and relieved. I was sick with doubt. How long will it take before everyone finds out that I'm not really Jewish?

"Remember," Mom said, "you can always transfer."

I spent much of that summer cleaning out my drawers and closet, taking inventory of the clothes I had. I'd need a winter coat and boots. I'd need desk supplies. I opened my toy chest to see if there was anything useful I could bring. Beneath the board games and puzzles were several half-empty bottles of gin, vodka, and Scotch.

✦ ✦ ✦ ✦ ✦

My speech coach Donna showed up at San Diego International Airport to say good-bye.

"You made it, kiddo," she said, clasping my shoulders with outstretched arms. "You're going to do great."

During the boarding announcement, Mom walked haltingly from the corner where she'd been sitting to the line that was forming by the departure gate. She turned her back to Donna and embraced me. My arms hung down like two steel booms.

"Take care of yourself," she said, kissing my cheek and blinking away tears.

I grabbed my carry-on bag. "Don't call me," I said, and then I boarded the plane.

PART FIVE:

THE COLLEGE YEARS, 1976–1981

THE CHEAPEST FLIGHT FROM SAN DIEGO TO New York's La Guardia Airport had a two-hour, predawn layover in St. Louis.

"I'll meet you for coffee!" Steven said when I called to say I'd be in the St. Louis airport from 3:30 to 5:30 a.m.

"At 3:30 a.m.?"

"Why not?"

He was waiting for me, bright-eyed and beaming. We hadn't seen each other since he and Dierdre had visited Mom and me in La Mesa a few years earlier. His hair was long and wild, a light-brown kinky globe around his head. He wore oval, wire-rimmed glasses, blue jeans, a T-shirt, and white sneakers. We hugged hard.

"You're so skinny!" he remarked.

"You look like a professor!"

"Almost there. I've still got a dissertation to finish."

The airport was deserted. All the snack shops were closed. Like two kids hunkering down to watch cartoons, we sat cross-legged on the floor outside a darkened Dunkin' Donuts.

"Sooo?" Steven began, a grin creeping across his face. "How does it feel to be a college freshman?"

"Scary."

"But exciting, right?" Steven was the one person who could unravel my tangle of emotions and find the muscle that held me together. He didn't dismiss my fears. He didn't indulge them, either.

"What if I made the wrong choice? What if Brandeis isn't the right place for me?"

"First of all, you won't know until you're there. Second, you can always change schools. Have you seen a course catalog? When you start choosing classes, call me. We'll go over them together!" His excitement was infectious. He made every contest feel winnable.

At 5:30 a.m., the lights in Dunkin' Donuts flicked on. Steven and I had talked for two hours without moving.

"I still can't believe you got up in the middle of the night to meet me," I said, pulling out my boarding pass.

"Sleep is overrated."

"You gonna go back to bed now?"

"Naaah. I'm gonna grab a cup of coffee and go to school. I have a lot of writing to do." He walked me to the gate. "I'll send you my table of contents. Send me everything you write. And keep me posted on school." He gave me a bear hug.

"I love you so much," I said.

"I love you so much, too."

✦   ✦   ✦   ✦   ✦

When I arrived at La Guardia Airport, Roy was waiting for me. He and Elena, who'd separated while still in L.A., had moved back to New York together, and gave their relationship one more try, but split permanently once they were back in the city.

He had offered to put me up in his one-bedroom East Village apartment for a few days before school started. He'd also promised to drive me there.

Roy's presence in my life, like his expressions of love, continued to be inconsistent. We'd go months without speaking and our conversations had lots of dead space. He never seemed to have much to say. He was often prickly and impenetrable. I couldn't navigate the distance between us. Yet, every now and then, he would surprise me with a random act of kindness, as he did when he'd agreed to be my "show-and-tell" a decade earlier, or when he'd surprised me with pierced earrings and then a kitten.

"I can take a bus directly to Waltham," I said as he put my suitcases into his car.

"No, I want to drive you. It'll give us a chance to spend time together."

✦ ✦ ✦ ✦ ✦

It felt good to be back in New York. I'd missed the seasons, especially the last days of summer, when maple trees started bursting with red and gold. My childhood friend Celeste took me to Macy's to buy a wool winter coat. Then she rounded up our old gang for dinner at a local pizzeria. Everyone looked the way they had five years earlier. In fact, little seemed to have changed. Kids still skated at Rye Playland. Woolworth's was still there. So were the greasers. No one's parents had divorced or died. Life had hummed along and now these girls whose bat mitzvahs I'd attended were also college bound.

"You haven't missed much," Celeste said. Everyone nodded. They said that I was lucky to have gotten out of Eastchester, as if moving to southern California had been a rollicking adventure.

"I practically had my own pool and went to the beach all the time," I lied, never letting on that I would have traded places with them in a heartbeat.

✦ ✦ ✦ ✦ ✦

Roy drove me to Brandeis on a gray, humid, late-August day. We rode the FDR Drive along the East River to the New England Thruway. I'd been looking forward to telling him about my life and learning about his. In the five hours it would take to get to Waltham, we could cover a lot of ground. I described the years in California, Doug's late-night visits, Mom's drinking, and my running away from home. He listened. At least, I thought he was listening. I asked him how he was doing. Then I asked about his relationships with Steven and Mom, his memories of my father, his decision to join the navy, and his plans for the future.

"Do we have to talk all the time?" he snapped. "Can't we just enjoy the silence?"

The sky was dark by midafternoon when we reached school. A storm loomed. The gloomy weather might have felt stirring amid majestic stone buildings draped in ivy but the Brandeis campus looked like a sterile, postmodern office park with white cinder-block buildings connected by mazes of narrow concrete walkways. There were few trees and very little grass. Like the weather, I felt bleak.

Roy carried my trunk to my second-floor dorm. "It's not what I expected," I said, trying to swallow the lump that had lodged in my throat. The campus architecture wasn't the only letdown; Roy didn't seem receptive to any more conversation, especially one about our hobbled relationship. He seemed eager to begin the drive back to New York. He wished me good luck, kissed me on the cheek, and left. Blinking away tears, I started to unpack.

Melissa, my roommate, had called me earlier that summer to introduce herself. She was from a wealthy Pennsylvania suburb. Her father owned a chain of hotels. She'd gabbed about her family, friends, and all the colleges that had accepted her. She'd sounded bouncy and warm.

We got off to a rocky start. We divvied up the room and made our beds. My empty trunk fit nicely at the foot of my bed and my single suitcase, underneath. Melissa had a ten-piece Gucci luggage ensemble with a matching umbrella but nowhere to stow it all.

"You don't have much, do you?" she asked, eyeing my half-empty closet. "Can I store my bags in your closet?"

She put away her dozens of dresses, jackets, coats, blouses, sweaters, pants, shorts, shoes, sneakers, and boots, and filled my closet with her empty valises.

"There!" she said, brushing her hands together as if she'd just wrapped up a day of installing sheetrock. Then, with one hand on her hip, she began scoping out wall space for her mirror and posters.

The venetian blinds covering our window caught her eye. "Oh, my God, those are disgusting!" she exclaimed. "We gotta clean these blinds before we can hang drapes."

She was right. Dutifully, I secured paper towels and household cleaner, and started wiping down the grimy blinds, one slat at a time as Mom had taught me, expecting Melissa to pitch in. But she just stood there. "You missed one," she said.

✦　✦　✦　✦　✦

Midway through our first week at school, Melissa introduced me to Rona, a girl from Michigan who lived at the far end of the hall. They had a similar look: short and petite, with perky brown bobs and a designer label on just about every item they owned. Each wore a shiny gold necklace: Rona's had a chai and Melissa's, her name spelled in Hebrew. In three days, they had become best friends.

"Rona and I have an idea . . ." Melissa began brightly while her new best buddy stood at her side, her eyes cast downward.

"We think you and Rona should trade rooms so she and I can room together!"

"But I'm all settled," I declared, feeling the swelling bruise of rejection. "And I just cleaned all the venetian blinds."

"We'll help you pack!" Melissa jumped in. "And we'll help you move!"

"Claudia's really nice, you'll like her," Rona assured me of her soon-to-be ex-roommate. "You guys have a lot in common."

"If she's so nice, then why don't you want to live with her?" I shot back.

"Because . . ." she stammered. "Melissa and I . . . we're like the same person. We're perfect for each other."

Wounded yet resigned, I complied.

"Don't take it personally," Melissa said over her shoulder as they left for lunch.

What Claudia and I had in common—besides having been snubbed by our roommates—was our low-income status. Claudia came from an Irish Catholic family. She was one of six children and her parents barely scraped by. Our relative poverty didn't bond us, however. Even the roommate switch seemed to insult her less than it had me.

"Whatehvaah," she groaned, rolling her eyes. Claudia didn't speak much. The flat expression on her pale face rarely changed. It was impossible to gauge her mood or know much of anything about her, including her physical size (the yardstick by which all girls measured each other) because she wore clothes that were at least a size too big.

"I was fat in high school," she shared in a moment of exceptional candor. "I keep my old clothes in case I get fat again." I revealed my own weight issues, hoping to establish common ground. But I couldn't endear myself to her and I tired of trying. She never bothered to reciprocate.

Claudia was animated and chatty around her two best friends, Sue and Sharon. Sue was Chinese-American. Sharon was African-American. Like Claudia and me, they depended on financial aid. I wanted to explain that even though I was white and Jewish, I was more like them than the wealthy Jewish kids of Reitman Hall, our coed dorm. But the three girls were a tight trio.

I couldn't find my niche. Most of the girls I met at school were like Melissa and Rona, wealthy and fervently Jewish. They weren't religious. But being Jewish was their identifier and their common denominator. It felt like seventh grade all over again. I met a handful of kids who didn't drip with designer labels, but still everyone paraded their Judaism, either with a Star of David necklace or a Hebrew-emblazoned T-shirt or Friday afternoon greetings of "Shabbat Shalom." I would politely decline invitations to join them for Shabbat dinner, feeling my self-consciousness resurge as they walked arm in arm to the kosher cafeteria and then to services. Instead, I hung out in my room with Claudia, Sharon, and Sue, who could have done without my company but against whom I did not measure myself.

✦   ✦   ✦   ✦   ✦

My financial-aid package included work-study. I had a range of on-campus jobs to choose from, and with five classes on my plate, I chose the one that paid the highest hourly rate so I could work the fewest possible hours. I became a custodian.

My daily assignment entailed cleaning the bathrooms of Sherman Hall from six to nine in the morning, Monday through Friday. My alarm clock jolted me awake at five. Half-asleep, I'd dress, pack my books, and dash the half-mile across campus to the all-girl dorm. In the building's basement office, I would punch a time clock with a crew of burly, chain-smoking maintenance men in coveralls and work boots. For the next three hours, I'd heave up and down four flights of stairs a steel bucket filled with sponges, disinfectants, rubber gloves, and a mop with toilet-paper rolls skewered on its wooden handle. I'd scour sinks and polish mirrors, tiptoeing around girls in plush terrycloth robes and bunny slippers. As they tweezed their eyebrows, blow-dried their hair, brushed on mascara, and glossed their lips, I'd scrub shower stalls and toilets, lifting wet, scummy clumps of hair from drains, emptying tampon containers, rubbing graffiti from walls, and scraping away remnants of the previous night's bulimic purges. Then I'd back out of the bathroom, mopping the floor as I went.

Scrubbing sixteen toilets, sixteen showers, and sixteen sinks every day was grueling. At the end of my shift, I'd put away my cleaning supplies, grab a quick breakfast in the cafeteria, and head to my 10:00 a.m. class. After dinner, I'd study in the library until it closed at midnight. Then I'd drag myself back to my room and continue studying by the light of a small desk lamp to avoid disturbing Claudia. I'd pass out by two and be up in a few hours to repeat the routine.

I liked working hard. What I couldn't take was the Sherman Hall girls' refusal to interact with me. They would enter the bathroom and barely acknowledge my presence. As I polished water faucets and rinsed toothpaste spit from the sink, they would avert their gaze, sometimes whispering under their breath. I wondered if seeing me clean their toilets mortified them. After all, I was their peer, an eighteen-year-old freshman, doing menial work. Vile work. Not the work of the privileged. Not the work of a Jewish college coed. I couldn't wait to finish my shift so I could merge anonymously into student life, except there was no anonymity for me as the custodian of Sherman Hall.

"Do you think you could leave some more toilet paper next time?" A girl's bellow shot across the crowded cafeteria. I didn't recognize her or the other girls at her table, but I knew the request was for me.

"Heyyy!" Standing now, she yelled louder. Heat rose from the bottoms of my feet to the top of my head. I wanted to melt into the linoleum tile floor. The query nailed me like a torpedo. "Tomorrow. Could you leave a couple extra rolls?"

Whatever the girls of Sherman Hall thought of me shouldn't have mattered. But it did. It reignited the shame I'd felt about being Jewish and poor. And the shame magnified the alienation I felt from these girls, my roommate Claudia, and pretty much everyone else in my dorm. I ached with loneliness.

✦ ✦ ✦ ✦ ✦

"Pssst." The sound echoed in the dormitory hallway. "Pssst."

A heavyset, grandmotherly-looking woman stood in a nearby doorway, beckoning. She wore a light-blue, button-down short-sleeved dress with a white collar and cuffs, support hose, and black lace-up shoes. Her gray, neatly coiffed hair framed her rosy round face. Her penciled-in eyebrows were dark brown and her lips, cherry red. The embroidered name "Marion" appeared just below her left shoulder. I approached her, dragging my bucket behind me.

"All done?" she asked, smiling. "How 'bout a nice cup of tea?"

I peered past the threshold into the large utility closet that she had transformed into a cozy sitting room, furnished with an upholstered club chair and an oval hooked rug on the white tiled floor. Against one wall was a cloth-covered table set for two. Mounted on the wall were shelves full of cups, saucers, and plates, a plastic tray with silverware, salt-and-pepper shakers, a sugar bowl, and napkins. Next to the table was a small cart with a hot plate, teakettle, and toaster-size television set. Above the cart hung a needlepoint that read "Bless This House."

"You can leave that outside," Marion said, pointing to my bucket. "No one's gonna bother it."

Marion offered me the club chair. I collapsed into its softness. "I hope you like Lipton," she said, pulling a teabag out of its paper packet. "Are you hungry? How 'bout a bran muffin?" She handed me a steaming cup of tea and a muffin on a flower-patterned plate. "I see you punch in every morning," she said, sprinkling sugar into her cup. "I'm here by five-thirty, with Charlie," she said of her husband, the head maintenance man. "We pick up muffins on the way. They're for the crew. I sure as heck don't need 'em!" she said, chuckling and patting her middle. "The boys need their energy. You, too. It's hard work, scrubbing bathrooms. I know."

Marion had worked for the maintenance department for forty-three years. She cleaned everything in Sherman Hall except the bathrooms. Twice a day, she took refuge in her little room. "I like to watch my soaps," she said with a mischievous grin. "I eat my sandwich or I have a muffin if my willpower's down. Sometimes I close my eyes."

Every morning at nine, Marion waited for me to come down the hall with my bucket in tow. As soon as I reached her door I'd hear her teakettle whistling. "I got the water boiled and a muffin all warmed up," she'd announce.

Over tea, we'd talk about simple things. Neither of us dug deep. Sometimes we'd watch the news. When winter came, she surprised me with two pairs of thick fuzzy socks from Filene's. "I knew you wouldn't have anything like these," she said. "Being from California." She was like the grandmother I never knew. Her kindness was a godsend.

Only once did I skip a visit. "I have to study for an exam," I lied.

"Ohhh, I seeee. Of course, I understand, school comes first," she said, turning off the kettle. "But tomorrow you'll come, won't you?"

"Sure." In truth, I didn't know if I'd manage to see her the next day because I was beginning to crumble beneath the weight of what would eventually balloon into a crippling depression.

It was late January 1977, and I'd just returned from winter break, which I'd spent with Elena, who generously put me up in her tiny Manhattan studio loft because I couldn't afford to fly home. Although she and Roy were estranged, we remained tight, tighter than I'd ever been with Roy. Even if I'd had the money, I wouldn't have gone home. I hadn't spoken to Mom in months and had no interest in seeing her. To her credit, Mom had honored my request not to call, although she'd caved on November 2, 1976, the night Jimmy Carter won the presidential election.

"I couldn't hold out anymore," she blurted as soon as I answered the phone. "I just had to hear your voice. How are you?"

"I'm watching the election."

"But how ARE you?"

"Fine."

"I just wanted to tell you that I spoke with my doctor and he says the diaphragm is the safest form of birth control."

"What? You called to tell me that?"

"I don't know if you're using anything or if you even need anything, but just in case you do . . ."

I didn't. I hadn't found anyone I was attracted to the way I'd been to Dean, although I thought I'd come close when I started dating the editor of the college newspaper, who looked at me one day and said, "I don't know if I'm straight or gay." Soon after, I met the electric-guitarist from an on-campus band, who invited me to his apartment for Friday night dinner. I was so lonely that the prospect of a fling felt enticing. But when he greeted me with a hearty "Shabbat Shalom!" it took every ounce of self-control for me not to pivot and run. Famished, I stayed long enough to scarf a chicken leg and then, feigning a headache, I took off.

I also developed a warm friendship with a bearded, guitar-strumming dorm mate who lived below me. Smart and funny, Billy reminded me of Steven. He was struggling to find his place at school, too. We spent hours commiserating and singing folk songs, and might have taken our relationship further had he not revealed his dream to marry, have a bunch of kids, and become a rabbi.

My alienation from Judaism made finding a boyfriend, not to mention making friends, impossible. I simply couldn't see beyond the wealthy kids who wore their Jewish identity like a headlamp. I couldn't dissociate Judaism from wealth, or escape the disgrace of my low-class youth. My shame tarnished everything.

Shame bloomed into arrogance. Scorn, I discovered, was the perfect antidote to envy. I didn't have to castigate myself for being a Jewish imposter when I could proclaim my superiority over anyone who bought into the hokum of Judaism—or any religious tradition, for that matter. I didn't recognize the self-deception. I couldn't see that I was trading one falsehood for another. Nor did I realize how my arrogance exacerbated my loneliness. I chose isolation over socializing with anyone whose relationship with Judaism I deemed ridiculous, which covered just about everyone.

I didn't share any of this with Marion. I never told her that I couldn't stomach the prospect of returning to school the following fall, that my first year at Brandeis would be my last. I continued having tea with her every morning, never explaining how Brandeis had reinforced for me the ugly stereotype that coupled being Jewish with being privileged, or why I had latched onto that stereotype in the first place. I had a feeling she wasn't up for any hard stories.

✦　✦　✦　✦　✦

All through spring semester, I regretted having returned to school. Mom began calling regularly.

"You don't sound right," she said.

"I hate it here."

"Okay, well, the school year's almost over."

"I want to leave."

"Finish out the year, then you can transfer."

"I want to drop out."

"You can do that, too."

I didn't. Instead, I grew despondent—too despondent to investigate other schools or plan anything other than scrubbing bathrooms and attending classes. Every morning, I dragged myself from Sherman Hall to the cafeteria to class to the library and then to my dorm to study some more. I was exhausted. I drank so much coffee that my hands shook. I felt ill. But I needed to work and finish school. I sought help from a wan counselor who advised me to go to the emergency room if I felt tempted to harm myself. Then I discovered the campus pool, where I swam furiously every day, determined to defeat my depression. To combat loneliness, I sometimes rode the campus shuttle into Cambridge or Boston. One day, on my way home, I stopped into a bar and had a glass of wine.

It wasn't my first experience with alcohol. It was, however, the first time I'd drunk alone, and in a bar, which made me feel very mature at eighteen, and which I couldn't have done in California, where the legal drinking age was twenty-one. It also wasn't lost on me that drinking probably was not the best outlet for the depressed child of a depressed alcoholic. And yet, I'd drunk in high school, with Mom's blessing, which she'd granted to demystify booze and help me establish a healthy relationship with it.

"If you're going to try anything," she'd said, "I'd rather you try it at home."

Instead of horrifying me, the invitation had raised my esteem of Mom—yes, she could be a nasty drunk, but she was also an unusually progressive woman who wanted me to learn responsible drinking. Why her alcoholism had not completely turned me off to booze, I don't know; perhaps it was because, with her permission, I had the chance to discover how good alcohol made me feel. The high was temporary, of course, and I was too conscious of her alcoholism to enjoy booze freely. But this didn't stop me from trying. And so, I treated myself to an occasional glass of wine and, like other college kids, kept a bottle of Paul Masson on the shelf above my bed.

The red-eye from Boston landed in San Diego at 4:30 a.m. on Thursday morning, May 5, 1977. It was the only flight I could schedule after my last exam. The day before, I had dragged my luggage into the classroom, taken the three-hour test, and cabbed over to Logan Airport for my 11:00 p.m. flight. Six hours later, I was sitting at Mom's kitchen table, facing platters of baked Virginia ham, cheese and crackers, and fresh fruit salad. Coffee was brewing.

"Have a little something," Mom coaxed.

"Um, it's a little early, Mom."

"There's ham."

"I'm not hungry, Mom. Besides, I don't eat meat."

"Since when? So, you're a vegetarian now?"

"No. I just don't eat meat." Still on the weight-loss seesaw, I felt desperate to lose the pounds I'd regained during my final, unhappy months at Brandeis.

"How about cheese? I got your favorites. Or have you cut that out, too? I can't keep up with you. . . ."

I shoved a thick slab of Brie and a Triscuit into my mouth.

"How about a little fruit salad?" Mom asked.

I hadn't missed her. If anything, my anger toward her had ripened. I'd fled Brandeis and landed in the next worse place.

"Where's Siam?" I asked, suddenly noticing the cat's absence.

Mom faltered. "I had to put him down."

"What? Why?"

"He had leukemia." It had been thirty years since her husband had died from leukemia but she could barely say the word. Her eyes filled. "He stopped eating and drinking. He wouldn't come out from under the chair."

"When did this happen?"

"Soon after you left."

"Why didn't you call me?"

"I didn't want to upset you. Besides, you told me not to call, remember?"

Now home, I was ambivalent about returning to college. I pondered transferring to UC–Berkeley to study journalism but felt so worn out that all I could think of was baking on the warm sands of La Jolla Shores.

"Submit your application anyway so you don't miss the financial-aid deadline," Mom urged. "Who knows? By the end of the summer, you might feel ready to go back to school."

Numbly, I followed her advice. Mom didn't push. In fact, she gave me all the room I needed to make up my own mind. She helped me weigh the pros and cons of taking time off.

"I just want you to be happy," she said.

I was happy to be back in La Mesa, where I'd been a curiosity but never an outcast. But I didn't want to live there. I especially didn't want to live with my mother, who was still depressed and drinking. The only way I could tolerate being home was by telling myself that it was temporary, which may be why, before summer was over, I was on a flight to San Francisco International Airport.

✦　✦　✦　✦　✦

With thirty thousand students, UC–Berkeley, or "Cal," was ten times the size of Brandeis—a city within a city. I could cross its sprawling campus a hundred times a day and never see the same face twice. And, to my delight, there were many different faces to see. To walk from the university's north to south end was to travel through a kaleidoscope of races and ethnicities, cultures, faiths, and rituals. On any given day, the air seemed to pulse with the preaching, dancing, chanting, and drumming of Christians, Muslims, Moonies, Sufis, Hare Krishnas, Hindus, and Buddhists, all offering words of inspiration to anyone who would listen.

The school had its Jewish population. It had a Chabad House and a Hillel. It had its wealthy students, too, Jewish and non-Jewish alike. But no one of any particular tradition or means stood out. Blending in here would be easy. What I didn't realize in the fall of 1977 was how easy it would be to get lost.

✦　✦　✦　✦　✦

The semester got off to a promising start. I scoured the work-study listings, fearing that I'd once again find custodial work to be the highest-paying option. Instead, I spotted an ad for a part-time wire editor at the school newspaper, *The Daily Californian*. The job entailed sorting through reams of dispatches from the Associated Press newswire machine and, using a pica ruler and pencil, laying out and headlining the most newsworthy items for the next day's paper.

I'd written a few creative essays for the Brandeis student newspaper but was no newshound, nor had I ever aspired to be a newspaper reporter. Yet, as soon as I entered *The Daily Californian* newsroom, smelled the ink, and felt the buzz of reporters furiously typing, while squeezing a receiver between their ear and shoulder, I knew that this was where I wanted to work.

The staff was full of Cal journalism students, all of whom seemed much older and more accomplished than I—maybe because they were pushy and loud and exuded confidence of a kind I hadn't known since my days as a high school speech champion. Every day from three to seven p.m., as I scanned the AP wire and laid out my section of the paper, I watched in awe as reporters flew out of the office to chase down stories and returned to rifle through their tall spiral notebooks and transpose scrawled shorthand into typed copy on deadline. Watching the speed and certitude with which they churned out their assignments both amazed and intimidated me. I was too insecure to imagine ever being able to write so fast and decided then that as much as I admired these reporters, I could never be one of them. Being the wire editor was enough. In fact, what mattered most was not to be scrubbing toilets anymore.

In the newsroom, as with every area of my life, I was easily enthralled and quick to idolize. Some part of this likely evolved from my low self-esteem and another part, from my need for someone to look up to. I still looked up to Steven, but he was in St. Louis steeped in his dissertation, and neither of us could afford long-distance phone calls. I needed someone closer whom I could put on a pedestal. I wasn't aware of this need, and I certainly never would have interpreted it as a need for a mother, or father, or even God. Instead, I set my sights on men. The perfect romance, I was convinced, would save me.

This misguided conviction drew me into dozens of disastrous and destructive relationships with men who, even if they had been kind, mature, or available, could never have sated my starved heart or healed my broken self. It would take years of therapy before I understood this. In the meantime, I began with Kyle.

✦　✦　✦　✦　✦

Kyle lived in my dorm at Berkeley. Tall and wiry with a mop of straight brown hair that covered half his face, he reminded me of an Afghan hound. I first saw him in the dorm's multipurpose room brilliantly playing Rachmaninoff's Piano Concerto No. 2 in C on a black baby grand piano. I loved this piece of music and stood mesmerized, watching his hands fly up and down the keyboard as his head and body alternately jerked and swayed to the music, his hair flopping in and out of his eyes. He seemed oblivious to the chattering students sauntering in and out of the room.

"Don't stop," I said, applauding, when he finished.

"No one's listening," he scoffed.

"I am. I'm your audience."

He smiled wryly. Then he continued playing, Paganini, Mozart, and Bach, each piece memorized and executed masterfully. I leaned against a wall, riveted. Finally, he stopped. I walked over to the piano. We introduced ourselves.

"Let's grab coffee," he said.

Kyle was sharp and had a biting wit. He also had a high school girlfriend who was a Cal student, and had just dumped him. He was angry, bereft, and determined to win her back. At the same time, he was flirting with me. I gobbled up every crumb of attention he tossed my way.

Kyle became my obsession. Our relationship was lopsided but not one-sided. He must have seen something in me, because he began appearing at my door late at night to slip into bed alongside me. Even though his visits usually followed a failed attempt to win back his ex, I convinced myself that he was falling in love with me, even when he poked his finger into my fleshy hip and said, "This, my dear, is lard, and I'm going to help you lose it."

He didn't have to help me. His words were motivation enough for me to starve myself. When he demanded that I see him exclusively, I gave him my word. When he said he needed me to accompany him on a visit to his mother's house in Sacramento, I consented, clutching the inside door handle of the two-seater chartreuse Porsche convertible that he gunned up Highway Five at a hundred miles per hour, crying as he sang to a blasting Boz Scaggs tape. And when he opened his mother's liquor cabinet and began chugging vodka from the bottle, I stayed silent, even though the scene hurtled me back a decade to the Saturday morning in Eastchester when I saw my mother do the same thing.

"Oh, Kyle, please don't start with the drinking now," his mother pleaded. Kyle and I had only ever gone out for coffee and I had never smelled liquor on his breath, so I dismissed the possibility that he was an alcoholic, even as he drank himself into a stupor, weeping until he finally passed out on the couch with me imprisoned in his grip.

Kyle's drinking probably saved me from what would have been a doomed affair. While I tried to rationalize his possessiveness, his criticality, and even his inability to let go of his ex, I could not tolerate his drinking. At nineteen, I was two years away from California's legal drinking age. No one ever suggested I get a fake ID, and I wouldn't have anyway. Being with Kyle was enough to prevent me from wanting to drink at all. Unable to admit my revulsion, I told him that I was not as ready as I'd thought for an exclusive relationship. With that, he shut me out of his life. "It's either all or nothing," he said the day after we returned from Sacramento. "If you can't commit, we have nothing to discuss."

I was not in love with Kyle. Actually, I was afraid of him. But his words and his vow to turn off the little trickle of romantic attention he'd dispensed tripped a switch, reigniting the feelings of abandonment and powerlessness I'd felt as a child. Panicked, I begged him to reconsider, to remain my friend.

"Friend?" he shot back. "I can't be just your friend. Jesus."

He acted as if we'd enjoyed a long romance and I'd callously ripped out his heart. He blamed me for ruining everything. His castigation was absurd. Nevertheless, it hit a nerve and accelerated the slow emotional tailspin that I'd been in for the past year but had yet to recognize.

✦ ✦ ✦ ✦ ✦

My preoccupation with Kyle made focusing on school more difficult than it already was, given that I really didn't want to be there. As I had done at Brandeis, I spent large chunks of time isolating myself in the library studying, although I usually ended up in the music room, listening to Beethoven symphonies through headphones, wondering how I'd landed back in school when I'd had no intention of returning. Though I usually made friends quickly, I couldn't find a kindred spirit. I formed some acquaintanceships with classmates, none of whom were Jewish, which spared me from having to explain what kind of Jew, or non-Jew, I was.

Then I met Judy.

Her deep voice grabbed my attention first. I twisted around in my chair and saw her sitting two rows behind me in a lecture on race and class in America. She wore baggy Levi's jeans and boys' black Keds sneakers. A pack of Marlboros bulged inside the front pocket of her plaid flannel shirt. Her blue plastic glasses rested low on her nose. Her complexion was creamy, free of makeup. A pencil jutted out of the makeshift knot of brown hair she'd twisted behind her head. Her look intrigued me, but it was her contributions to class discussions, her knowledge of politics, and her dedication to social activism that made me want to know her.

Judy was from Beverly Hills. Her father was a lawyer; her mother, a social worker. Aside from their zip code, however, nothing suggested her family's wealth. In fact, she seemed uncomfortable with her privilege. "My parents never blew money on designer clothes or cars or vacations," she told me over coffee one day. "They didn't send us to private school or fancy summer camp. My brother and sister and I paid for the things we wanted. We had to work."

Judy's parents were social activists. They worked as literacy volunteers. They collected clothing for the homeless. They ran food pantries. "We'd sit around the dinner table and talk about what we could do to make the world a better place," she said, lighting a cigarette. "The littlest things—volunteering in a soup kitchen or helping a kid from an inner-city school learn how to read."

As she spoke, I spotted it, glimmering on a silver chain beneath the open collar of her shirt: a tiny Star of David. I was shocked. She was nothing like the Jewish girls I'd known. She bought her clothes at Goodwill. She never mentioned having gone to Hebrew school or becoming bat mitzvah.

"You're Jewish?" I asked, confused by the sudden connection to her that I felt. How could I feel connected to her when we had grown up so differently? I couldn't possibly tell her about Mom's drinking, or about our sleeping on the floor, or living on welfare.

"I'm Jewish, too," I stammered. "I mean, I was born Jewish, but I've never really been Jewish . . ."

"What do you mean you've never really been Jewish?"

"I never went to Hebrew school or became a bat mitzvah. We never belonged to a synagogue."

She drew deeply on her cigarette and blew smoke rings into the air. "My parents never belonged to a synagogue. They didn't give a shit about Hebrew school."

A smile spread across my face and my shoulders relaxed. I described the lavish meals Mom had once cooked for Rosh Hashanah and Yom Kippur, the challah that I'd lacquered in sugar, the prayers she whispered over the candles. I explained how Mom seemed to lose interest in those rituals the more depressed she became and the more she drank. I detailed our descent into poverty.

"We had to go on welfare," I said, staring into my coffee cup. I told her the story of our move to La Mesa and the unexpected relief I experienced from being the only Jew in town. I told her of Uncle Doug breaking his word about being able to take care of us, about having to go back on welfare.

"Being on welfare was pretty awful, but at least I didn't have to worry about what other Jewish kids thought of me. Plus, I finally got have the Christmas tree I'd always wanted, and I got to celebrate Easter." I drained my coffee. "After a while, I felt like I wasn't Jewish anymore. I felt like I didn't qualify. But I didn't miss it. In fact, when I left Brandeis, I wanted to be anything but Jewish."

Judy leaned across the table. "I went to Beverly Hills High with a lot of other rich Jewish kids who all went to chichi tennis camps and had their own cars, and fancy-schmancy bar and bat mitzvahs." Without taking her eyes off mine, she pulled the pack of cigarettes from her shirt pocket. "But here's what my parents taught me: Being Jewish has nothing to do with money or Hebrew school or going to synagogue. It's about tikkun olam and doing mitzvot."

"Tikkun olam?"

"Repairing the world."

"Mitzvot?"

"Commandments to act well, to do the right thing by others. It is our greatest responsibility."

I winced at my ignorance.

"That's not the part of being Jewish you ever saw," Judy said, squeezing my hand. "You didn't grow up with the kind of supportive parents and advantages I had. You grew up with a single mom who was overwhelmed and depressed. How were you supposed to learn about being Jewish? Who was going to teach you?"

✦ ✦ ✦ ✦ ✦

Judy and I grew close. Her generosity and compassion allowed me to reveal my deepest shame and feel safe. More important, she gave me hope that I could find a way to be Jewish. She taught me through social action. Together, we withdrew our money from Bank of America to protest its investment in apartheid South Africa. We marched for reproductive rights. We rallied against nuclear weapons. On Friday nights, we welcomed Shabbat with Gallo wine and tofu burgers on challah. The ritual felt awkward to me.

"I don't know the prayers," I said, apologizing for my silence.

"You don't have to," she said. "Just close your eyes and say whatever words make sense to you."

"I'm not sure I believe in God."

"Me, neither. But there isn't just one way to be Jewish. You'll find yours."

Near the end of the fall quarter, Judy met David.

"This is Daveeed," she gushed in a foreign-sounding accent when I ran into them in the middle of campus.

✦ ✦ ✦ ✦ ✦

David was bearded and swarthy. He wrapped his long, thick, wavy black hair behind his head in a blue and white print bandana. Tufts of black chest hair pushed through his unbuttoned shirt collar, partially obscuring the chain that held a silver chai. "Daveeed is making aliyah," Judy crooned, entwining her arm in his.

"Aliyah?"

"He's moving to Israel."

"Why?"

"Because it's the Jewish homeland," David said.

Homeland? I thought Queens was my homeland.

"When are you going?" I said as they nuzzled noses. "When are you *going*?"

"I'm not sure," he said, reaching for the pack of Camels in the side pocket of his army-issued cargo pants. "I want Judy to come with me."

Once Judy and David moved in together, I had to compete for her time. It was a match I couldn't win. Judy was too newly in love to dedicate herself to our friendship as she once had. I relied on her heavily for emotional ballast, especially while I was entangled with Kyle and trying to figure out what kind of relationship I wanted or didn't want with him. It was particularly painful to see her so deeply in love with a man who clearly loved her, while all Kyle gave me was an all-or-nothing ultimatum. Rejecting it and him should have been my obvious choice, but it wasn't. My hunger to be wanted and loved was too intense for me to think clearly. Once he nixed the possibility of a friendship, however, the choice of whether to even try and salvage it was gone. Although we'd never been together in any healthy sense, we were now completely estranged. I felt devastated, while Judy, who'd been my rock, was missing in action.

Like an insidious black mold that had been dwelling inside me for years, depression began its slow, steady creep. My concentration in school continued to falter, my drive to succeed waned, and I finished the quarter with mediocre grades. If I were going to survive at Cal, I would have to move out of the dorm because I couldn't bear the thought of running into Kyle. I stopped by the housing office and spied an ad for a small apartment a couple of blocks away from campus. It was a quaint, second-floor walk-up in a well-kept turn-of-the-century building. It had high ceilings and polished wood moldings; clean, nondescript brown carpeting; and a small but functional utility kitchen. It came with a dark-green, slightly worn, but very comfy antique sofa, which fit nicely beneath the bay window on one wall, and a wooden dining-room table with four chairs on the opposite wall. At the far end of the living room was a large window that overlooked San Francisco Bay. Technically, the apartment was a one-bedroom, although the so-called bedroom, which shared one door into the living room and one into the bathroom, barely fit a double-size mattress. Still, the hundred-eighty-dollar monthly rent was cheaper than the dorm, and would be cheaper still if I found a roommate.

Judy had a friend named Phyllis who had just transferred to Cal from UCLA and was looking for an apartment. We liked each other well enough and decided that she would take the tiny bedroom and pay a hundred a month for rent. Meanwhile, I set up my double mattress in the corner of the spacious living room, and decorated it with a patchwork quilt and pillows to try to make it look like a daybed. Sleeping in the living room didn't bother me because neither Phyllis nor I had a boyfriend or required much privacy. She was a biochemistry major on a premed track, spent most of her time in the library, and preferred eating out to cooking at home. It was the ideal arrangement. I had the monetary advantages of a roommate without having to compromise too much of my solitude. And solitude was what I wanted.

Because Phyllis was hardly ever home, she didn't care how I decorated the place. I bought a cheap lamp, kitchenware, houseplants, and posters of my favorite Matisse and Picasso prints from the Berkeley flea market. I set up my stereo and speakers, and stacked records, books, and a few knickknacks on the built-in bookshelves. Not since my days of hunkering down inside my snow fort had I felt so cozy and content, safe inside the near-silence of my refuge.

In mid-November, the second quarter began. Now that I had a place of my own, I expected to feel calmer and more focused in school. I saw Judy infrequently and made a couple of new friends I'd meet occasionally for coffee. But I didn't feel the same peace I'd felt when I first moved into my apartment. The silence that I'd initially relished was starting to feel burdensome. Instead of soothing me, it was amplifying the noise in my head. And there was a lot of noise.

There had always been a lot of noise: echoes of shame and rage, mostly about my mother's drinking and neglect that I'd buried for years in academic achievement and speech superstardom. Now, there was noise about Kyle—even though he had wounded me, I missed him and wondered if not committing to a relationship with him had been a mistake. In the stillness of my apartment, the cacophony thundered.

It didn't help that Mom had begun calling me on weekend afternoons, drunk. I heard the slur in her speech instantly. I hated her for that. I hated her.

"Isssso good to hear your voice. How ARE you?"

"I can't talk now."

"I missss you. How'sss school?"

"Fine. Busy."

"Whensa good time for me t' call?"

"I don't know. I'll call you." I didn't call her. Weeks would pass. She'd call again. Perhaps she felt remorseful. Or perhaps she was so lonely that she was willing to risk rejection. I felt guilty for not wanting to talk to her. The guilt made me hate her more.

✦　✦　✦　✦　✦

A few days before Thanksgiving, she called to say that she and Louise, her next-door neighbor, were coming to visit. "We're coming for Thanksgiving!" She sounded unusually sober.

"Louise invited me along on her trip up to San Luis Obispo to see her sister," she told me. "We're passing through Berkeley, so we thought it would be nice to have Thanksgiving together!"

"I've got midterms. I don't have time to cook."

"You don't have to cook. We're going to bring Thanksgiving to you!"

Gutless, I relented.

Phyllis flew home to Los Angeles for Thanksgiving, and on that day, I cleaned my apartment and set the table for three. Mom estimated that she and Louise would arrive at five p.m. By seven, I hadn't heard from them. By nine, I began to worry.

At nine-thirty, Mom called. "We hit terrible traffic. You must be starving. We're almost there."

They arrived after ten, each hauling one side of an ice chest crammed with a complete, cooked, and frozen Thanksgiving meal, along with a tablecloth, sterling silver candlesticks, and Cold Duck.

"Oh, dear," Mom said with a frown as she pulled the huge, half-frozen turkey from the ice. "I took this out of the freezer two days ago. It should have thawed by now." We lit my efficiency oven and jammed the bird inside. "Give it half an hour," Mom said, sounding hopeful. She warmed the iced-over cranberry sauce, string beans, and sweet potato pie on top of the stove, stopping every few minutes to poke her finger inside the turkey's cavity to see if the stuffing was warm.

"How 'bout a little Cold Duck while we wait?" Thankfully, she liked the idea of Cold Duck better than the drink itself and took only a couple of sips.

It was nearly midnight by the time we sat down to eat our lukewarm meal. The clang and scrape of forks and knives on plates were the only sounds in the room.

"Evelyn, you're the only person I know who can serve a delicious Thanksgiving dinner that's been precooked and frozen!" Louise gushed, breaking the silence.

A better person would have appreciated a hand-delivered, homecooked Thanksgiving dinner. And I might have, had it come from someone other than my mother. But I had too much pent-up fury to feel anything but hatred. I'd done everything I could during the past two years to escape her orbit and now here she was, serving a tepid holiday feast that I had to keep assuring her was delicious. I was still taking care of her.

Halfway through the cheesecake dessert, Louise said, "We'd better get going."

"You're getting back on the road now?" I asked.

"We booked a motel for tonight but we'll be on the road first thing in the morning. We should be at my sister's by early afternoon."

"You keep the leftovers," Mom directed. "You won't have to cook for a while."

It was nearly one in the morning when they left. I was exhausted but too agitated to sleep. I put away the food, washed the dishes, and poured the remaining half-bottle of Cold Duck down the kitchen drain.

No single factor—not Mom's drunken bouts, the humiliation of scrubbing toilets at Brandeis, Kyle's bullying and abandonment, losing Judy's affections, or eating a cold Thanksgiving dinner at midnight—caused my eventual collapse. But Thanksgiving was the tremor that set it in motion, loosening a psychic avalanche that flattened me under mounds of debris. In the days immediately following Mom and Louise's visit, I couldn't stop crying. I couldn't sleep. I couldn't eat. I couldn't get out of bed. I didn't shower. I didn't brush my teeth. My legs were gone, and I was clinging to the last piece of stable ground, with nothing solid or safe below me.

Phyllis was still in L.A., so I stayed under the covers all weekend, rocking, sobbing, and screaming into my pillow. My mind was a movie reel playing backwards, then forward, then backwards again, rehashing the same scenes over and over, chewing on itself: You rotten miserable thing. You ruined my life. Had I ruined Mom's life? Or had she ruined mine? I wanted to stop the images but I couldn't. I tried to lose myself in sleep, but even when I managed to doze off, the movie reel became my dreams.

On the Saturday after Thanksgiving, I called Judy. "I haven't slept in days," I told her, crying. "I don't know what's happening. I'm so tired."

She brought over some marijuana and a small portable television set. "Take a few hits of this and you'll sleep like a baby," she said. "And watch TV. It'll distract you."

I smoked the joint that night. Almost instantly, my heart started to race. I could feel it hammering in my chest, ramming into my ribcage, then ballooning into my esophagus and up into my throat. I couldn't breathe. I tried turning on the TV. The knob wouldn't move. Is this the right knob? Do I turn it right? Do I turn it left? Do I pull it out? Push it in? What's wrong with this TV? What's wrong with ME? Relief, once so close, was gone. A new wave of tears crashed over me. I paced the living room, up and down, up and down.

I crawled onto the green sofa. Is the sofa shaking? Is the room shaking? Is it me? WHAT'S WRONG WITH ME? You should go out, take a walk. You haven't been outside in days. Go to a bookstore. I willed myself to move but couldn't let go of the sofa. I was holding on for dear life, as if in a car spun out of control, digging my nails into the cushions. Maybe I should call someone. Maybe I should call Judy. It's Saturday night. She'll be out. Besides, I've called her too much already. Who else can I call? I thought of calling Steven, my greatest champion, my clearest voice of reason. Steven understood me better than anyone, but I doubted that even he would be able to stop this nightmare. How can I explain what is happening? Where do I start? I checked the time. It was eleven-thirty at night. When will the morning come? When will this be over? What if it never ends? How can I make it stop? I could kill myself. That would stop the noise in my head. But how should I do it? Slit my wrists? Turn on the oven and put my head inside? Maybe I should just let the apartment fill with gas.

What if I fail? I curled into a ball and wedged myself into the sofa. Another rush of tears, and then finally, sleep.

I awoke with the sun shining through the bay window, warming my face. It was Sunday morning. Phyllis would be back by late afternoon. Winter quarter started the next day. I had a full schedule of classes. I didn't think I would make it through the day. I called Judy.

"I don't know what's going on," I spluttered through tears. "I can't eat. I can't sleep. I can't stop crying."

"I'm coming over," she announced. Judy and David lived nearby. Within minutes she was at my door.

"I was up most of the night," I said. "The pot freaked me out. I tried to watch TV but I couldn't turn on the set. I think the knob is stuck. I didn't want to break it."

She kneeled down and turned on the news. "You just have to turn it hard," she said, with a soft smile. "You wouldn't have broken it. And even if you had, it wouldn't have mattered. It's a TV." She put her arms around me.

"I'm sorry I keep bothering you," I said, weeping fully. "I don't know what's wrong with me. I feel like I'm losing my mind."

"Don't apologize," she said, brushing tears off my face. "You're in pain. Tomorrow we're going to talk to Walter."

✦　✦　✦　✦　✦

Walter Beecham was the bespectacled, bearded social science professor in whose class we'd met the previous quarter. He was also our advisor. Walter cared deeply about his students. He often stayed after class to talk with anyone who needed his ear. When I first arrived at Berkeley, he had counseled me about classes. I'd confided in him about my hellish year at Brandeis and my ambivalence about returning to school. I'd also told him a little bit about my life, which may be why he didn't look totally surprised when Judy and I walked into his office Monday morning.

"Andrea's in crisis," she said before I could get the words out. "She needs help."

I described the previous days of insomnia, the nonstop crying and suicidal thoughts. "I think I'm having a nervous breakdown," I said wearily.

Walter removed his glasses, placed his hands on my shoulders, and looked at my eyes. "You're wiped out," he said gently. "Okay. This is what I want you to do: I want you to withdraw from school today. Do it right now. Go to the registrar's office as soon as you leave here and fill out a withdrawal form. It's easy. They won't ask you any questions. They're used to students taking time off. Whenever you're ready, if you're ready, you can come back." As he spoke, he scribbled a name on a scrap of paper. "Then, I want you to call Helen Salter." He pressed the paper into my palm. "She's an excellent therapist and a friend. Call her today."

Helen insisted on seeing me the next day. "Can you come first thing in the morning? I don't want you to wait."

She lived in a Berkeley arts and crafts house a few blocks from campus. The minute I rang the bell, she opened the door and led me into her study. It was a small room filled with brightly colored tapestries and pillows from Africa and South America, as well as Judaica. In fact, I noticed a mezuzah inside the doorframe of her office and the house.

"Sit anywhere you like," she offered. Her voice was warm. So were her gray eyes and full-mouthed smile. She looked to be in her mid-forties, short and heavyset, with neck-length salt-and-pepper hair that she wore with bangs and a center part. Something about her felt familiar, as if I'd known her my whole life. Perhaps it was her New York accent, or the way her thick thighs rubbed together when she walked. Or perhaps it was the Star of David around her neck.

"Tell me what's going on," she said.

For nearly an hour I spewed my story, beginning with the events of the past week and reaching all the way back to Rego Park and the horrid Sunday morning visits with Milton. Helen listened intently, leaning forward in her chair, her elbows planted on her thighs, her chin resting in her hands. When she said our time was up, I couldn't believe that an hour had passed. I didn't want to leave.

"I'd like to see you three times a week," she said, registering my concern. "Don't worry about the money right now. I have a sliding scale. Pay me what you can." As she walked me to the door, she placed a hand on my shoulder and turned me toward her. "I need to know that you'll call me if you have any thoughts of hurting yourself. Promise me," she said, searching my eyes for agreement. "If you can't, then I'll have to hospitalize you right now." I gave her my word, shaken by just envisioning another night like the one I'd just had. "Okay. I'll see you in a couple of days. I'm trusting you to call me, day or night."

For the next six months, I saw Helen three times a week: twice privately and once in group therapy. I had initially resisted her suggestion of attending the group. I had no interest in revealing my emotional wreckage to strangers. But Helen insisted that hearing others' struggles would make it easier to share and accept my own.

"You'd be surprised how many people twice your age struggle," she assured me. "You're way ahead of many of them. You'll see."

The group of men and women, all of whom were at least twenty years older than I, welcomed me warmly. They'd been working together for a year or so and knew each other's stories. Some suffered with depression. Some were recovering alcoholics. Others had failed marriages or histories of destructive relationships. As Helen had predicted, listening to their stories made me feel less isolated and ashamed.

When I finally gathered the nerve to share my story, everyone responded with empathy and praise. I was, they all agreed, so much more together than they had been at my age. I hardly felt like I was together, but their words emboldened me and gave me hope that I would come through this nightmarish chapter of my life.

For the next year, I dedicated myself to therapy and to getting better. My withdrawal from Cal in December 1977 marked the end of my financial aid, including my work-study job at *The Daily Californian*. And so, in the same week that I began therapy, I began frantically job hunting. A speed-reading company offered me eighty dollars a day to canvass community college campuses around the Bay Area and pitch their classes to students. The work was lame, but it paid the bills.

I told Mom, Roy, and Steven about my breakdown and withdrawal from school, and they were one-hundred-percent supportive. Steven started calling me weekly to see how I was doing, while Roy wrote occasionally. Mom let me know that as far as she was concerned, I could leave school indefinitely. "I just want you to be happy," she'd said during one of our infrequent chats. It was a line she'd repeated throughout my life, and it was the best gift she could have given me. But it did not dilute the rage I felt when she called on weekend afternoons, after she'd been drinking. I stopped answering my phone after noon.

Once Helen felt confident that I was no longer a danger to myself, she suggested that I see her only twice a week, once privately and once in group. She relocated our private sessions to a soundproofed studio where she had begun practicing a therapeutic technique that encouraged me to yell, bite into a thick towel, and pound on foam furniture to help me release my most submerged feelings. When I'd first started therapy, I was too self-conscious to cry in front of Helen, let alone smack a foam-rubber bat against a mini-fridge-size foam-rubber cube while grunting and emitting other primal sounds. After all, I had worked all my life to bury my deepest self, disguising my anguish in academic achievement.

Yet, week after week, Helen would encourage me to close my eyes, slow my breathing, and call up memories of my mother, my father, and my childhood. Once, she placed the rolled-up towel in my arms and told me to rock it like a baby, as if I were the baby. I scoffed at the idea, ridiculing it as hippy-dippy Berkeley therapy. Then I tried it. It was the first time I wept openly in her presence.

Pain, manifested in its rawest form, can resemble madness. And if someone had told me that at twenty years old, I would be a temporary college dropout spending an hour a week thrashing foam furniture while I screamed and wept, I would have thought it insane. But it was in a soundproofed room, flogging foam rubber and hollering my guts out, where I reluctantly and achingly excavated the pieces of my past, and cleared a path to healing.

It was a long, slow journey, and just a couple of months into it, I recognized two things about my life that had to change: I had to find a more enjoyable and interesting job, and I had to leave my apartment. Phyllis and I got along fine, but she was never home, and although that setup had been ideal when she'd first moved in, it wasn't working anymore. I was too isolated. I was lonely. I needed to have people around me. I wanted to be back in the world.

I found a job making soup and sandwiches at the Stuffed Inn, a popular deli on the hilly north side of campus. My shift began at seven a.m., when I would open the restaurant, make vats of pea and vegetable soup, halve hundreds of avocados, slice pounds of lunchmeat and cheese, and mix tubs of egg salad and tuna fish. The work was mindless, but at least it wasn't solitary. At ten a.m., my coworkers, who included students, artists, and activists, would arrive. One would make a pot of coffee. Another would turn on the stereo, and we'd drink coffee, wipe down tables, dance, and sing to the sounds of Bob Marley, Stevie Wonder, and the Grateful Dead. Around eleven-thirty, the regular lunchtime crowd of students and professors would start lining up to study the chalkboard menu that listed sandwiches named for American authors. What made tuna on rye a "Hemingway" or roast beef and Russian dressing on a Kaiser roll a "Fitzgerald" I never understood, but I memorized these and every other combination, just as I mastered the art of making industrial-size quantities of soup and de-pitting avocados. When my shift ended at two p.m., I'd walk home tired but content, reeking of onion, my fingernails green with avocado.

I loved my job, especially my coworkers—the poets, musicians, social activists, and college dropouts who, like me, were trying to figure out the next steps in their lives. I didn't share their passion for Jerry Garcia, reggae, or marijuana, but we enjoyed each other's company, and often hung out at cafés drinking cappuccino and talking about our futures.

In my immediate future was a plan to end apartment living and move into a communal household. One day, one of my work buddies showed me a "roommate wanted" ad on the restaurant bulletin board: Two men and a woman, all in their late twenties, were looking for a second woman to move in to their rambling Tudor two blocks from the Stuffed Inn.

Mike and Audrey were graduate students at Cal. Felix ran his family's business restoring antique carousel animals. He was dark-haired and bearded with a pale Irish complexion. Mike, also bearded, had sandy brown hair and wore wire-rimmed glasses. Audrey was a willowy, curly-haired brunette who wore a silver chai. "Oh, you're Jewish?" I said, blurting out the obvious. "Me, too." I don't know what inspired this announcement, especially since I'd shelved my Jewish exploration when Judy and I drifted apart. But something about seeing Audrey's chai and learning that Mike was Jewish made me feel connected to both of them.

Why did the fact of their or anyone's Jewishness create this sense of connection? It defied logic. It defied my history. I had spent my youth beaming jealousy and contempt on every Jewish kid I knew. It was the best strategy I had for dealing with my shame. My friendship with Judy had encouraged me to explore my Jewish self, but since my breakdown, I had reverted to my old default of being nothing—until I met another Jew and felt that peculiar sense of fellowship. It baffled me, feeling esprit de corps with people simply because they were Jewish, being drawn to members of the tribe that I'd eschewed.

Talking about my connection and conflict with Judaism was difficult, because from the outside it probably seemed easily surmountable. You want to be Jewish? Be Jewish! But it wasn't that simple, because to be Jewish would have required tremendous self-acceptance—acceptance of my history, ignorance, and shame. It would have required me to feel comfortable inside my skin, which I did not, and yet, I did want to be *something*. I wanted to be part of something. Not a communal household or therapy group but a larger, spiritual community that could open a window onto life's meaning and, perhaps, inner peace. The Berkeley campus was full of people offering such communion. Could I be a Jew for Jesus? A Hare Krishna? A Buddhist? A Baptist? Perhaps. But why would I feel any more legitimate claiming one of these traditions as my own rather than Judaism? I ignored the question and obvious contradiction.

One afternoon as I was leaving the restaurant, I saw a man reading at a corner table. I'd seen him before, sitting alone with his book and cup of tea. He wore loose-fitting cotton pants and a tunic, and wooden beads around his neck and wrist. His wire-rimmed glasses made him look learned, and when he removed them to invite me to chat, I saw gentleness in his eyes.

He said he was studying Buddhism, that he'd been drawn to its teachings on suffering, detachment, and compassion. I, too, felt drawn. These were exactly the ingredients my inner-peace-seeker needed.

"I'm thinking of becoming a Buddhist," I told Judy when I ran into her a few days later.

"A Buddhist?" Her gaze narrowed.

"It makes so much sense. Detachment. Compassion. Self-acceptance."

"You can become a Buddhist," she said, looking at me squarely. "But in your blood, it's not who you are."

She was right. I could no more authentically anoint myself Buddhist than Baptist. Of course, I could have educated myself about any one of these traditions, just as I could have educated myself about Judaism, the tradition into which I had been born. But I didn't.

✦　✦　✦　✦　✦

My year away from school was essential, difficult, and rich. It was a year of self-exploration, of climbing out of my suicidal abyss, and, with Helen's help, raking through the past twenty years to understand what had led me to it. I spent session after session mourning the father I never had, excoriating him for failing me so miserably, spewing anger and hatred toward my mother for her drinking and abuse, grieving a childhood that ended while I was still a child. It was harrowing but liberating work.

My depression and loneliness, anxiety and rage, obsession with success and validation were making sense, even if they didn't disappear. It would take many more years and ill-advised attempts at romance, including a dead-end fling with my roommate Felix that culminated in my needing to find a new living arrangement, before I learned to discipline my demons.

Some of that discipline came from exercise. I swam laps at the university pool. I started running. I also started writing. I'd long written poetry and kept a journal, but I was no longer interested in rehashing personal angst. I wanted to write about other people's struggles. Walking to and from work during the past year, I recognized the faces of many who were struggling, from the homeless sleeping in doorways on Telegraph Avenue or languishing in People's Park; to the women hunched on blankets, cradling their babies while begging for spare change; to the mentally ill sparring with imaginary combatants—people who seemed more disenfranchised than I had ever been as an impoverished Jew with an alcoholic mother. I wondered why their lives had unraveled and what had sustained them, however marginally. What would their resurgence require? What accounted for their meager survival amid overwhelming adversity? Or were they beyond hope? Where, I wondered, does a person even begin to search for such a thing as hope?

The embattled folks I saw every day weren't thriving, but neither did they seem to have given up. Even my mother, who'd endured catastrophic heartbreak, hadn't given up. When depressed and drinking, she still pressed on. Learning not to quit was the lesson she had instilled in me every time she put the salt shaker in my hand and told me to go after robins. Was that how I'd survived my collapse—by seeking help instead of ending my life? I was too intellectually moored to credit anything divine for my survival. Yet, I ruminated about the misfortunes and survival of others. Someday I would write about them. I would tell stories of human struggle and triumph. It would be my way of scratching a spiritual itch.

I no longer had my work-study job at *The Daily Californian* but I'd stayed in touch with the editor, who welcomed—and paid for—a couple of essays I wrote about street life in Berkeley.

"I'm published!" I exclaimed to Steven, whom I called the day my first article came out. "And they paid me for it!"

"Send it to me! I want to see everything you write."

Emboldened, I began sending story ideas to the editor of a monthly called the *East Bay Express*. John Raeside liked my ideas but what he really needed was a dance critic. "Can you write about dance?" he asked. I loved dance and had taken some classes at Cal. Though I would have preferred writing about street people, I wasn't about to turn down an assignment, especially when it included complimentary tickets to performances and paid thirty bucks an article.

"Writing is writing," Steven said. "Keep it up."

And so, my freelance writing career and my new life began.

Although Audrey said she didn't care about my affair with Felix, Mike said I'd broken the cardinal rule of communal living and demanded I move out, even though on most nights Felix escorted his long-term girlfriend past my room and up to his, both of them smiling at me as I sat, humiliated, in the stairwell.

Mike didn't care about any of that. And Felix, having lived in the house longer than anyone, had no intention of leaving. So, feeling ashamed of my own sleazy behavior, I relented and joined a new household.

Carol, Alex, Dan, and I hit it off instantly and lived well together for a few years. We shared Sunday dinners, as well as Passover Seders and Rosh Hashanah celebrations, which Carol, whose parents had survived the Holocaust, insisted on. Not since my childhood encounters with my great-aunt Vera had I met anyone remotely touched by the Holocaust, and the sadness of it briefly inspired me to try to resurrect my Jewish journey. It didn't last.

In the winter of 1978, a couple of months after moving into the new house, I returned to school. I decided that studying journalism would be the best approach to becoming a writer who wrote about human struggle.

"You don't need a journalism degree," the dean of Cal's journalism school said when I showed him samples of my freelance work. "You've already got clips. Just keep doing what you're doing."

Realizing that I wasn't thick-skinned enough to be a news-breaking reporter, I sought guidance from my advisor, Walter Beecham.

"You're interested in human struggle and social justice," he said. "Why not major in social science?"

"Because I want to be a writer," I said.

"You can still be a writer. You already are."

His words reflected more confidence in me than I had in myself, and infused me with the determination to make them true.

Time away from school had given me valuable perspective. I studied what I loved, didn't suffer over grades, and did fine. Three years later, in June 1981, at age twenty-three, I graduated. Mom flew up from San Diego to attend the ceremony. I'd avoided seeing her since her Thanksgiving visit, but didn't have the heart to forbid her from coming. Neither my roommates nor I kept liquor in the house, so her drinking wasn't an issue. When she suggested extending her stay, I told her I had to start looking for a job.

An aerobics studio in Berkeley hired me a week later. In 1981, the fitness craze was sweeping California, around the same time that I was becoming a workout junkie, having discovered that exercising often was an ideal distraction from depression. I taught between ten and fifteen classes a week, which supported me while I continued freelance writing. It was an exhausting way to make a living. I would ride my ten-speed through the early-morning Bay Area fog to the studio, teach one or two classes, ride home, try to write, and then cycle back to the studio at the end of the day to teach again. Teaching provided a steadier income than writing, and I was often too tired to think about anything besides soaking my overused body in a warm bath.

The writer's life, such as it was, was tougher to sustain than I'd imagined. Not only did it exact more time and energy than I had, but it also required a certain amount of isolation, which made me feel lonely. I didn't like being alone. After three years of therapy, there was still a lot of noise in my head, which I quieted by running or swimming. The only time I was at peace alone was when I was working out. Exercise had become my religion.

As for my spiritual restlessness, I soothed it in my new community of aerobics teachers and students. A couple of students, who happened to be Jewish, became my close friends. I didn't seek out Jewish women. But something kept drawing me to them. This did not happen with men, perhaps because I met so few. Those I was drawn to were usually gay or not available.

I sorely wanted a relationship. I had such trouble meeting men that I even placed an ad in the "personals" column of the *San Francisco Bay Guardian*. I received dozens of letters from eager suitors, some of whom I met, none of whom turned out to be Mr. Right. The few relationships I did have were almost always brief, tempestuous affairs with men twice my age who were going through divorce (or who claimed to be going through divorce) or on the rebound. Luckily, I felt no pressure from my biological clock. I wasn't interested in ever getting married or having children.

"Have you considered contacting your father?" Helen ventured as I griped about my failed love life. "You see the pattern, right?" she asked gingerly. "The older men?"

"I don't know where he lives," I protested, like a child trying to weasel out of homework. "I don't even know if he's alive."

"Ask your brothers," she pressed. "They might be able to point you in the right direction."

"Why does it matter?" I challenged. Just thinking about speaking with Milton Kott scared me. "I've forgotten that I even have a father."

"No, you haven't."

✦ ✦ ✦ ✦ ✦

I went to the university library and found the New York yellow pages. Roy told me that Milton had once co-owned a sports-fishing supply store on East Nineteenth Street in Manhattan with a man named Harry Eiseman. The store was called Eiseman & Kott. I turned to the Es and saw the store's display ad in the middle of the page. Too timid to call, I wrote my father a letter.

One week later, I received his reply.

"I don't know if I'm more shocked or overjoyed to hear from you!" he'd scrawled. He ended every sentence with an exclamation mark. "When can we talk?!"

I wrote back and once again he responded fast, this time enclosing two photos of himself in a jacket and tie. His silver hair was nearly gone. He looked heavy. His face was crooked and red. He was in his seventies now and must have assumed that I wouldn't recognize him because he'd drawn a circle around his head with an arrow labeled "me" pointing to it.

Milton wrote to me for the next several weeks, always including pictures with his letters. The pictures went backwards chronologically. In one, he was eating an ice-cream cone, and in another, he had a drink in his hand, looking as I had remembered, trim and dashing, with dark eyes and silver hair gleaming. He also sent pictures of me as a toddler on a tricycle and then, as a baby. He proposed that we speak on the phone. "I'll call you next Monday, four p.m. California time!" he wrote.

There's nothing to be afraid of, I told myself. He can't do anything to you over the phone.

I recognized his voice immediately when he called.

"Is this Andrea Kott? The one and only Andrea Kott? The daughter of the one and only Milton Kott?" He had the same hambone humor. "This is your dad. I don't mind telling you that I cried when I read your letter. I showed it to everyone in the store."

I struggled to start the conversation. "How've you been?"

"It's so nice that you wrote to me. Have you been getting my letters?"

"Yes."

"Did you look at the pictures?"

"Yes."

"Did you see the one with the arrow pointing to my face? Funny, eh? Like you wouldn't know it was me! It was Phil's idea. My friend Phil, he's the guy next to me in the picture. Such a kidder."

I pulled out the first picture that Milton had sent of himself in a jacket and tie. He was standing next to a man his age. They were holding hands.

The conversation lasted less than five minutes, and in that time, Milton never told me how he'd been. He didn't ask anything about me, either. In fact, he seemed to be talking to himself. After going on and on about how delighted he'd been to hear from me, he moved to get off the phone.

"When can we talk again?" he asked. "How 'bout next week? You call me this time. Call collect."

Feeling disappointed, I agreed. A week later, I dialed his number.

"Andrea?" He sounded half-asleep.

"Did you remember our phone date?"

"Of course I remembered. You can call me anytime. And you call collect."

"I did. You accepted the charges. Should I call back?"

"Nothing doing. What do you want to talk about?"

"Oh, I don't know . . . about you and me I guess . . . and about my mother . . ."

"Your mudda. Whadda piece a work she was, lemme tell you. That woman had to knock back a coupla Scotches every night just to get to sleep."

"Did you ever remarry?" I ventured.

"Now you listen to me: I don't ask you about your personal life and don't you ask me about mine!"

His explosion stunned me. Suddenly, I was back in Parson's toy store hearing his open hand slam the counter. At twenty-three years old and living three thousand miles away, I was quaking.

"Hey, we can't do all this catching up on the phone!" he blurted, adopting a new persona. "Why don't you fly out here? I would love to see you! I can send you a ticket!"

I imagined being alone with him, something my mother had always tried to shield me from. "It's not a good time," I lied, eager to hang up. "I just started a new job. And my mother's coming to visit—"

"Your mudda, whadda piece a—"

"I gotta go. Sorry. I'll call you again."

I didn't call, and he didn't, either. He might have been a harmless old man like the one in the photo with his face circled. But he sounded bitter and unhinged. I destroyed his letters and tried to forget about him, as I had attempted to do with Judaism. I kept the pictures, however. Maybe someday I'll change my mind and fly east to meet him.

Three years later, Milton was dead. The call came at 11:15 P.M. California time.

"Is this Andrea Kott?" The connection was crackly.

"Yes."

"Is this Andrea Kott, daughter of Milton Kott?"

"Yes, it is."

"This is Jack Bunker, Ms. Kott. I am your father's attorney. . . ."

"Yes?"

"Your father died this morning. I'm sorry to be the one to have to tell you."

I mashed the receiver against my ear. I opened my mouth but no sound came out. Your father died this morning. Milton had been a stranger to me. He had been unloving, vindictive, and mean. But he was my father. I wept, not for who he was, but for who he'd never been.

"He was ill," Jack Bunker continued. "He'd had heart surgery a few weeks ago. I brought him home from the hospital. I didn't hear from him for a few days so I stopped by. I found him lying on the floor next to his bed. Facedown. I'm sorry to be the one to have to tell you."

"Nobody told me he'd been ill."

"Well, you two weren't exactly pen pals."

The next day, I called my mother and brothers. I couldn't hold the news of Milton's death by myself. Jack Bunker had already called them.

"Thank God," Mom said, exhaling deeply. Neither her divorce nor moving to California had eased her torment. Once we'd settled in La Mesa, her fear of Milton seemed absurd. But I couldn't reason her out of it. Like anger, fear was something that Mom gripped like a shield. She never seemed to feel safe. Mom didn't even believe that Hitler was dead. She insisted he was not only alive but also planning another Holocaust. At least she believed that Milton was dead, and she rejoiced like the Munchkins who found Dorothy's smashed house on top of the Wicked Witch of the East.

Steven reacted blandly to Milton's death. "Good for Mom," he said. "That's one worry she can put away. You must feel relieved too, right?" It was uncharacteristic of my brother not to probe more deeply. Despite our intimacy, however, Steven and I had never talked much about my father, or his. The few times I'd asked about Leslie, he'd shot back terse, one-word answers, which seemed to say, "Let's not go there."

Roy hadn't been any more eager to talk about his father, but he never masked his sorrow about having lost him. On the rare occasions that I'd broached the topic, he'd close his eyes and shake his head slowly, as if Leslie had just died. Roy seemed more angry than sad about his father's death. But he never pretended to be over it. And he insisted that Steven wasn't, either.

"Mom never told us that our father was sick," Roy had said when he visited me in Berkeley earlier that year, one of his rare, random attempts to reach out. "She either said he was away on business or visiting family in Hungary. After he died, she took us to a lake for a picnic. That's where she told us. I remember her turning to me and saying, 'You're the man of the house now, Roy.' I was seven. Steven was five. The whole time she talked, I was picking up grasshoppers and snapping off their heads. Steven sank down into the water until it covered his head."

Like Mom, Roy seemed to carry heartache everywhere. He blamed it for his failed romances and overall unhappiness. He said that losing a parent at such a young age had permanently scarred him. He called it a primal injury, the kind that could handicap anyone, no matter how despicable a parent may have been.

Roy must have thought a lot about my fatherlessness because soon after we learned of Milton's death, he offered to fly me to New York.

"Milton had a younger sister, Shirley," he said. "Maybe you'd like to meet her. I'm sure Jack Bunker would give you her number. I believe she lives near Coney Island with her husband and daughter. They're your family."

Until that moment, I had never considered that I had another half of a biological family—aunts, uncles, and cousins I'd never met. My fantasy about discovering a loving father had faded but I started spinning a new one, a dream about finding love in this newfound family. Drawing a deep breath, I phoned Shirley.

"I was expecting your call," she said. Maybe it was grief that made her sound chilly and flat. Or maybe she thought I was angling for a slice of Milton's estate.

"I was thinking of coming to New York," I said timidly. "I thought we could meet."

"We met a long time ago but you probably don't remember. Call us when you get here. We'll give you directions to the house."

✦ ✦ ✦ ✦ ✦

On a raw day in February 1984, I rode the D train toward Sheepshead Bay. Through a grimy subway car window, on an elevated section of track, I spotted the sign for the Cyclone roller coaster that Steven and I had ridden twenty years earlier. I got off at Coney Island, walked down a flight of stairs to the street below, and called Shirley from a pay phone. The winter wind burned my fingers. "Wait for us by the turnstiles at the bottom of the stairs," she instructed. "We'll recognize you."

Minutes later, a diminutive, platinum-haired woman wrapped chin high in a mink coat approached me. She was the female version of my father, with gleaming white teeth, piercing dark eyes, and bushy charcoal eyebrows.

"Andrea? I can't believe it. The last time we saw you was when you were an infant, just days old, right, Stan?" she said to the heavyset man beside her. She cupped my face in her hands. "You have your mother's cheeks. But you have your father's smile."

Shirley and Stan shared a two-family, red-brick rowhouse with their daughter Heddy, a thirty-year-old cosmetology student who lived in the apartment upstairs. Their house was spotless. Heavy clear plastic covered the living-room sofa and chairs. In the small kitchen was a square table, draped in a vinyl cloth. The table had four chairs and place settings. In the center was a plate with chocolate daisy-shaped cookies. "Are you hungry?" Shirley asked. "Your father loved these cookies. Your mother, she wouldn't touch a cookie. Not ever. Always watching her figure."

If I had ridden a spaceship and landed on another planet, this would have been it—not because of how people or things looked but because of how surreal it felt to be sitting elbow-to-elbow with next of kin I never knew existed. Do they love me? Could they? Could I love them? Is blood enough to bond us?

We sipped coffee in awkward silence. Heddy nibbled a cookie, picking off sugar granules with her long pink fingernails. Obese with a tight perm, she looked like a fat-faced Little Orphan Annie, squinting beneath layers of heavy blue eye shadow. Stan, a cab driver in his late sixties, was obese, too. He worked the night shift and kept checking his watch. Shirley, nearing seventy, looked like a ballet mistress with her hair twisted tightly behind her head.

"You sure you won't have a cookie?" she coaxed.

Heddy helped herself to another. Stan refreshed his coffee. This is my family. My aunt. My uncle. My cousin. The wall clock ticked.

"Your father was so thrilled to hear from you," Shirley began, sounding forlorn. "He showed us your letters."

"He wanted to see you," Stan chimed in.

"Oh, he always wanted to see you," Shirley said, the pitch of her voice climbing. "But your mother . . ." She said mother like it left a bad taste in her mouth. "Evelyn had it out for Milton from the very beginning."

Stan nodded in agreement.

I felt cornered like a mouse. "I guess Milton never paid my mother any alimony or child support. . . ." I didn't guess. I knew. I knew how vicious my father had been. I knew how pummeled my mother was. But I was sitting in a minefield, afraid of stepping on a wire.

"She wouldn't let him see you," Shirley spat, her eyebrows knitting together. "She brainwashed you against him! He never had a chance!" Like a summer day turned stormy, the room suddenly felt airless and dark. "You were just a child, I know," she resumed, calmer. "The failure of that marriage had nothing to do with you. But boy, was your mother a case. And your grandmother—oh, my God . . ." She dabbed the corners of her red-lipsticked mouth with a napkin. "We were so happy when you wrote to him. And your father was beside himself. He kept hoping you'd fly out here. He would've paid for the ticket. Why didn't you come?"

My reasons had felt right at the time. But now I felt foolish and sad for having dropped the ball. Maybe Milton did love me. Maybe I would have discovered that if I'd visited him. But maybe not.

"I'm sorry," I said limply.

"I know you are," Shirley said. "Come downstairs. I have some pictures you might want."

She led me to the basement. "This was more your father's room than anyone else's. That was his favorite chair," she said, pointing to an oversized brown-leather recliner in the corner of the wood-paneled room. "He spent Saturday afternoons in that chair, watching TV." She handed me two Polaroids of Milton sitting in the chair. It swallowed him up. "These were taken a few days before he went into the hospital. He had a bad heart, you know."

He looked old and pathetic behind the heavy, black-rimmed glasses that covered half his face. In one photo, he held the glasses in his hand. His eyes were red and moist. His mouth hung in a thin frown. His red polo shirt, open at the collar, revealed his thin, shriveled neck. His legs were matchsticks. A wet spot encircled the half-open fly of his white pants. I felt sorry for him. This was the man I had been afraid to see?

Shirley and I returned to the kitchen. It was four-thirty and dark outside. "Would you like more coffee?" she offered.

"Thank you, no. I better head back to the city."

"We'll take you to the station."

She wrapped herself in her mink coat and slid next to me in the backseat of the car. I didn't want to stay any longer but I felt sad about leaving, doubtful I'd be seeing them again anytime soon. Stan parked the car and they walked me to the turnstiles. I took my time hugging them and they hugged me back. I kissed each of them on the cheek and they kissed me.

"I'm so glad we found each other," Shirley said. "Let's not be strangers."

I'd hoped that by meeting Shirley and Stan I would learn something deep about the person my father was, something that might have helped me understand, even forgive, his malice. I'd long suspected, for example, that he was gay and closeted, which would have explained his rage toward my mother, and later toward me when I asked if he'd remarried. But neither my brief correspondence with him, nor my visit with my aunt and uncle, revealed anything about him or his life, leaving me without the closure I'd sought. To me, he would always be a mystery and a monster.

✦ ✦ ✦ ✦ ✦

I spent the flight back to Berkeley thinking about my new family and trying to figure out when I could see them again. I planned to write and thank them for opening their hearts to me. Before I wrote, Roy called.

"Did you ever ask Shirley about Milton's will? She's the executor, you know. You and Mom might have some money coming to you."

"I just met her, Roy. We're still getting to know each other. How can I ask her about money?"

"Milton never paid Mom alimony or child support, Andrea. You and she are entitled to some portion of whatever he had."

"I'm sure Shirley knows that. Let's wait and see what happens."

"No, don't wait. Once the will is read in probate court it will be hard to ask for anything."

"It's hard now."

"It will be harder."

I'd just found Shirley. I didn't want to alienate her.

"Find out about the will," Roy pressed. "Do it for Mom."

That day, reluctantly, I called.

"I figured I'd be hearing from you," Shirley said, her voice steely.

"You did? Why?" I asked, feeling guilty.

"Your mother. I'm sure she's been wondering about the will."

"Well, sort of . . ."

"Yeah, I figured your mother put you up to this. You'll get something, don't worry."

"When will you—"

"We'll figure it out."

That spring, Jack Bunker read my father's will in a Long Island probate court. My mom, brothers, and I were not present, though we'd each received a copy of the will in the mail. "In consideration of Evelyn Kott, my stepsons Roy and Steven, and my daughter Andrea," it stated, "for whom I make no provision . . ." I reread the sentences, looking for a typo. Again and again, I read. Milton had disinherited us all.

I'd been disowned. I felt too angry and hurt to care about the money. Still, I wondered: Had Milton already cut me out of his will by the time he'd started sending me photos? Or had it been an afterthought, a response to feeling spurned, a final act of retribution for my not coming to see him? I wondered if Shirley knew that I'd been cut out, and why she'd been so quick to guarantee me something. Maybe she hadn't planned on giving me anything.

Word of our disinheritance spread among Mom's small circle of friends and relatives, all of whom began calling me. "Your father was a good-for-nothing," each of them said, as if reading the same script. "A rat! A louse! He never gave your mother a dime. He owes her!"

Roy called to tell me that he and Steven had hired an attorney. "We're going to court on Mom's behalf." She wouldn't have to appear, he said. She'd been through enough. "You,

Steven, and I will give the deposition." It didn't matter whether I consented or refused. Either way, I would have felt like a traitor.

Weeks earlier, I'd been hugging Shirley and Stan at the Coney Island subway stop. Now, we sat at opposite ends of a long oak table in a windowless conference room in a Brooklyn courthouse. I tried to catch Shirley's gaze to convey my conflict and remorse. She averted her eyes. The attorneys asked why we were contesting the will. I spoke for the record, robotically. Shirley and her family whispered to each other like children telling classroom secrets.

"I told you I would give you something," she hissed as we all filed out of the room. "I didn't have to come to this." She whisked away with Stan and Heddy. I never spoke with any of them again.

In the end, the court awarded Mom, my brothers, and me a total of eighteen thousand dollars, which we split four ways. My brothers said that Shirley never would have coughed up that much. For them and for Mom, the settlement was a win. I felt gypped. Sure, the money came in handy and kept me afloat while I built my freelance career. But it came at the expense of my relationship with Shirley, the only link to my father that I would ever have.

By 1984, at age twenty-six, I was contributing to a number of national women's magazines. I was writing about health and fitness, which were becoming my specialties, building a portfolio of national clips, and meeting editors. As I proved my capability, I took on assignments to write about a wide range of subjects, including business, auto racing, and even Russian politics. My expanding portfolio led to more work.

My combined income from teaching, freelancing, and writing occasional advertising copy allowed me to afford my own apartment, a three-hundred-thirty-dollar-a-month one-bedroom in a rundown turn-of-the-century building in a not-so-good part of Oakland. Living with Carol, Alex, and Dan had been great, but it had also run its course. I was older now and more emotionally resilient. With plenty of friends, I was eager to live alone.

My love life continued to be a series of poor choices. Therapy, and my attempts to come to terms with my father, had helped me understand these choices, which continued to feature older, unavailable men. But it didn't stop me from making them.

The exception was Will, a ponytailed computer typesetter whom I met in the advertising department of Emporium-Capwell in San Francisco where I was a freelance copywriter. Nearly six feet tall, Will carried much of his three hundred fifty pounds in the massive thighs he'd built during his powerlifting days. Despite his excessive weight, his teddy-bear face, green eyes, and warm smile melted me.

At thirty-six, Will was ten years older than I. A fanatical reader with an encyclopedic knowledge of global history, philosophy, and politics, he'd chosen leftist activism over college, and spent his twenties working as a community organizer and protesting the Vietnam War. His passion for social justice inspired me. Born into wealth, he loathed all forms of elitism and inequality, and happily gave cash to the homeless, sometimes as much as twenty dollars at a time.

"Here ya go, brother," he'd say, pressing a bill into a stranger's hand.

"How can you do that?" I'd ask in a tone of moral superiority. "He's just going to spend it on booze."

"So what? If I were sleeping on a subway grate, I'd probably like a bottle of Thunderbird to get me through the night."

Will's heart was bottomless. His sense of humor was wicked. He made me seize with laughter. He loved me sweetly.

"Hi, hon," he'd say over phone in the middle of the day.

"Umm, I'm working right now . . ."

"I know. I just called to say hi. I miss you."

Later, at the sound of my key in the door, he'd cheer.

When our four-year, on-again, off-again relationship began, I adored Will, and the feeling was mutual. But our relationship lacked one crucial ingredient: heat. When it came to sex, Will could take it or leave it. It's not that he didn't like sex; he just didn't crave it the way I did. I didn't lust for him, but I wanted him, and I wanted him to want me. His affection was constant yet platonic. Instead of seducing me, he'd muss my hair or rope me into a slap-and-tickle fest. He didn't reject my advances, but he didn't initiate any, either.

From the beginning, we were like an old married couple: talking, laughing, and holding hands. We liked the same movies, plays, and food. We cared about the same political and social causes. The problem was I didn't want to be part of an old married couple. I wanted to be like the women I saw at the café where we had breakfast on Sunday mornings, their hair still wet from the shower that they surely had taken with a partner after untangling themselves from love-soaked sheets. Will and I never showered together. Our sheets were always pitifully dry.

Will said he wanted to spend the rest of his life with me, although he had no interest in marriage. Part of me loved the idea of growing old with him. I'd even fantasized marrying and having a child together. But another part of me knew that I was too young and libidinous to commit myself to someone who was so erotically detached and fell fast asleep at night after a quick and uneventful cuddle, leaving me alone with a jumbo pack of M&Ms and David Letterman. After two exasperating years of aching for passionate love, I made my first attempt to leave.

Ending my relationship with Will was hard because, aside from sexual incompatibility, we were well matched. Our sorry sex life was all we ever fought about. I chastised myself for being childish and shallow, giving up the truest love I had ever known or might again. But I was twenty-eight years old and unwilling to relinquish my dream of true romance. I didn't want a best friend. I wanted a lover.

I also wanted out of my feast-or-famine freelance life. My body was worn out from teaching. I hated writing advertising copy. And writing for women's magazines wasn't giving me the experience I needed to learn to cover the social issues that I cared about. The best way to acquire such experience would be to work as a daily reporter. It was time to get a newspaper job.

Every week, I poured over the want ads in *Editor & Publisher* and mailed letters with copies of my resume and clips to papers all over the country. The bulk of newspaper jobs were on the East Coast, which suited me, since I'd been feeling nostalgic for New York and wanted to be near my brothers. Steven had finished his Ph.D. and accepted a job teaching English literature at Western Connecticut State University in Danbury, and Roy, who surprised me periodically with a phone call or invitation to meet for dinner, had remarried and moved to Brooklyn.

Mom still lived in La Mesa. At sixty-two, she had retired early from UCSD. We'd advised her against retirement, afraid that she'd become isolated. But she couldn't tolerate her job anymore, and assured us that she'd be fine. She did quit smoking. But she drank more. The dress she'd bought for Roy's wedding could not hide the bloat she'd acquired from alcohol. No amount of makeup could obscure her puffy face and eyes, which she could barely open. And nothing would stop her from leaving drunken soliloquies on my answering machine on weekend afternoons. I had every reason to leave California.

Part Six:

The Newspaper Life, Norwich, and Beyond:

1986–Present

At TWENTY-EIGHT AND WITHOUT A JOURNALISM degree, I had slim odds of landing a newspaper job. Competition was fierce, and aside from my stint as the *Daily Californian*'s AP wire editor, I had no daily experience. Plus, I was relatively old to be starting out in newspapers. I would be lucky to get an offer anywhere. Still, I applied for every job for which I thought myself remotely qualified, preparing for the possibility of having to relocate to some no-man's-land in the middle of the country. When Fred Granger, the executive editor of the *Norwich Bulletin*, invited me for an interview, I felt like I'd hit the jackpot.

The *Bulletin* was a thirty-thousand-circulation daily located in the tiny Connecticut shore town of Norwich. I was unfamiliar with the geography of the state and had blindly assumed that because it was small, its towns would be in close proximity to each other, and that I'd be a stone's throw from Kent, where Steven and Dierdre lived. But Norwich was a two-hour drive from Kent, a three-hour drive from Manhattan, where I had friends, and just about as far from other metropolitan areas. This didn't dampen my interest in the job. Even Granger's concern about my leaving "Bezerkely" for Connecticut's staid southeastern shore didn't scare me off.

"What do you know about southeastern Connecticut?" the grizzled and bearded editor asked me over lunch.

"Nothing," I confessed.

"Oh, well," he said, tilting his head back to take a long slow swallow of Scotch. "You'll learn."

I should have listened. He must have known how staggeringly difficult it would be for anyone to move from a progressive, diverse, and vibrant city to a conservative, homogeneous backwater. But he needed an editor, and if I was willing to uproot myself, then he wasn't about to discourage me. Meanwhile, I worried that this could be my last shot at establishing a steady writing career and that if I didn't seize it, I would end up an aging aerobics instructor and occasional magazine contributor, with arthritic knees and a forever unstable income. So, in the spring of 1986, I became the features editor of the *Norwich Bulletin* and did not allow myself to think about how radically my world was about to change.

✦　✦　✦　✦　✦

At first glance, Norwich seemed charming: a quaint New England mill town with centuries-old white-clapboard houses and churches with tall steeples. Just beyond its charm, however, was desolation. The mills had long since closed, and most of the downtown was shuttered and deserted, save for the newspaper office, a café that operated between noon and two p.m. only, a decrepit grocery store, and a skanky bar. Downtown Norwich reminded me of a deserted town in a bad Western movie, where the only movement came from the occasional tumbleweed blowing down the street. Few residents, aside from the *Bulletin* staff, seemed to be younger than sixty-five. Suffice it to say, it wasn't a great spot for single twenty-somethings like me.

What's more, there was no sign of Jewish life. Although I'd ceased my Jewish journey years earlier, I'd left behind many friends in Berkeley whose Jewishness had attracted me. None of these friends was religious. Few observed the holidays. But the fact of their Jewishness had made me feel connected to them in a way that I hadn't felt connected to anyone, despite my paltry knowledge about Judaism. Living in Norwich nixed my chances of finding such connection. And not having that option, for reasons that I could not name, felt like a deprivation. Suck it up, I told myself. You want to work in newspapers? You want to write about human struggle? Pay your dues.

I dove into my new job with gusto, set on being the best features editor the paper had ever seen. I spent twelve hours a day in the newsroom reading the AP wires—now computerized—assigning photography, editing reporters' stories, and pounding out deadline pieces, keeping my ears attuned to the police scanner for potential breaking news. I learned fast. My supervising editor praised me. Even Granger, who pickled himself at every lunch and spent late afternoons cloistered inside his windowed office swigging Jack Daniel's, gave me an outstanding performance review.

But I was miserable. My days were long and I had no life outside of work. I jogged around the local elementary school track but couldn't connect with the stroller-pushing mothers I met. The one woman I befriended at my new pool moved away. I looked for compatriots at the gym but found only men who seemed miffed at having to share weights. I avoided socializing with colleagues because it meant hanging out in the seamy local bar. It's not that I didn't drink. I did. In fact, I started drinking too much, and alone.

For me, more than one glass was too much. Like Mom, I had a low tolerance for alcohol: One glass made me lighthearted and fun; two glasses made me drunk. Getting drunk didn't make me nasty. It dialed down my misery. But misery returned in the morning with a whiff of my boozy breath. I disgusted myself. Thankfully, this kicked some sense into me—so did a coworkers' praise for my weight loss after a bout with flu. Illness had killed my desire for liquor, drinking had made me fat, and for me, being fat was as good as hitting bottom.

That I was so acutely aware of my drinking behavior assured me that I did not have a problem. I could control my alcohol intake. I just needed to cut back. I recognized the risk of drinking, but I would not deny myself the lift that it brought. Besides, as one who instantly craves what she can't have, I knew that swearing off liquor would make it an obsession. I chose instead to walk the tightrope between enjoying its gentle buzz and closely minding the voice of caution in my ear.

Fortunately, my drug of choice was exercise. I worked out fiercely seven days a week. On weekends, I ran on the beach in nearby Watch Hill, Rhode Island, then swam, and napped in the late-summer sun. Occasionally, I escaped to New York City to visit a friend. Being there cheered me up. I'd leave feeling resolved to tough out my job for a year, or at least until I found a better one. But once I saw signs for Norwich on the highway home, dread clutched my stomach.

I had to get out of there.

Reuniting with Will gave me added incentive. We had parted as loving friends, which made separating particularly heart-rending. Our phone calls grew more frequent and tearful. Nine lonely months in Norwich and the approach of my twenty-ninth birthday clouded my memory of how frustrated I'd been in our relationship, and convinced me to give our love another try.

Will visited during Christmas. "I could find work in New York City in a second," he said as we cuddled in bed at a Red Roof Inn near the Hartford airport where he'd landed an hour earlier. We stayed up late drinking brandy, which eased us into a level of intimacy that we'd rarely shared in Berkeley. "I've already made a few phone calls," he told me the next morning, as I made a cup of hotel-room coffee. "There's plenty of work in Manhattan." I felt thrilled yet apprehensive. Was the passion we'd just shared the 'new us'? Or was loneliness propelling us toward disappointment and disaster? And what about my dream of living in New York City? During the week of Will's visit, I landed a job as a general assignment reporter at the *Jersey City Journal*, which was as close to Manhattan as I could get. I wasn't sure if taking the job and reuniting with Will were wise choices, or if I was settling.

✦   ✦   ✦   ✦   ✦

On a frigid day in January 1987, just nine months after arriving at the *Norwich Bulletin*, I drove a packed U-Haul down I-95 to Jersey City. I was ecstatic, more about leaving Norwich than about moving to Jersey City. Still, I had high hopes. I'd rented a one-bedroom apartment on the second floor of a refurbished brownstone, which had a view of the Manhattan skyline. I was thrilled to be returning to civilization. In a month, Will would drive across country and find a new job. Together, we would set up house.

Much of my job at the *Jersey City Journal*, a sixty-thousand-circulation daily, entailed covering municipal government, which meant filing late-night dispatches about town council, school board, and various other city meetings. By proving myself a capable city reporter, I'd hoped my editors would eventually allow me to write columns about Jersey City's poor and homeless, many drug-addicted, some of whom took shelter in the newspaper's lobby. Unfortunately, the paper was not keen on supporting my dream of writing about social inequality and human struggle.

"Do you want to be a reporter or a social worker?" one exasperated editor snapped, when I unintentionally frowned at an assignment to cover a crooked city administrator. I didn't want to be a social worker. But I wasn't a born newshound. I lacked the guts to sniff out scandal, let alone stare it in the face. I kept at it, though, while I started looking for another job.

The job I wanted was at the *Advocate*, a small daily in Stamford, Connecticut. I'd met the editor there before going to Norwich. She'd liked my clips and said I'd be perfect to write the weekly "My People" column, which featured stories about people and issues in the community. She promised to call me as soon as the job opened up. She told me to stay in touch.

Meanwhile, Will and I resumed our old-married-couple rhythm. Because I worked longer hours than he did, he kept house, grocery-shopped, planned weekend outings, and minded our two rescued cats. When a ruptured lumbar disc hobbled me, he withstood my pain-fueled tirades. After my surgery in March 1988, he nursed me back to health. Whether I was ill or well, he doted on me.

"You're my bunny," he'd croon.

We were each other's bunnies. But we weren't lovers.

In his kindness, Will would chat with my mother whenever she called. They'd met just once, when I brought him to a family wedding. Mom couldn't fathom what I saw in him, which I attributed to her dismay at his weight. Will, on the other hand, saw in her what I couldn't: someone who wanted to give me her love.

"I don't know why you don't want to talk to her," he said.

"Because she was an abusive parent and is an alcoholic."

"She obviously wants to have a relationship with you. You should give her a chance."

"You can't possibly understand what it was like for me as a child, having had her as a mom, screaming at me all the time—"

"But you're not a child anymore. Don't you think it's time to let it go? She won't be around forever."

"She still drinks."

"If I had the kind of life she's had, I'd probably drink, too."

Mom's drinking had always troubled me but even more so as I faced my own uneasy relationship with alcohol. I'd been vigilantly monitoring my intake of booze, which I used for pain relief before my back surgery.

"I think I might have a drinking problem," I confessed to Will one night as I mixed a double Bloody Mary.

"You don't have a drinking problem," he countered. "You're having a drink at the end of the day like most people do."

"I'm drinking every night."

"You're having one drink."

"I'm having one huge drink. Every night."

"You're in pain. You're not swigging booze from a bottle in a brown paper bag. Give yourself a break."

Aside from having an occasional beer, Will wasn't a drinker, nor did he have a family history of alcoholism. He equated problem drinking with destitution, but I knew from observing Mom, who wasn't a bottle-in-a-brown-paper-bag alcoholic, that problem drinking could be less blatant than that.

"My mother is an alcoholic."

"You're not an alcoholic."

"Not yet."

"You're not close to being an alcoholic. But if you're worried about it, stop drinking."

Surgery nixed my pain, and once again, I quit drinking excessively, but I didn't stop altogether because alcohol smoothed my edges like nothing else. I was willing to endure my conflicted relationship with it in exchange for the short-lived relief it provided. I adhered to strict, self-imposed rules about when I could and couldn't imbibe: never before six o'clock at night, never in lieu of exercising first to ease stress, and never when I was depressed. Though drinking eased my anxiety, it compounded my depression, as it did Mom's. I would not be like her.

✦ ✦ ✦ ✦ ✦

Mom called every couple of weeks, always on weekends, and more frequently during my bad-back bout. Now retired, she was surviving on her pension and Social Security—Milton's and her own—which kept her comfortable. Her only friends were Louise, the neighbor next door, and a nephew from her first marriage who lived with his family in San Diego. When she wasn't with them, she was in her apartment alone. She didn't take classes. She didn't see theater. She didn't participate in community activities. Her life sounded solitary and sad, but the slur of her words repulsed me too much to care.

Steven called me at work on an April morning. He wanted the name of the neurosurgeon who'd recently operated on my back. "I must have a ruptured disc, too, but my doctor can't see anything on my X-rays to explain the pain I'm in," he said. My surgeon invited Steven to send him his X-rays. After reviewing them, he suggested Steven get an MRI.

The MRI revealed a melon-sized tumor hidden inside the curve of his tailbone. "It's called a chordoma—a tumor of the spinal cord," Steven told me with characteristic matter-of-factness. "It's slow-growing but benign. What a relief."

Steven needed surgery. The operation would be complicated and long. To reach the tumor, doctors would have to cut him open in the front like a door and in the back like a four-pane window. The best hope of permanently removing the grisly mass was to excise everything it had attached itself to—namely, Steven's tailbone and the surrounding nerves, which controlled his bowel, bladder, and sexual function. It was a gruesome choice to have to make.

"I just want them to get rid of it," he said.

The fifteen-hour procedure took place in June 1988 at the New York University Medical Center. Steven had insisted that we not call Mom. "She'll make it about her," he said. Dierdre, Roy, and I paced the hospital halls until late into the night, waiting for word that Steven was in recovery.

Steven couldn't have visitors in intensive care, but as soon as he moved into a private room, I rushed to see him. Before entering, I froze. He was sitting in a wheelchair, his hands folded in his lap. A tangle of plastic tubing snaked out from beneath his blue hospital gown. A bag of urine dangled at his side. He was facing a panoramic window that framed the Brooklyn Bridge, yet he seemed to be staring into space. How much does he know about his illness? How much does he want to know? I had done some research. Few chordoma studies existed, but those I found reported an average survival rate of ten to fifteen years. No one beat this disease. But I would not share this information with my forty-four-year-old brother, who would not entertain a conversation about anything other than positive outcomes—the same brother who, upon learning of his father's death, had submerged his five-year-old self in a lake. Swallowing tears, I turned and left.

✦   ✦   ✦   ✦   ✦

In mid-July, Will and I visited Steven at home in Connecticut.

"I'd better prepare you . . ." Dierdre began.

She'd been waiting for us. Before she could continue, Steven emerged from the house. He was skeletal. His T-shirt and shorts flapped around his twig-like limbs. His legs looked like pipe cleaners planted in clown shoes. A baseball cap sat low his head. He shuffled over to me and wilted onto my shoulders. He cried.

"You're so skinny," I said, feeling stupid for stating the obvious.

"I'm afraid to eat," he whispered. "I don't want to have to go to the bathroom."

He hobbled to the bedroom. I followed and found him lying on his side, tucked into a fetal position, keening into his pillow. Although he'd known in advance about the physical deficits that the surgery might cause, no amount of preparation could have blunted the horror of his loss.

"Who would want this body?" he sobbed. I rested my hand on his shoulder and cried, too.

I called Steven every day for months. The calls didn't last long because all he did was weep into the phone. Even when he mustered the energy to speak, our conversations were brief.

"How are you feeling today?" I'd ask gently.

"Not so good. Down day."

There were many down days. Pain wracked his body and his mind; he had no idea what functions, if any, he'd regain.

"I don't recognize myself anymore." Then the tears would come, both his and mine. I felt impotent, useless.

For as long as I could remember, I'd worried about losing Steven. I could not bear the thought of life without him and so I'd worried, I suppose, to prepare for the loss, should it come. In fact, I used to tell friends that if I ever lost my brother, they would have to lock me in a thickly padded room where I could scream and hurl myself against the walls to deal with the heart-shattering grief. Now in my thirties, watching Steven battle disease, I felt sure that if he did not survive, I wouldn't either.

✦　✦　✦　✦　✦

"Let's go to the Caribbean," Will suggested in October. "We need to get away. And you need a break from Steven."

He wasn't wrong. But I could not go twenty-four hours without checking in with my brother. Even from the heavenly island of St. John, I called him daily, slumping helplessly inside a pay phone as he wept.

In time, and with the aid of catheters, rubber gloves, and antiseptics, Steven learned to do for his body what it had once done for him. It would take nearly a year for his postoperative pain to subside; nerve pain from the tumor never left him. Still, he felt strong enough six months after surgery to resume teaching, and to finally tell Mom about his illness. He said she was more wounded than angry that he had withheld the news, but she had plenty of anger for me, as she had all my life.

"I can't BELIEVE you didn't tell me about Steven. How could you NOT have TOLD me?"

"He asked me not to!"

"But what about ME? Did anyone even THINK about ME?"

"That's the point, Mom. It wasn't about you!"

Steven allowed Mom to visit him at home in Connecticut a few months later, sometime around Christmas. Given the friction between Mom and me, I decided to stay away. Steven and I spoke regularly anyway, sometimes every day.

"Annndreaaa," he whispered over the phone one afternoon while I was at work. "I had an erection! They said I'd never have one again!" I was overjoyed for him. "See? This disease is not life-threatening," he asserted. "It's life*style* threatening."

I hoped for a miracle. I hoped that he was right.

✦ ✦ ✦ ✦ ✦

Two weeks after Will and I returned from St. John, the *Advocate* hired me to be assistant features editor and columnist. This was the job I'd been hoping for, and I agreed to start on November 1. I prepared to move to Stamford—alone.

"The only thing that's changing is our living arrangement," I told Will, feeling guilty for lying. Will had turned his life upside-down to create a life with me in Jersey City. He had left the Bay Area, work, and colleagues that he adored, spent days driving across the country, and threw himself into the freelance job market, all to be with me. Now, I was leaving him again.

I'd had high hopes for us. But the lack of passion that had frustrated me in Berkeley resurfaced in Jersey City. I'd expected that vacationing on a Caribbean island would ignite a fire between us. But after a few attempts at lovemaking under a sagging mosquito net, we resumed our companionable, passionless partnership. I wanted out. I also wanted the freedom to pursue a sexy political activist I'd interviewed for a story.

Dennis was smart and flirty, and called me at work regularly. Over time, our phone friendship evolved into occasional beers at a local pub. Dennis was everything that Will wasn't: strict about diet and exercise, an avid marathon runner, and infatuated with me. He was also unfaithful. He lived with a woman whom he said he wanted to leave, and pressed me to plunge into an affair. Drunk on his attraction, I was sorely tempted. But I would not cheat on Will, nor would I be the "other woman." The *Advocate* job gave me an excuse to make a quick and permanent exit.

"Oh, right," Will shot back. "You're moving out after two years and telling me that things between us aren't changing. Gimme a break." It was the first time I'd ever seen him angry. "Good luck at your new job," he said as I handed him my apartment key. "And do me a favor. This time, when you realize you've made another wrong move, don't call me."

It didn't feel like the wrong move. Not at first, anyway. I knew that laying out the weekly bridal page would be part of the job, but it seemed like a small price to pay to have my own column. Every week I would get to write about someone in the community with a compelling story. To me, the most powerful stories were the ones that needed telling, stories of people battling racism, poverty, mental illness, or addiction. The *Advocate* covered Fairfield County, one of the wealthiest counties in the United States, the county had its own population of recovering crack addicts and homeless people, and I made it my business to find them.

"Mark loves your column," my boss Roslyn Ross said of the executive editor. "But he's wondering if maybe you could lighten it up a little."

"Lighten it up?"

"Yeah, maybe write about something more upbeat every now and then, like the Junior League?"

"The Junior League? Do you really think that our readers need to read about privileged people like themselves? Shouldn't we be enlightening the public about the people in this community they probably don't even know exist, like the homeless sleeping in the train station?"

"Yes, but you can't hit readers over the head with this stuff every week, Andrea," Roslyn said. "It gets to be too much. Instead of snubbing your nose at high society, why don't you look at it as sociology?"

I liked Roslyn. She was the first Jew I'd met since leaving Berkeley. I'd felt the rush of familiarity when we met and wondered if she might be the inspiration I needed to resume my Jewish journey. But Roslyn was nothing like Judy, my former soul mate in Berkeley and Jewish mentor. Judy had rejected the wealth and privilege that I'd associated with being Jewish. To her, being Jewish was about social action. Roslyn, on the other hand, with her large diamond wedding ring, lunchtime jaunts to Bloomingdale's, tales of Caribbean vacations, and lavish wedding, seemed like a poster child for material advantage. She may very well have been a mensch. After all, she'd chosen journalism, which is a form of public service. But my past hardships and resentments clouded my ability to see past her pricy possessions. I wrote her off before I even got to know her.

✦ ✦ ✦ ✦ ✦

The *Advocate* was the last square on the checkerboard of my consumer newspaper career. I loved writing my column. But I deplored the days I spent laying out wedding and engagement pages, which always included phone calls from pushy mothers insisting that I run their daughters' photos large.

Six months into the job, feeling like a failure and fearing the resurgence of depression, I returned to therapy. Instead of talking about my career frustrations, however, I ended up talking about my loneliness, my failed relationships with Will and now Dennis, who cheated on me as he had his former girlfriend, and my rage toward my mother.

"These things are not disconnected," the therapist said.

"Huh?"

"You've had a lot of disappointments in men, in your mother. They go way back. Your mother's drinking, for one. Have you ever dealt with the pain and anger it caused you?"

"No."

"I suggest starting there."

She steered me toward Al-Anon, a spinoff of Alcoholics Anonymous, founded to help people cope with the alcoholics in their lives. She said that my anger toward my mother had informed all my relationships, most notably with myself. It had certainly poisoned my relationship with men, including Will. He wasn't an alcoholic, of course, but the frustration of not being able to enjoy with him the kind of love that I wanted had disappointed and enraged me. I knew that if I wanted a shot at healthy love, I was going to have to deal with my rage, which meant that I was going to have to tackle my feelings toward my mother.

Al-Anon gave me a forum to vent, listen, and learn. It taught me that I did not have to shoulder the responsibility for my mother's ruined life, that I hadn't caused her alcoholism and couldn't fix it; all I could do was admit my powerlessness over it and hand the rest up to God.

Those words, about handing it up to God, made me cringe. God, which some Al-Anon attendees call a "higher power," is a touchstone of the twelve-step program. I still didn't know if I believed in God. I had trouble wrapping my mind around the concept of an all-powerful deity intervening in my life, but I wasn't prepared to dismiss the existence of a force in my heart, as in my mother's, which could serve as a moral guidepost or sounding board.

Either way, I wanted to feel better and decided to swallow my discomfort. At the end of every meeting, I forced myself to join in the recitation of the Twenty-third Psalm:

> The Lord is my shepherd; I shall not want. He maketh me to lie down in green pastures: he leadeth me beside the still waters. He restoreth my soul: he leadeth me in the paths of righteousness for his name's sake. Yea, though I walk through the valley of the shadow of death, I will fear no evil: for thou art with me; thy rod and thy staff they comfort me. Thou preparest a table before me in the presence of mine enemies: thou anointest my head with oil; my cup runneth over. Surely goodness and mercy shall follow me all the days of my life: and I will dwell in the house of the Lord forever.

The words felt stilted. The only way I could say them was with my eyes closed. In self-imposed darkness, I found their meaning: No matter where I was, in life as in death, God would be with me.

The words, when I didn't resist them, gave me peace. It was wonderful to feel that I was not alone and, more important, to consider that Mom's drinking was in God's hands, not mine. After spending half my life hiding liquor bottles and bargaining with my mother about her drinking, I was slowly beginning to understand that the only thing I could control was my reaction to it. This reasoning made sense, and I was eager to see if it would help me repair our relationship. To find out, I invited her to stay with me for one night during her East Coast Christmas visit.

"Be careful," my Al-Anon friends warned. "You're just beginning to understand your anger. It's still loaded."

"I know," I said, impatiently. "I get it. I'll be fine."

✦ ✦ ✦ ✦ ✦

After flying east to see Steven, Mom visited Roy and his new wife, Joan, in New Rochelle. I'd seen her infrequently since returning to the East Coast a few years earlier. She always stayed with my brothers when she visited. I'd make an appearance but had never offered to put her up, until now.

She took a train from New Rochelle to Stamford, where I met her. We went to a small Italian restaurant. The maître d seated us and asked if we cared for a cocktail.

"Nothing for me, thanks," I said.

"Scotch on the rocks, please," Mom requested.

My body tensed. I felt like I was the seven-year-old who had to beg her mother not to drink until she went to bed. Get a grip. You're not seven. You're thirty-one. She's having one drink. She sipped her Scotch and smiled at me.

"This is lovely," she said. I nodded and smiled, and searched her face for signs of wooziness. She isn't drunk. And even if she were, there's nothing you can do about it, I reminded myself. You can only control your reaction to it.

Mom nursed her drink. She asked about my new job and how I liked living in Stamford. She kept trying to engage me in conversation. She seemed nervous. Her eyes began to droop a little, and her speech to slur. I gave clipped answers to her questions. Finally, our food came. We ate in near silence.

"This really is so lovely," she said again.

As soon as we entered my apartment, I blurted, "I don't keep Scotch in the house."

"I don't need any more Scotch."

"Or gin."

"I'm fine, sweetie."

"Or vodka."

Before I could stop myself, I erupted. Mom hadn't even removed her coat when I laid into her for all the years of her drunken abuse. It was a sucker-punch that she didn't see coming, and it even surprised me.

She looked aghast. "We just had such a lovely dinner!" she exclaimed, as if to say, "Don't do this, Andrea. Don't ruin our one evening together." But I was on home turf, a bull out of the gate, pawing the ground, my head down, my nostrils flared. I charged.

"I've been going to Al-Anon, and now I know why I've been so miserable for all these years!" I began.

We stood face to face in the entryway just inside the front door. Mom looked suddenly small.

"Do you have any idea what your drinking did to me?" I scolded. Just as I had once withered beneath her verbal pounding, now she withered beneath mine. "What were you thinking?"

"I did the best I could!" she wailed, cowering like a frightened animal. The more tremulous she looked, the more savagely I attacked. I was on fire. I wouldn't fall for her tears, her sob story.

"You ruined my life!" I roared. "That's what you used to say to me, remember? How could you have said such a thing? Do you know the damage you did? You're the one who ruined my life. MINE!"

We screamed at each other about whose life had been harder, who had suffered more. It was two-thirty in the morning when we finally stopped. Mom slumped against the wall, still in her coat, sobbing. We staggered to bed. I gave her the bedroom. I slept on the couch, tasting what I thought was sweet revenge.

The next morning, I found her sitting in the kitchen, puffy-eyed. She seemed neither angry nor apologetic.

"I made coffee," she offered with a feeble smile. "I snooped around a little. You know, you could use a few nice pots and pans."

"I'm good, thanks."

"Let me buy you something."

"Mom, really, it's not necessary."

"I know it's not necessary. It's something I want to do. Why don't we go shopping before you take me to the train?"

We had breakfast, got dressed, and went to the mall. She bought me an expensive wok. We never discussed the fight.

"I love you very much," she said before the train doors closed.

Guilt devoured me. Although I tried telling myself that Mom had deserved every ounce of my fury, I could not forgive my own cruelty. Whatever initial satisfaction I'd enjoyed paled against the memory of her cowering in the corner, her eyes frozen in fear.

Meanwhile, Mom, who still lived in San Diego, tried reaching out, sending what little money she could spare, or calling. She called on weekends, usually in the early afternoon, which was late morning on the West Coast, late enough for her to have had at least one drink. I knew better than to answer my phone if it rang any later than three p.m. Instead, I'd screen my calls and lower the volume on the answering machine to avoid hearing her long, slurry messages. When I did answer, the conversations were always the same:

"When can you visit?"

"I don't know, Mom."

"It's so good to hear your voice. You don't call."

"Yes, I do, Mom."
"No. I call."
"I gotta go, Mom."
"You do that. You go."

✦ ✦ ✦ ✦ ✦

In the spring of 1989, less than a year after arriving at the *Advocate*, I left. It wasn't just the job that wasn't working for me; it was my life. Three times in three years I'd moved in search of the newspaper gig that would make me happy, and each time I'd failed to find it. I'd failed at love. I'd failed at forging peace with Mom. Our confrontation about her drinking and verbal abuse, which I thought would exorcise my anger, had filled me with self-recrimination. Despite enlightenment from therapy and Al-Anon, I remained deeply unhappy. I had to change course.

I decided to quit newspapers. I'd never considered myself a real journalist anyway. I was simply a writer who wanted to use my skills for social good. I took a job at a Manhattan consulting firm that promised to train me to write grants for nonprofits but then canned me after four months because of my inexperience. With a yearlong lease on a Brooklyn apartment and no income, I panicked.

"I got fired," I told Steven over the phone as I packed up my desk.

"All right! Now you're free for lunch!"

I couldn't laugh. "Steven, what am I gonna do?"

"Andrea, relax. It will all work out."

He sounded calm and reassuring, my rock of a brother who was now facing his mortality, living from MRI to MRI, knowing that his tumor could return at any time. He'd never tolerated pity, not for me or for himself. He downplayed his suffering, which became the yardstick by which I measured my own. However scary my career crisis felt, it wasn't the end of the world.

Freelancing and unemployment checks sustained me. I joined a local Al-Anon group and notched up my fitness routine, biking every Sunday across the Brooklyn Bridge to Central Park, where I lapped the six-mile loop five times before biking home and collapsing. In the spring of 1990, a Manhattan-based medical trade paper hired me. I'd given up on newspapers but *Medical Tribune* allowed me to write about health and medicine, which I had come to love. I moved to a two-room, third-floor walk-up on the Upper East Side, joined the YMCA, began running the Central Park reservoir, and started my life anew.

✦ ✦ ✦ ✦ ✦

Mom was starting a new life, too. She might have drowned in a bottle of booze had her sister and brother-in-law not invited her to move into their Florida condo in the summer of 1990. After decades of not speaking, they'd reestablished contact, thanks to Aunt Lila, who recounted the story years later.

"One day I just decided enough is enough and I picked up the phone," she began. "I said, 'Evy, this is Lila, your sister. Evy, twenty-five years is long enough. You're gonna be seventy. I'm gonna be sixty. It's time to let it go.'"

Miraculously, Mom did. She and Lila grew close. They spoke often. She made several trips to Florida. "Eli and I didn't want her living alone anymore," Lila told me. "I mean, who did she have in San Diego to take care of her, your uncle Doug? The truth is, Andrea, she wanted to be near you, Roy, and Steven but she couldn't get off her you-know-what to make the move. So I said, 'Evy honey, listen to me. Instead of spending all your money on airfare, why don't you move in with Eli and me? We have plenty of room. You'll have your own bedroom and your own bathroom. You won't have to be alone anymore. And you'll be near the kids.'" Lila didn't seem to know about Mom's drinking.

Moving to Florida turned Mom's life around. My aunt and uncle hired her to work part-time in their hospital gift shop and wouldn't let her pay rent. Between her salary, pension, and Social Security, she lived well. She leased a car, bought new clothes, and flew to New York every few months to see my brothers and me.

Living in only two rooms was my excuse for not hosting Mom. She'd stay with Roy, who had a large home in New Rochelle. I preferred seeing her there, on neutral territory.

Each time I saw her I was amazed at how well she looked: thin and tan in a crisp cotton blouse and white slacks. Her hair was short and frosted. Delicate gold hoops dangled from her newly pierced ears. She wore makeup. Her eyes sparkled.

"You look sensational!" I said one Sunday when we all gathered for brunch.

"Thank you! I do water aerobics every morning."

She'd quit smoking ten years earlier, and since Lila and Eli didn't drink, she'd mostly quit that, too. At Roy's, however, she joined everyone for cocktails. I grew taut, scrutinized her every move, and waited for her to turn sloppy. She didn't. She didn't even get mean, just boozy enough to make me want to leave.

✦　✦　✦　✦　✦

She called me often.

"Come to Florida!" Her voice was upbeat, clear.

"I'd love to, Mom. But I'm so busy right now."

"How 'bout a quickie visit? I'll buy you a ticket."

"I don't need you to buy me a ticket, Mom." Now that she had some disposable income, she kept trying to send it my way, a hundred fifty here or there. The money felt like a trap. I couldn't accept it and then push her away. On the other hand, not accepting it was as good as rejecting her.

"You're my daughter. I want to help you."

"I don't need help."

"I want you to be happy."

"I am happy."

"Are you? How's work? Are you seeing anyone?"

"Work's good, and no, I'm not seeing anyone."

"You will. You're smart and beautiful."

"I'm also thirty-two."

"You're young! Don't be in such a hurry. You'll find someone. I promise."

She capped every conversation with an invitation for me to call whenever I needed to talk. I felt guilty for not going to see her. But I wasn't ready.

Then Lila started calling me.

"Why don't you come visit her, doll? Florida living agrees with her, I'm telling you. She's making friends. We all go out to lunch. We go to theater. We play mahjong. She's happy. But she doesn't stop talking about you. She wants so much to see you. At least return her calls."

✦ ✦ ✦ ✦ ✦

It was noon on Sunday, November 17, 1991, when my phone rang. I was getting dressed for a run in Central Park. I couldn't wait to feel the autumn sunshine on my skin and decided to let the machine pick up. I heard Mom's sober voice and grabbed the phone.

"I just wanted you to know that I'm sending you a little something," she said shyly. "I got a tax refund. It's not much but I figured you could use it."

"I don't want it—"

"Let me help you—"

"I don't need your help!"

"You don't have to spend it. Put it away for a rainy day."

"Mom, please stop sending me money!"

"I already mailed it."

I should have been grateful but I was furious. I had been inching my way back into our relationship at my own pace and didn't want to feel beholden to her. She can't buy me, I muttered to myself as I laced my sneakers. I won't cash the check. I'll tear it up. Irate, I grabbed my keys. Just before closing the door, I spied my Walkman on the kitchen table. I used it in the gym but never for jogging because I needed to be able to hear cars and bicyclists around me. But I was agitated. I needed to hear something other than Mom's voice in my head. Just this once. I snatched my headphones.

I cranked up the volume and started zigzagging from my apartment on Seventy-sixth Street, up Third Avenue, over to Lexington, and up to Park and Eighty-first. I hesitated at a flashing red "Don't Walk" sign. I can make this, I thought, and sprinted from the corner to the median. Did it. The sign continued flashing. Impatiently, I jogged in place. My body pulsed with anger. I needed to move. The opposite corner was a hop away. If I go right now . . . Music thrummed in my ears. All I could hear were tires screeching as I stepped off the curb.

I awoke to a crowd of onlookers staring down at me. What happened? Why am I lying on the ground? I struggled to remember the moments before I lost consciousness.

"Oh, my God, I can't believe I did that," I groaned, recalling my split-second decision to dart across the street and the grunt I emitted as a car plowed into my right thigh, catapulting me through the air and onto a sidewalk where I now lay, unable to move. From the corner of my eye I saw blood pooling near my head. I began to cry.

A police officer towered over me. "Ma'am, you have no ID. Who can we call to meet you at the emergency room?" I mumbled the name and number of Jenna, a friend who lived nearby. An ambulance arrived.

"We're going to roll you onto a stretcher," one of the EMTs began, "but first we have to straighten you out. It may hurt a little. Are you ready? One, two . . ."

They snapped my body straight. I passed out.

✦   ✦   ✦   ✦   ✦

My eyes opened to the fluorescent lights of the X-ray room at Lenox Hill Hospital. I felt the cold blades of surgical scissors slicing through my windbreaker. Shit. That's the windbreaker that Will bought me. I floated in and out of consciousness. The steel table dug into my burning bones. I passed out again.

A dark-haired, gentled-faced man with wire-rimmed glasses smiled at me.

"I'm Dr. Fine," he said in a voice that sounded far away. "It looks like you've broken your pelvis. . . ."

My pelvis? Shit. How will I finish my run with a broken pelvis? I won't be able to run tomorrow either. . . .

"You may also have some internal bleeding. We're going to take some more X-rays. . . ."

Everything went black.

✦   ✦   ✦   ✦   ✦

Roy and Steven stood at the foot of my bed in the intensive care unit.

"How did you know I was here?" I asked. "What time is it? What day is it?"

"It's Sunday," Roy said. "It's almost five. Your friend Jenna called me. Luckily, she knew my name and that I live in New Rochelle. She looked me up."

"Oh, Andrea," Steven said. He moved to the side of the bed, slid his hand under mine and cradled my fingers. "Thank God you're alive."

Thanks to my relative youth—I was thirty-three—and fitness, my injuries were not life-threatening. I had four nondisplaced fractures in my pelvis, one each in my collarbone and sacrum, and several in my ribs. My eyes were blackened, bruises covered my shoulders and back, and a mango-size swell formed at the site where the car's fender had rammed into me. Morphine and Valium numbed my pain and blurred time. With every blink, another day passed. I asked my brothers not to tell Mom about my accident, but she found out when she called me at home and spoke with my upstairs neighbor, who was feeding my cat. She was at the hospital the next evening.

"Who told you I was here?" I asked guardedly.

"Your neighbor."

"I didn't want to worry you." In fact, I didn't want her to make my pain hers.

"Lots of luck," she said with a laugh. "I always worry about you. I'm your mom."

I was too dazed to push her away.

The day after Thanksgiving, the hospital discharged me. A pair of hulking ambulette drivers hauled me, strapped into a wheelchair, up three flights of stairs to my apartment. They transferred me to the loveseat in my living room and took the wheelchair away. Then Mom arrived with a set of soft flannel sheets. She gave me a pain pill, covered me with a blanket, and put the new sheets on my bed. I flashed back to Rego Park and her tucking me under a heavy down quilt on the velvet sofa when I was sick. She fussed over me just as lovingly now. "Get some sleep," she said softly, as she helped me into bed. "I'll call you tomorrow."

For the next month, I dragged myself around on crutches. I couldn't lift my legs, so leaving my apartment was impossible.

Friends brought me newspapers and groceries. A visiting health aide bathed me. A physical therapist taught me how to bear my weight and walk. I hated being dependent. More than anything, I hated not being able to live the parts of my life that defined me—work and working out. Without them, I didn't know who I was. I felt pathetic and lost.

I'd spent the past few years running but getting nowhere. I wasn't becoming the writer I aspired to be. I wasn't doing socially meaningful work. I'd hurt Will. I'd behaved monstrously toward my mother and still hadn't reconciled the rage I felt toward her. I'd simply tried to stifle it with work and exercise.

I abhorred stillness. "Have you ever tried meditating?" my new therapist asked after listening to me complain about the constant noise in my head. He was a kindly, ponytailed, and bespectacled man in his seventies who wore a string of brown wooden beads around his neck. His office was filled with statues of the Buddha.

"When you get home at the end of the day, before you do anything else, try sitting quietly and listening to your breath."

I tried. Twice. Then I gave up and went to the gym. Listen to my breath? What would that accomplish? Sit quietly and be with myself? For what? You can be a Buddhist but it's not who you are.

No, I couldn't be a Buddhist. I couldn't be a Jew. I certainly couldn't meditate. All I could do was chase my tail, except I didn't know that I was chasing my tail—until the car hit me.

That I hadn't died was a miracle. I'd never believed in miracles or anything otherworldly. I still didn't know if I believed in God. Yet, as I recuperated inside my tiny apartment, I was no longer sure that I didn't.

The last time I'd thought about God had been in Stamford, during my days in Al-Anon. I recalled the peace I'd felt after reciting the Twenty-third Psalm. I needed that peace now. I'd forgotten the Lord's Prayer but pondered God, not as the dark and handsome hybrid of Roy, Paul McCartney, and my Ken doll, but as a steady, reassuring presence. "I believe in God in my heart," Mom had said in Rego Park. Her words rang true. I liked the idea of God in my heart—of God as conscience, the spark behind the impulse to act well and the knowing in my gut when I didn't.

It would have been an ideal time to delve into Judaism. Many of my friends were Jewish. None of them was religious but they all embraced their Jewish identities. Denying my Jewish heritage had been easy around non-Jews, but it felt oddly painful among these women who loved the tradition for the guidance and wisdom it provided. In their company I felt connected yet alienated, envious, and confused. By blood, I was Jewish. In my mind, however, I was an imposter: a low-class, white trash, welfare kid who didn't feel entitled to claim it as a birthright. What would it take for me to feel like I belonged?

I returned to work in January 1992. Within a couple of months, I was swimming and running. But I couldn't shake the terror of the accident. I couldn't stop reliving it. I couldn't stop crying.

"Why am I falling apart now?" I sobbed during one of my Saturday calls with Mom.

"You're coming out of shock."

"But it's been months! I keep seeing the car smashing into me."

"Trauma takes time to surface. You steeled yourself to survive. Now you're feeling the pain."

"I don't want to feel it now. I want it to be over! I want to get on with my life!"

"You have to go through it to get past it, sweetie. And you will. But it's going to take time."

✦ ✦ ✦ ✦ ✦

If anyone knew about surviving trauma, it was my mother. She had suffered family upheaval, widowhood, domestic violence, and poverty, and still managed to take care of my brothers and me. At times, she managed more. "I want you to be happy," was all she'd ever say when I described friends' parents prodding them toward lucrative careers, or marriage and motherhood. Mom never prodded. What she did do, when she could, was tell me how much she believed in me. Her cheerleading was quite a contrast to her abusiveness. But, like all humans, Mom was complicated, something I didn't appreciate until now. All I saw back then was her misery and anger, not her efforts to love me. Except for one day, when, at sixteen, as I sobbed in fear of failing at my one dream—becoming a writer—she rested her hands on my shoulders and said, "So, you'll be a writer," as if it was a done deal and my success, a given.

Sadly, for most of my life, Mom couldn't move past her pain and used alcohol to numb it. Moving in with Lila and Eli forced her to forgo her nightly boozing. This didn't rattle her, as I would have expected. In fact, she seemed to be reaching the other side of sorrow. Still, I felt wary. Our harrowing years had outnumbered our happy ones. Who could say that she wouldn't lapse back into depression and drinking?

I accepted her caring as I could, in small, nourishing doses. At first, I spoke only of my broken body, of the swelling that had yet to resolve, and how alien it felt to walk with a cane. In time, I opened up. I shared frustrations about my career and about being single at thirty-three. "When you're not looking, you'll meet someone," Mom said, chuckling. "In the meantime, live your life. You're smart, you're talented, and you're beautiful. You have so much to offer. Stop beating yourself up. It's such a waste of time."

For the first time in decades, she filled me with hope, as she had when she put a salt shaker in my hand and sent me outside to achieve the impossible—stop a robin in its tracks—with the simple promise that I could.

✦ ✦ ✦ ✦ ✦

By spring, I felt like myself. My body had healed. I was dating. I was happy. I'd decided to leave *Medical Tribune* to pursue a master's degree in public health so that I could write for nonprofits whose mission was helping underprivileged people. I'd work through August, visit Mom, and start attending Columbia University's Mailman School of Public Health in the fall. I had just registered for the graduate entrance exam when my phone rang.

"Hi, sweetie." Mom's voice sounded faint.

"What's wrong? You don't sound right."

"Oh, nothing. I'm just getting over a little pneumonia."

"A little pneumonia? Didn't you just have pneumonia?"

"A month ago. The doctor said I'm catching it on airplanes."

"When was the last time you flew, Mom?"

"Right after your accident, I guess. November?"

"Mom, it's May."

"Well, I guess I never got rid of it. I must need a stronger antibiotic."

"Mom, you can't live on antibiotics. You need to have someone to look at your lungs."

She called me two weeks later.

"I took your advice. I saw a pulmonologist."

"And . . . ?"

"It seems I have a malignancy."

"Where?"

"My lungs."

On Saturday morning, June 6, 1992, I took a cab from the Graduate Record Examinations (GRE) testing center to LaGuardia Airport and caught a flight to Fort Lauderdale. Mom and Lila met me at the terminal. They had once looked alike, both short and round. Now Lila was svelte. She wore white slacks, a white tunic, and gold sandals. Her once-curly chestnut-brown hair was platinum blond, straight, and cut up to her earlobes, with a middle part and bangs. Her perfume and makeup were heavy. Mom wore white slacks and a silk flowered blouse. Her mousy gray hair was flat. She wore no makeup or perfume. Her bones cut into my chest when I hugged her. An odd-looking fist-size bulge protruded just beneath her jaw. With every breath she coughed. With every cough she gagged. It was hot and humid. She was shivering.

I stayed in Florida for a few days. I brought Mom to doctor appointments. I swam in the condo pool while she rested on a chaise longue and listened to Beethoven's Sixth Symphony on the Walkman Roy had bought her. In the evenings, after Mom turned in, I walked with Lila. I told her about life after Rego Park: Mom's drinking and depression, her abusiveness, and our decent into poverty.

"I wouldn't have survived without Steven," I said. "Roy disappeared, first into the navy, then in L.A. He kept his distance. Steven was my rock. He was always there for me. He saved my life."

"No wonder you and your brothers haven't called or visited Mom," Lila said. "Eli and I kept asking each other, what could Evy have done that her kids don't want to see her?"

As we walked, I explained how difficult it felt, even now with Mom dying, to forgive her.

"She was having such a hard time when you were a little girl," Lila said. "That's why she sent you to live with Eli and me. But, honey, if I had known she was drinking like that . . ." She paused for a moment. "I had no idea."

"No one did."

"If I had known, I never would've sent you back." She wrapped her arms around me and we hugged tight. "What a mistake. Biggest mistake of my life."

The summer of 1992 was dizzying. I spent much of it flying back and forth to Fort Lauderdale to visit Mom. When I wasn't traveling, I was hustling freelance writing assignments. In between, and when I least expected it, I fell in love.

Erik and I met on a June evening at a meeting about end-of-life care, of all things. I'd covered the issue for *Medical Tribune*. Erik, a philosophy professor, had just accepted a position at the Hastings Center, a biomedical ethics research institute that had been my main resource. I noticed him as soon as he entered the room. He reminded me of my brother Steven: bearded, bespectacled, and professorial. I sat down next to him and peered at his nametag.

"Why don't I know you?" I asked, flirting. "I know everyone at the Hastings Center."

"Because I haven't started yet," he flirted back, his soft brown eyes pulling me in. "I start in September."

We had dinner that night and the next. Contrary to Mom's advice, I didn't play it cool. I liked Erik and had a powerful crush on him. I dove in headfirst.

"I need to tell you that my mother is dying of lung cancer," I ventured as we finished our meal. I was not about to waste my time getting to know him if the interest wasn't mutual, or if he couldn't handle my mourning. "I'm telling you because who you see tonight might not be who I am in a week or two."

With his eyes fixed on mine, he finished his wine, leaned forward, and said, "We'll go through it together."

✦ ✦ ✦ ✦ ✦

Erik was unlike any man I'd ever met. He didn't shy away from the emotional complexity of relationship. He didn't avoid difficult conversations. He didn't ask me to act happier than I felt. He didn't want me to censor myself or sugarcoat my life stories. When he asked how I was, it was because he really wanted to know. He wanted to know everything about me, including the shame I suffered over my lack of Jewishness; the son of a Holocaust survivor, he had plenty of his own.

Like many survivors, Erik's father, Henri, emerged from the Holocaust deeply ambivalent about Judaism, and he passed his ambivalence on to Erik and his two brothers. He and Erik's mother, Rachel, who wasn't Jewish, raised their sons as Jews, even though they did not belong to a synagogue, send the boys to Hebrew school, or require them to become bar mitzvah. Erik said that in his family, being Jewish meant celebrating Passover and Chanukah, decorating a Chanukah "bush" (Christmas tree), and listening to his father talk about the Holocaust.

In graduate school, Erik read the Torah as part of his studies in philosophy. He still didn't know Hebrew, however, and could not take time away from his doctoral work to learn it. Between not knowing Hebrew and lacking the matrilineal link to Judaism, he said he never felt authentically Jewish, despite his deep knowledge and love of the tradition. Instead, he felt ignorant and ashamed. "If I'm ever lucky enough to have children, I won't make their Jewish education optional," he insisted. "I would never want my kids to feel like they couldn't be Jewish." Though I had no intention of ever having children, I agreed with him completely.

Falling in love while my mother battled stage-four lung cancer felt like the ultimate disconnect. One weekend I would be in Erik's arms and the next, holding Mom's hand as her oncologist drained blood-tinged fluid from her lungs. From one week to the next I bounced from elation to grief. The life I'd dreamed of was beginning, while my mother's death loomed.

✦　✦　✦　✦　✦

The weekend after I met Erik, I returned to Fort Lauderdale. Mom was thinner, frailer. She'd enrolled in a clinical trial for a chemotherapy drug.

"You sure you want to go through with this?" I asked, wishing she'd opt for hospice care.

"Absolutely. It's the only chance I've got to beat this thing."

On Sunday, the day before I was scheduled to fly home, Mom suggested that we go to the beach.

"How can you? Are you sure?"

"Of course I'm sure. I can rest on the beach as easily as I can at the pool. C'mon. Let's go."

We packed peaches, grapes, and a thermos of iced tea. We parked near the boardwalk and laid our blanket on the sand in the shade of a palm tree.

"I'm wondering if you'd mind . . ." I began, feeling uneasy. "I'd like to go for a run."

"Of course I don't mind. Go!"

"Will you be okay by yourself?"

"Of course I'll be okay! Maybe I'll walk a little."

"It's so hot . . ." I cautioned.

"I'll be fine."

"I won't be long."

"Take your time, sweetie. Enjoy."

I headed down to the water's edge, dodging children and boogie boards. I'd forgotten my watch and set my sights on a distant jetty. It's about half a mile away. I'll run there and back in twenty minutes. I breathed in the ocean, and followed seagulls and pelicans as they skimmed the turquoise waves. The wind warmed my face. My mind relaxed. It felt good to be away from the sounds of Manhattan, the subways and sirens. I was thirty-four and happy at last, excited about starting graduate school, and in love. I hadn't told Mom about Erik yet but I knew she would like him.

I thought of her, walking alone, and my stomach tightened. I should go back. But I need this run. I'm not going far. She'll be okay. I looked behind me to see how much distance I'd covered. I tried to locate the spot where I'd left her, but all I saw was a mosaic of swimsuits and umbrellas. Just a few more minutes. I plodded on, each footfall sinking into silky sand. The crowd was thinning. Almost there . . . I checked behind me again. I was a million miles away. How long have I been running? It felt like hours. How long will it take me to get back? The jetty was close. But something told me to turn back.

I swung around and picked up my pace, running near the water for firm footing. I searched the crowd for the print of Mom's bathing suit, the bow on her hat. Nothing looked familiar. I lumbered through growing mounds of scorching sand. I snaked around beach blankets. I stumbled over rocks and sandcastles. I sidestepped children squealing as ocean spray splashed their legs. My legs grew heavy. My breaths came hard. My mouth was hot. My throat burned. Sweat stung my eyes. The ground buckled and blurred. Why had I run so far? Sprinting now, I raced to the boardwalk, anticipating the lights of an ambulance or police car. My chest pounded. I flared my nostrils and opened my parched mouth, starved for air. Then I saw her, inching toward me, holding onto a fence with one hand, wiping her brow with the other.

"Are you all right?" I gasped.

"Just a little out of breath," she said, panting.

I put my arm around her and supported her elbow. She was trembling. We inched our way to a shaded playground. I steadied her onto the back of a giant stone turtle.

"Put your head down," I said. "I'll get you water."

I brought her a glass of ice water from the snack bar. As she sipped, I peeled off the running tights I'd worn over my bathing suit and doused them in a nearby fountain. I carried them dripping and spread them across her sweat-slicked back. She shivered. After a few minutes, I helped her over to our blanket and gently lowered her down. I handed her the thermos of tea. She gulped thirstily. Then I put my arms around her and buried my head in the crook of her neck. Together, we wept.

✦　✦　✦　✦　✦

On the flight home, I cried quietly in the well of the airplane window. I felt a powerful urge to pray. But I didn't have the language of prayer. And I didn't know whom to pray to. God, if I even believed in God, was at best a feeling in my heart, not a director of life events. God can't save my mother or rewind the clock to give us another chance at loving each other. So, what's the use in praying? I didn't know. All I knew was that I craved a connection to something larger than myself, to words and rituals that could guide me through this impending loss and its aftermath. I mouthed a made-up prayer.

The next day, I bought a book about Judaism. Aloud I read: Baruch Atah Adonai, Eloheinu Melech Ha'olam. Blessed are You, God, Ruler of the universe. The words stuck in my mouth. Ruler of the universe? I balked at the image. Then, as I'd done when I first recited the Twenty-third Psalm, I closed my eyes and surrendered to the sadness. I could not hand this anguish up to God. But praying helped me feel less alone.

Two weeks after Mom and I walked on the beach, Roy and I visited her in the hospital. (Steven, although still in remission, could not handle all the traveling.) She had just begun receiving the experimental treatment and awakened disoriented after two days of drug-induced sleep. I pulled a chair close to her bed. I fed her applesauce.

"Mom, I think I've met the man I'm going marry." I felt silly, attempting to cheer up this dying woman. Still, I expected her to be happy for me.

She stopped eating. "Just take it slow. Don't be in such a hurry."

By the next weekend, she was comatose. She never awakened.

✦ ✦ ✦ ✦ ✦

Mom hadn't wanted a funeral. Maybe she didn't want people to fuss over her. Or maybe she didn't believe that she would succumb to her cancer. She must have considered the possibility, because she'd conveyed her wish to be cremated, which Lila and Eli honored. Then they sat shiva. I did not return to Florida to sit with them. I attended the memorial that Roy and Joan hosted a month later.

Waiting so long to formally mourn Mom felt wrong. I would have preferred the immediate solace of family and friends. I wanted ceremony to help me work through my grief. The secular gathering that eventually took place at Roy's home was more like a Sunday brunch than a memorial. People gaily shared memories of my mother in between bites of lox and bagel sandwiches and sips of mimosas. I wanted to talk about her death, about its mystery and permanence. I wanted to commune with others over this shared loss and the incomprehensibility of mortality. There was no such talk. My mother had been gone just a month, but her closest friends and relatives had seemingly moved on. Why couldn't I? Had I known then that Jewish tradition gives us a year to mourn, I might have better tolerated the sadness that trailed me during the months to come. Indeed, there was much about Judaism that I was about to learn.

On October 3, 1993, a year after my mother died, Erik and I married. We had agreed to end our respective legacies of Jewish alienation and shame by beginning our life together with a traditional Jewish wedding (minus the chair dance). Unfortunately, finding a rabbi to marry us was complicated and harrowing.

Two rabbis said that Erik would have to "convert" to Judaism to officiate at our wedding. Despite his quirky Jewish upbringing, his identification with Judaism, his knowledge and love of the tradition, these rabbis pointed to his mother's non-Jewishness as proof that he wasn't "really" Jewish. This had always pained Erik deeply: to feel Jewish in his bones but to know that, because his Judaism had not traveled to him through his mother's blood as Jewish law requires, he wasn't considered a member of the tribe. We both felt alienated and angry.

Then we met Rabbi Miriam, a freelance rabbi who agreed to marry us as long as we promised to create a Jewish home. Erik and I had different ideas of what constituted a "Jewish home"—a disagreement that would later cause tension between us. We did agree, however, that we would never pass on to our children the ignorance and shame that had informed our own ambiguous Jewish identities.

And so, on a sunny and crisp Sunday afternoon, we stood among two dozen of our closest family and friends, and exchanged rings and vows beneath the chuppah that Roy, Steven, and Erik's brothers Josh and Karl held high. Erik wept as his father, Henri, chanted the seven blessings, and I wept as the rabbi invoked my mother's memory as a blessing. We repeated prayers after her, and sipped wine from a crystal goblet, which she then wrapped in cloth and handed to Erik, who stomped on it to a resounding "L'Chaim!"

✦　✦　✦　✦　✦

One year later, a few months after receiving my master's degree in public health, I gave birth to our daughter, Sophie, and two years after that, to our son, Ben. More than marriage, having children had never been on my agenda. I'd hardly had a childhood of my own, let alone a model for how to parent. Besides, I'd grown up taking care of my mother and wasn't keen on the idea of having anyone (except a mate) depend on me ever again. But Erik had been resolute. He wanted children.

"I will never meet anyone like him again," I'd told my therapist as I thrashed over two terrifying prospects: diving into motherhood or losing the love of my life. I dove. It was an unsound way to enter motherhood, but fortunately, next to marrying Erik, it turned out to be the best decision I've ever made.

Having Sophie and Ben gave me a mandate to commit myself to my Jewish education so that I could set a good example for them. If I was intent on sending them to Hebrew school someday—and I was—then I would have to make Jewish learning part of my life, too. Erik wanted a Jewish education for our kids, but he still felt too ashamed over his lack of Jewish knowledge (specifically

Hebrew) to tackle his own learning, so he relied on me to lead the way. I contacted the rabbi of our local synagogue.

"We want to create a Jewish home and eventually send our children to Hebrew school," I began.

"Very good."

"The truth is, I need a little Hebrew school of my own."

"Come sit with me on Wednesday mornings for an hour and we'll study Torah."

"But I haven't joined the temple yet."

"That's okay. Just come. You have plenty of time to join."

Every week, I joined the rabbi in his study and read a transliterated blessing that he chanted in Hebrew before we delved into the week's parshah, or Torah portion. I was self-conscious about being thirty-six years old and knowing so little about Judaism. I was even more self-conscious about reading transliterated text without knowing its meaning. But the rabbi, kind and thoughtful, heartily encouraged me, never losing patience with my steady stream of questions.

I loved my Jewish exploration. I began attending Friday night Shabbat services as the next step of my journey. Erik, however, wanted no part of synagogue life.

"I don't read or understand Hebrew," he said.

"Neither do I."

"It doesn't bother you the way it bothers me. I've read Torah. I should know Hebrew."

"It does bother me, but I try to ignore it."

"I can't ignore it. And I can't stand that most of the people sitting in that synagogue are probably reciting prayers without even knowing what they're saying. I can't do that."

"But we promised Rabbi Miriam that we would create a Jewish home."

"Creating a Jewish home doesn't mean sitting in temple and saying words you don't understand. We will live good and meaningful lives. We will give our children a Jewish education.

We will teach them to be mensches. I can't think of anything more important in Judaism than that."

We had this argument many times before I finally accepted that creating a Jewish home would fall to me. I resented this for a while. Then I decided to focus on my own Jewish education, and on Erik's support and gratitude that I was making Judaism part of our family life.

Truth be told, I didn't feel comfortable in this synagogue, either. The sanctuary was dim and uninviting. The seats were hard and the stained-glass windows, instead of filling the room with colorful light, were gloomy. The rabbi who had been so personable during our Torah study sessions was joyless during services. None of the worshippers seemed glad to be there, nor did anyone welcome me or invite me to sit with them. Not being able to afford the yearly twenty-five-hundred-dollar membership dues didn't help. Although Erik and I were not remotely poor the way I had been growing up, his academic salary and my earnings as a part-time freelance writer left us no disposable income.

The rabbi, in his well-meaning attempt to bring me into the community, offered me a reduced-rate membership, assuring me that the temple extended this courtesy to all families of "lesser means." I reluctantly accepted the offer. Cloaked in welfare-kid shame, I delivered a meager dues payment to the temple secretary, who was either unaware or disapproving of the temple's flexible financial arrangements.

"Is that all you're paying?" she said, squinting and holding up my check to the light as if it were a counterfeit bill. I fought the urge to bolt from the room and, beneath my shroud of Jewish imposter-hood, I relayed the rabbi's invitation to pay what I could. With a smirk and a "Hrumpff," she stuffed the check back into its plain white envelope, which she threw into a file folder. I was now officially a temple member. But in the eyes of some, I would never belong.

My interaction with the secretary stained my view of the temple. For a few months, I attended Friday night services, peering through downcast eyes for an isolated seat in the back of the sanctuary, where I tried to conceal my unfamiliarity with prayers and songs. I felt ashamed to be there alone amid families and couples, too ashamed to introduce myself to anyone, and too insecure to acknowledge anyone's interest in meeting me. A familiar pang of humiliation returned. I stopped going to services and let my membership expire.

Although I abandoned any hope of the synagogue becoming my spiritual home, I would not forgo my determination to give Sophie and Ben a Jewish education. Erik and I agreed that a firm educational foundation would inoculate them against the kind of shame we had suffered over our confused and uninformed Jewish identities. Fortunately, the synagogue's nursery school, which was open to nonmembers and non-Jews, became a wonderful source of Jewish learning for Sophie and Ben. Every Friday, they brought home a small challah roll and two Shabbat candles. I would prepare a traditional meal of roast chicken and vegetables, and we would say the blessings as we lit the candles, shared grape juice from the Kiddush cup, and tore off pieces of challah. If I couldn't prepare a proper Friday night meal, then we'd have "pizza Shabbat" and say HaMotzi over the crust. These rituals felt foreign to me, and practicing them, however informally, felt awkward. But the kids loved them, so I did not reveal my discomfort. I did not want to do anything to dampen their excitement.

In order to create a Jewish home and set a positive example for Sophie and Ben, I knew I would have to acquire a more formal Jewish education. I tried reading the Torah on my own, but lacked the patience to decipher the meaning of its antiquated text. I read a few books about Judaism. I took a class. The enormity of what I needed to know overwhelmed me. The more I learned, the more I realized I needed to learn. This included some understanding of Hebrew, which I'd need to be able to recite and understand the blessings that my children were learning. Some may have risen to such an educational challenge, excited by the opportunity to help enrich their children's religious learning, but I felt paralyzed, ashamed not only of my impoverished legacy but also of my ignorance. I have time, I rationalized. The kids are too young to notice how little I know. I can get by on what little I know until they're older. Then I'll deal with it.

In the meantime, I went through the motions of creating a Jewish home. I prepared the same meals for Rosh Hashanah and Yom Kippur that my mother once made, and, as she had, I invited Sophie and Ben to cake their challah in sugar. I still dreaded Passover, thanks to memories of my orthodox great-uncle El's interminable Seders. But in the company of Erik's family, which included a growing brood of nieces and nephews, Passover was raucous and rich. And, with my father-in-law, Henri, leading the Seder, I felt a new urgency to understand its importance.

I developed a special affection for Henri, whose trauma from the Holocaust informed his work as a psychoanalyst for socially and economically marginalized families, as well as his lifelong crusade against prejudice. Henri was less ambivalent about Judaism than he had been as a young father. At sixty-five, he was not devout, but he was proud and grateful to be Jewish.

Henri's painstaking journey from ambivalent to proud Jew, his resilience, and his commitment to healing the world inspired me. The Seders at his Philadelphia home were nothing like those of my childhood, with my bullying uncle El glowering at me every time I wiggled in my seat. They were forums for discussing world events, politics, human bondage, both physical and spiritual, and acknowledging our obligation as Jews to help free anyone who was in any way enslaved. They opened my eyes to what being Jewish could mean.

As Sophie's fifth birthday approached, my desire to belong to a shul returned. I wanted her to have someplace to attend Hebrew school. And I longed for a like-minded Jewish community. I visited a different synagogue, one known for its political and social activism. The prospect of paying dues still troubled me, but I scheduled a meeting with the rabbi anyway.

"Andreaaaaa???" the salt-and-pepper-bearded man said as he emerged from his study. I couldn't believe my eyes! It was Billy, my guitar-playing friend from Brandeis. "What happened to you? I came back to school sophomore year looking for you and you were gone! Where'd you go?"

"Berkeley."

"Ahhh, I should've figured," he said, his eyes crinkling at the corners as he smiled. "You radical, you."

"Brandeis wasn't right for me. But you! You're a rabbi! What about all those kids you wanted?"

"Three is plenty, don't ya think? And such a blessing! And you?"

"Two."

"So, what brings you to my temple?" he asked, peering over his wired-rimmed glasses. "Need a rabbi?"

"I want to enroll my daughter in Hebrew school."

"Great! How old is she?"

"Five."

"Five's a good age. A perfect time to start."

"I hate to ask, but . . . membership. How much does it cost?"

"First year's on us. We want families to get a feel for the place. Everyone ends up staying."

"I haven't had much luck with synagogue membership . . ." I began. "I've been trying to educate myself, but I still don't know very much about being Jewish."

"No need to apologize," he said. "You'd be surprised how many people walk in here for the first time since their Hebrew school days. Or for the first time ever. Something about having kids—"

"And death," I added.

"Death?"

"I lost my mom five years ago. I wanted to pray but didn't know how."

"You can learn here. Why don't you come to Shabbat services tonight? Meet the congregation. You can say Kaddish."

"I don't know Kaddish."

"You'll learn."

"And I'm not exactly mourning anymore . . ."

"We say it for everyone."

"I have so many questions. . . ."

"Questions are good. Judaism is all about questioning." I relaxed in my chair and noticed that he wasn't wearing a yarmulke. "Israel actually means 'wrestling with God.'"

"Yeah, well, I have questions about God, too. Sometimes I believe that God is in my heart. Other times, I'm not so sure I believe in God at all."

"My feelings about God change all the time," he offered. "That's okay. We Jews are always questioning. And learning." He got up to leave and took my hand. "I have to write my sermon for tonight's service. Maybe I'll see you?"

"Maybe."

"Keep asking questions. Shabbat Shalom."

"Shabbat Shalom."

✦ ✦ ✦ ✦ ✦

That evening, I returned to the temple. I pushed open the heavy sanctuary doors and stepped into a light-filled room with floor-to-ceiling windows. Rows of folding chairs angled toward the bimah and Holy Ark, which held three velvet-covered torot. I bowed my head, hearing my breathing in the room's sacred hush. People ambled in. Greetings filled the air. Children ran around. A man with an easy smile approached me.

"Are you new? Welcome. There's a seat next to mine. Come sit."

Billy entered. He still wore no yarmulke but had wrapped a white tallis around his shoulders. The cantor picked out a melody on his guitar. People pulled their children onto their laps. Chatter turned into chanting. A gentle hum filled the room.

"Everybody!" the cantor called out. "Dai di dai, dai, dai, dai-di-di-dai."

Tentatively, I joined in.

"Shabbat Shalom," Billy said over the chanting.

"Shabbat Shalom," the congregation replied.

"Please turn to page six, and rise for the sh'ma.

I leafed through a stapled booklet and mouthed the transliterated prayer: Sh'ma Yis'ra'eil Adonai Eloheinu Adonai Echad. Then I read the English translation at the bottom of the page: "Hear, O Israel: the LORD our God, the LORD is one."

I looked around the room. Everyone knew the prayer by heart. Some said it with their eyes closed. Others belted it out through wide smiles. I shifted my weight from one foot to the other. How can I say these words if I'm unsure about God? Billy's words replayed in my head: My feelings about God change all the time, and that's okay because Judaism is all about questioning. But did everything have to be in Hebrew? How would I ever understand anything?

Toward the end of the service, the rabbi roamed among the worshippers, his hand outstretched, inviting people to speak the names of loved ones in need of healing. The room turned quiet. Names punctured the stillness. I thought of Steven, now out of remission, his tumors spreading wildly. I could not rally the courage to utter his name. Then the congregation sang, "Mi shebeirach avoteinu, M'kor habracha l'imoteinu. May the source of strength who blessed the ones before us help us find the courage to make our lives a blessing, and let us say, amen."

I wept uncontrollably. A woman put her arm around me. I cried harder.

Through my tears, I sang, "Mi shebeirach imoteinu, M'kor habracha l'avoteinu. Bless those in need of healing with refuah sh'leimah, the renewal of body, the renewal of spirit. And let us say, amen."

The service closed with the mourners' Kaddish. People rushed through it, seeming to say it in a single breath. "Yitgaddal veyitqaddash shmeh rabba . . ." I couldn't keep up, even with the transliteration. I closed my eyes, and followed the rhythm: "Yit'barakh v'yish'tabach v'yit'pa'ar v'yit'roman v'yit'nasei . . ." At the end of prayer, people hugged and wished each other Shabbat Shalom. Billy found me standing awkwardly by myself.

"You made it!" he said. "You'll stay for kiddush?" He led me into an adjoining room with tables full of dessert platters and challah. "This is my old friend Andrea Kott," he said to anyone whose arm he could grab. "We knew each other in college, can you believe it? She's thinking of becoming a member. She has a daughter in kindergarten." I eyed the door. "We look forward to meeting Sophie," he continued, as I put on my coat. "And to seeing you again."

✦ ✦ ✦ ✦ ✦

Sophie began Hebrew school that year, 1999, and, Ben, two years later. Every Saturday morning while they attended their programs, I attended Torah study. In the synagogue library, a dozen other congregants and I passed a box of rugelach around a U-shaped table and discussed the week's parshah. We questioned. We debated. Sometimes we argued. Billy encouraged us to dig deeply into ourselves as we searched for personal relevance in the text. I loved it.

"Fantastic!" Steven said when I told him about my participation in Torah study.

"Really? I thought you rejected Judaism."

"No, I never rejected it. I lost my chance to become bar mitzvah after working so hard, and I never bought the whole God thing. But I always loved the tradition."

"I'm not always sure about the God thing, either."

"That's okay. There's more to Judaism than that. Keep studying. And keep me in the loop. I love hearing about what you're learning."

As Sophie and Ben received their Jewish education, I received mine. I learned the aleph bet (Hebrew alphabet) and began to recognize words. I sang in the temple choir. I joined social action projects. I corralled Erik and the kids to help make sandwiches for the Midnight Run, serve lunch to the indigent elderly, and paint signs protesting the U.S. invasion of Iraq. We even traveled as a family to Washington, D.C., to march against the genocide in Darfur.

"You're being Jewish," Billy commended.

"Being Jewish? What's the difference between being Jewish and being a good person?" I challenged.

"You were born Jewish, but that doesn't automatically make you a mensch. You are learning to be a mensch by doing mitzvot. And you are teaching your children." He studied my face. "Being Jewish is not about what we're born into. It's about the good deeds we do."

Good deeds I could do. But is that all it would take to make me Jewish? Despite the warm and vibrant community I discovered at the synagogue, and despite the nourishment of my spiritual appetite, being unable to afford full temple membership undermined the feeling of legitimacy that I craved. The financial "arrangement" that the temple offered gave me a feeling of déjà vu, rekindling the shame I'd felt watching my mother collect food stamps and government cheese. Billy maintained that ours was not the only family in need of assistance. Still, the display of material wealth among much of the congregation made me feel that I would never be worthy of the tribe.

When I confided this to him, he said, "You're the only one standing in your way."

I suspected he was right. And yet, memories of childhood poverty were not all that undergirded my discomfort and ambivalence. The liturgy offended my feminist sensibility. And mouthing transliterated prayers or even stumbling over what little Hebrew I'd learned seemed dishonest, because I still could not comprehend its meaning. I went through the motions of chanting and praying, watching myself watch myself, feeling like a fraud. Nevertheless, I persevered.

"How can I insist that Sophie and Ben get a Jewish education if I don't do the same?" I asked Erik, who joined me when his own discomfort didn't dissuade him. "We owe it to them. We don't want them to grow up like we did." And so, whenever they complained about going to Hebrew school, which they eventually did, I'd say, "It is important to know who you are. You are Jewish. It is your heritage. Question it. Struggle with it. Reject it if you must. But know what you are rejecting."

✦ ✦ ✦ ✦ ✦

If anyone had told me during my darkest days in Berkeley or Norwich that I would eventually live in my own house with my husband and our two children, the loves of my life, I would have thought them crazy. I never dreamed I'd have my own family. In fact, I'd sworn my aversion to marriage and motherhood. They turned out, however, to be among the things that would heal me.

Our life was hectic and rich, filled with afterschool sports, music lessons, Hebrew school carpools, and family hikes, bike rides, and trips to the beach. And yet, family life did not come easily to me. The only marriages I'd ever observed had been my brothers'. And the only parenting I knew was my mother's. My young life had been a fight for survival. It left me needy, controlling, selfish, and afraid, above all, of abandonment. I knew nothing about the negotiations that healthy family life required, or how to respond calmly to its natural complexities and conflicts. What came most naturally, unfortunately, were impatience, rage, and the impulse to yell. I never hit. But boy, could I shout. I had a live wire in me that stress or sadness easily tripped.

Like most two-career couples with young children, Erik and I had our share of stress. He worked long hours and often traveled, while I juggled full-time parenting with working from home as a freelance writer and editor for public health nonprofits. We also had more than our share of sadness. Throughout Sophie and Ben's early school years, my brother Steven was dying.

By 2000, Steven's cancer was out of control. Every MRI identified new tumors, wrapping around his ribs, strangling his sciatic nerve, and penetrating the membrane around his brain. They grew inside his body and then pushed their way out. One engulfed his vocal cords, making it look like he'd swallowed a tennis ball. He underwent repeated operations to remove tumor-riddled bones and flesh, a piece of collarbone, some ribs, a tiny chunk of skull. His pain became so severe that once he nearly overdosed on painkillers.

"Everything about this disease says 'quit,'" he'd say one day, only to rally the next. When walking became difficult, he used a cane. When one leg went numb, he wore a brace. When the watermelon-sized growth protruding from his left hip made sitting in a chair impossible, he bolstered himself with pillows. When surgeons removed half of his vocal cords, he wore a microphone headset so students could hear his remaining croak-of-a-voice. "I look like Madonna!" he quipped after class one day. "Now all I need are fishnets and conical breasts!" How could he joke? How could he want to go on living? Where did he find the courage?

"This isn't courage," he'd say flatly. "This is my life."

In his last years, Steven's hope teetered. Standing, sitting, walking, and sleeping became unbearable. Drugs barely reached his pain.

"This is no life," he'd say, before swallowing a handful of pills and falling into a drugged sleep, only to awaken in time to teach, saying, "I think I'm going to beat this thing."

Those were the worst days. I'd agonize over Steven's refusal to let go, and then find myself rooting for him to hold on. I couldn't bear to lose him, yet I couldn't bear to hope. I could only wish he would stop hoping, so that his suffering would end. But I knew he wouldn't. Hope, after all, was keeping him alive, and living was what mattered most.

I prayed for Steven to die in his sleep so that his suffering would end. I didn't believe in an almighty God who intervened in life events. Even if I had, it was a selfish prayer because I was really praying for my own suffering to end. So, I switched gears and prayed for the strength to be a better wife and mother. I'd become combative with Erik and short-tempered with the kids, exploding at the slightest infractions. I'd been hurling my grief at everyone.

One night as I prayed, I heard a voice: *You've been doing a lot of asking. Where's your gratitude?*

Some might have called the voice conscience. I called it God. I listened. I couldn't remember the last time I'd expressed my appreciation to Erik for his love and support, or considered how lucky I was to have two children who were happy, healthy, and safe. Yes, I was losing my brother. But Judaism, as Billy had once explained, valued life above all else, just as Steven did. You cannot forsake your family in the shadow of Steven's dying. From then on, I said prayers of thanks every night for my family, their health, safety, and love.

In early February 2004, a couple of weeks before he died, Steven said, "I want someone to say Kaddish for me."

"Kaddish?"

"Yes. People think of it as a prayer of mourning, but it's actually a celebration of God. It's a wonderful prayer. I love the rhythm of it. Yitgaddal veyitqaddash shmeh rabba . . ."

"Since when do you know Kaddish?"

"I used to know all the prayers. I had to know them to become bar mitzvah, even though I never did. I think I can still say the sh'ma," he mused, looking toward the ceiling. "Sh'ma Yis'ra'eil Adonai Eloheinu Adonai Echad. Hear, O Israel, the Lord is our God, the Lord is one."

I felt dumbstruck. There was so much about Steven that I didn't know and would never learn. "Since when do you celebrate God?" He didn't answer. He was getting sleepy. I changed course. "Do you remember the Moses pendant that Grandma gave you?"

"Of course."

"Why'd you stop wearing it?"

"I think I took it off when I was painting the apartment in Eastchester and just never put it back on. How's Torah study going?"

"I haven't been in a while," I said, disappointed that he'd changed the subject. "I'm struggling . . ."

"With what?"

"God."

"What do you mean struggling?"

"I don't believe in God as an all-powerful deity. The only God I've ever believed in is in my heart. I'm not sure how Jewish that is."

"It doesn't matter." His eyes looked heavy. "God or no God, you're Jewish. You'll find a way of being Jewish that works for you." He began dozing. I gathered my things. "Where are you going?" he said, prying open an eye.

"I've got to get home to Sophie and Ben. I'll be back tomorrow."

"Wait." He marshaled what little strength he had to stand. "I want to hug you."

We wrapped our arms around each other. I rested my cheek on his bony shoulder, dampening his neck with my tears.

✦　✦　✦　✦　✦

Steven died a few minutes before midnight, on February 24, 2004, in a Connecticut nursing home, with Dierdre, Roy, and me at his side. Cantor Jonathan, to whom I'd grown close in social action projects, including protesting the U.S. invasion of Iraq, graciously agreed to conduct Steven's funeral. In his rich tenor voice, Jonathan recited the Twenty-third Psalm, first in

Hebrew and then in English. I bowed my head, expecting to feel comfort from the now-familiar words: Yea, though I walk through the valley of the shadow of death, I will fear no evil: for thou art with me. . . . I felt no comfort. I rose to say Kaddish. I closed my eyes and listened for the rhythm. I could not hear it. I could not celebrate God.

The day after the funeral, Billy called. "I hope you're planning to sit shiva."

"I hadn't planned to."

"You should sit, even if it's just for a day."

"But I haven't been to temple in weeks. I haven't been to Torah study. I quit Hebrew." In truth, I didn't want people to see me grieve.

"People will want to reach out to you. Give them a chance."

The temple sent out an email announcing the shiva at my home. A handful of friends from Torah study came. They let themselves in through the unlocked front door and joined me in the living room, where I sat looking at family photos. When I talked about Steven, they listened. When I was silent, so were they. It wasn't my job to entertain. They had come to take care of me. I'd expected to feel awkward, but instead, I felt embraced. At the end, we said Kaddish. I said it every night for the next month, even though I had to read the transliteration from a book. It felt good to say the prayer that had been so meaningful to my brother; it was hard to feel grateful, however, especially in the light of day, when I awoke to the starkness of his absence.

For the next few months, I felt like a ghost of myself. I feared that I would never come back to life.

"Jewish tradition gives us a year to mourn," Cantor Jonathan said several weeks later. "You have to go through all four seasons without your brother to make the emotional shift. You have to experience spring without him, then summer, then fall and winter. Give yourself time."

Billy encouraged me to attend the upcoming Yizkor (remembrance) service on the last day of Passover. "We observe Yizkor four times a year, on Yom Kippur, the final day of Sukkot, Passover, and Shavuot," he explained. "In the course of living, we all lose someone." He put a hand on my shoulder. "We have folks in this congregation who've been coming to Yizkor for years. They're healing. But grief, like healing, is fluid. It comes and goes. Come to Yizkor. It might help you feel less alone."

Only half a dozen people attended the service. The sanctuary felt cavernous. I sat near the back, hoping no one would see me cry. Billy arrived with his guitar. I was afraid he was going to urge me to move closer to everyone. He just smiled at me. "Even though we return to our lives, we never stop grieving for the people we've lost," he said as he strummed. He began to sing. People joined in. I wept freely.

✦ ✦ ✦ ✦ ✦

In the coming years, with Sophie and Ben both attending Hebrew school, my synagogue participation increased. I rejoined weekly Torah study and resumed my Hebrew studies. I participated in social action. With renewed fervor, I observed Rosh Hashanah and Yom Kippur.

Like marriage and motherhood, the High Holidays healed me in a way that I never could have anticipated. I still had a wavering belief in God and found much of the liturgy offensive. But none of this mattered to me during the Days of Awe, the ten days of introspection and repentance between Rosh Hashanah and Yom Kippur when I contemplated my sins and vowed to make amends through prayer and tzedakah (charity). I loved these days for the forgiveness that they offered and for their directive to be a better human being. Most of all, I loved them for the opportunity they gave me to teach Sophie and Ben what I was finally learning, to replace self-preoccupation with a larger purpose, tikkun olam, repairing the world by performing mitzvot.

For my family and me, the most meaningful part of Rosh Hashanah was Tashlich, the ceremony of atonement, when we cast off the "sinful" parts of ourselves. After the conclusion of services, we walked with our fellow congregants to a stream near the temple, each of us carrying a small piece of challah. Every morsel of challah that we tossed into the stream represented the part of our character that had caused us to sin. Even Erik, despite his discomfort with synagogue participation, seemed to appreciate the chance to throw away his most ignoble qualities.

One week after Rosh Hashanah came Yom Kippur. Like muscle memory, the reverence I'd felt when my mother prayed over the candles returned when I lit them with Erik and the kids. As a child, I had thought that if there were ever a time when God was watching me, it was on Yom Kippur. That's how I felt the first time I attended a Kol Nidre service.

Kol Nidre is one of the holiest and most beautiful of Jewish prayers, sung after sundown to mark the beginning of Yom Kippur. As the cellist played the prayer's plaintive melody, I bowed my head and closed my eyes. Although I sat among hundreds of worshippers, I felt alone in the room with God. I prayed for forgiveness, even though I had come to understand that true atonement required face-to-face apology. It was too late for me to apologize to Mom but not too late to apologize to Erik, Sophie, and Ben for anything I had done during the year to hurt them, or for them to do the same.

However deeply these rituals nourished me, I still could not overcome the humiliation I felt whenever the synagogue's financial secretary called to see if my family still needed a special financial "arrangement" to make our membership affordable. I tolerated the embarrassment long enough for Sophie and Ben to complete Hebrew school.

Neither Erik nor I had required or expected the kids to become B'nai Mitzvah. We were shocked when each voluntarily undertook the work involved, including the rigor of memorizing and interpreting portions of Torah and haftarah. And when they, on their respective days, read from the unfurled Torah scroll and shared their understandings of the ancient text, we wept with joy because we knew that they had not inherited our painful Jewish legacy. Their experience of being Jewish had neither burdened nor isolated them. Their connection to the tradition had been free of self-consciousness and conflict. Their Jewish identity had flourished and they embraced it proudly, without ambivalence or apology. They felt at home in their Jewish skin.

This was what I wanted, to feel at home in my Jewish skin. To some, including Billy, it seemed simple: I was born Jewish, and therefore, I am Jewish. So, why were there so many years when I couldn't feel Jewish?

"You're the only one standing in your way," Billy had said. I knew he was right. But I was stuck. Calling myself a Jew didn't feel right but neither did denying my Jewish heritage. Despite my best efforts, I could not convince myself that I didn't care about or had no stake in my Judaism. I could not negate who I was. I wanted to feel Jewish without reservation, but I didn't know how to begin.

Money complicated things. Once Sophie and Ben started college, we simply could not afford temple membership, even with "an arrangement." Angry at the resurgence of shame I felt over our inability to make a financial contribution, I left the temple. During my five years away, I started writing this book. I approached it as a journey, hoping that it would reveal the roots of my ambivalence and alienation from the tradition that is my birthright. It has done that, and so much more.

Writing this book has helped me understand the trajectory of my life, how the hardship of my youth informed the individual

I have become, for better and worse. It has helped me articulate what it is about Judaism that I love, and clarify, even just a little, what being Jewish means for me. It has helped me see that being Jewish has nothing to do with class or material wealth, and everything to do with how I live my life; that Judaism is a tradition more of action than of belief; that where I pray is not as important as the fact that I pray; that just wanting to heal the world is not as meaningful as the steps I take to help others; that a true apology is a personal one; and that being a mensch requires me to forgive others.

It would not have been enough to understand these things in isolation, however. This book was intended as a journey, and journeys need destinations. Ambivalence was not the ending I wanted. I didn't want to keep hanging in a state of limbo. I needed a finishing point, a sense of closure. To achieve that, I would have to test out my newfound clarity, to see if the understanding I had gained through writing would allow me to join the Jewish community that I craved but had shunned. I would have to risk the discomfort of mumbling prayers that I did not yet understand, or rely on transliteration because I'd forgotten what little Hebrew I'd learned. I'd have to listen to the liturgy without the insecurity, financial and otherwise, that masquerades as contempt or defensiveness. I'd have to accept the offer of reduced temple dues. Most important, I'd have to commit myself, once and for all, to a course of study about Judaism. I could no longer blame childhood trauma, ignorance, or shame for my feeling disenfranchised. If I wanted to belong, then I would have to stake my claim and walk back through the synagogue doors. I would have to get out of my own way.

I started by sitting with Billy. I told him about my struggle and my journey. He listened with care. I said that my financial situation hadn't changed. "Has this community ever not welcomed anyone because of their inability to pay?" he asked rhetorically. We both smiled. "It's good to have you back," he said. Next, I sat with the cantor, who immediately invited me to a program that the temple was having on aiding undocumented immigrants. He added, "Come back to choir!" It was as if I'd never left.

During my years away from synagogue, I'd done my own volunteer work, mostly teaching English to low-income, often undocumented, immigrants and refugees. I'd also worked in soup kitchens, donated to food pantries, and lobbied for humanitarian political causes. Doing these activities felt good, but doing them alone did not; neither did observing the High Holidays. Despite the celebratory meals that I cooked for my family, and the ad hoc Tashlich ceremony that we performed at a nearby stream, the Days of Awe felt amiss without belonging to a larger community.

Family and community are central in Judaism. According to Rabbi Bradley Shavit Artson, the dean of the Ziegler School of Rabbinic Studies at American Jewish University, "At the very beginning of the Torah, God tells us that it is not good for a person to be alone." As Rabbi Artson writes, "To be a human being means to be in dialogue and in relationship with other human beings. There is no identity separate from everybody else. From the very moment we are born, we are involved in relationships that help us understand who we are and help us grow into who we can become. It is not possible to be a person and to be alone."

Although I did not feel alone when I was with my family, as a Jew I did not feel complete. In synagogue, around the Torah study table, or under the high-topped tent where we worship during the High Holidays, I am part of my other family, an enduring community. Yet, I am Jewish not simply because it's my legacy, but also because it's who I want to be.

There are moments in synagogue or Torah study when the wisdom of Jewish teaching exhilarates me, when I feel renewed after conveying an apology, casting my most sinful traits into a stream, or performing mitzvot. These rituals ground me. They inform my perception of what it means to be a good person, a mensch. They nudge me out of self-preoccupation, and toward people and communities whose need for healing is greater than mine.

This is not to say that I embrace everything that Judaism teaches. But if I've learned anything on my Jewish journey, it's that Judaism offers multiple lenses for viewing life, its many challenges and dilemmas. It encourages learning and debate, especially when it comes to God. As Billy told me years ago, Israel means "to wrestle with God." And I do continue to struggle, but I trust that in Judaism, with its invitation to question and doubt, my struggle has its place.

✦ ✦ ✦ ✦ ✦

A couple of Pesachs ago, Erik's parents, my brother Roy, and his eldest son, Justin, joined Erik, Sophie, Ben, and me for our yearly Seder. Roy and I had made some headway in bridging the gap between us but we didn't really begin growing close until 2008, when he learned that he had lymphoma. That's when we started spending more time together, walking our dogs, meeting for swims, and sharing family dinners. He became a regular at our Seder.

At this particular Seder, it was time to sing Dayenu (die-ay-new), the song that celebrates liberation, Torah, Shabbat, and the many other miracles that God gave to the Jews. The song is an expression of gratitude to God; it says that just one of the miracles that allowed the Jews to escape slavery in Egypt would have been enough, dayenu, and yet, there were so many. It compels us to look for the miracles in our lives, and to keep our eyes open for reasons to be grateful.

Dayenu is so upbeat that it's impossible to sing it without tapping a foot, bouncing and smiling. "Day, Day, Enu, Day, Day,

Enu, Day, Day Enu, Dayenu DayeNU!" With every chorus, we slapped our open hands on the table and stomped our feet.

"Day, Day, ENU, Day, Day, ENU . . ." I heard my father-in-law belt out the words.

"Day, Day, Enu, Day, Day, Enu . . ." I heard Roy and Erik.

"DayEnu DayeNU . . ." I heard Sophie and Ben.

"DAYENU, DAYENUUU!!!" I scanned the room and saw that all the windows were open. We were singing so loudly that the whole block probably heard us. I didn't care. I wasn't embarrassed. I was filled with joy. And I felt proud. As I sang louder and louder, I felt a catch in my throat and my eyes fill at the sound of my voice, at home.

EPILOGUE

ON APRIL 4, 2017, AFTER AN EIGHT-YEAR BATTLE with lymphoma, my brother Roy died.

His death did not come as a surprise. I had expected it to sadden me. I had not expected to feel devastated. Although we had come a long way from the days when we barely spoke, we never got as close as Steven and I had been. But this was my second and last sibling to die. My mother was long gone. My father had always been gone. I felt orphaned.

As I had done after Steven's death, I sat shiva for Roy for an evening. One friend, looking at the family photos on the coffee table, noted one picture in particular: It was of my mother, Roy, and me; I was about five months old, sitting on Mom's lap, smiling at Roy.

"Look at you adoring him," my friend said. It dawned on me then that I had become so used to Roy disappointing me that I had forgotten how dearly I'd loved him.

"When did you stop adoring him?" my friend asked.

I had to stop and think. "I guess it was when my mother started falling apart. Roy moved to Los Angeles. I used to think he wanted to get as far away from us as he could. But maybe he really just needed to get away from my mother."

Only as Roy's life was ending did it occur to me that he hadn't intended to leave me behind. He'd simply tried, in his own flawed but human way, to gain as much distance as possible from the memories of losing his father, being shipped off to an all-boy boarding school where his classmates harassed and beat him and Steven for being Jewish, living under the watch of an abusive stepfather who molested them, and Mom's helpless dependence. I suppose that moving to L.A. was his ticket to survival. He saved himself the best way he could. Unfortunately, I was the baby he threw out with the bathwater.

Looking back, I recognized how Roy had, in fact, tried to demonstrate his love for me over the years. He drove me up to Waltham, Massachusetts, for my freshman year at Brandeis. He added a leg to a business trip so he could see my new digs at UC–Berkeley. He hand-delivered a bag of warm bagels to Erik and me on the morning of our wedding. He went out of his way to meet me for early morning swims at the YMCA or across Great Pond in Wellfleet, Massachusetts, where both of our families vacationed. He joined me for dog walks. He drove from his end of Westchester County to mine to watch Ben play lacrosse. And he schlepped his weakening body into Manhattan to catch a ten-minute play that Sophie directed. We were working hard to get to know each other. We were getting closer.

One summer afternoon, several years ago, Roy left a message on my cell phone, asking me to call him. I was vacationing on Cape Cod with Erik, our kids, and Erik's family, and I feared that Roy's illness had taken a critical turn. I found a quiet spot and called him.

"There's something I need to say to you," he began. I braced myself. "I joined a men's group a few months ago. I have Joan and the kids, but I don't have any close male friends, and I thought this would be a good way to find some." Impatiently, I shifted in my chair. This is why you wanted me to call you?

"During our last meeting we did an exercise to build intimacy. It was very difficult for me. We had to share the names of five people who we'd hurt and had never apologized to. You were first on my list." I stared at my phone in disbelief. I almost didn't recognize the voice coming out of it.

"I actually owe you three apologies," Roy continued. "The first is for pressuring you to join Steven and me in contesting Milton's will. If we hadn't pushed you, then Shirley might not have shut you out, and you might have had a relationship with her, which could have been healing for you." I thought of dismissing his concern, telling him that he didn't need to apologize. But the truth is, I had felt angry and sad about having lost the chance to know my father's family. I continued to listen. "Second, I apologize for not being there for you when you were young. You needed both Steven and me to help you cope with Mom, but I was too busy dealing with my own issues. I was too immature and selfish to be there for you. Third, I apologize for being impatient and angry with you so much of the time. You always reminded me of Mom—the way you looked and spoke. Every time I saw you, I saw her, I saw Milton, and I felt my life fall apart all over again. I had to get away. But I abandoned you, and I'm sorry."

Roy finished speaking. For a minute, we were both quiet. His honesty stunned me. It rekindled the anger I'd felt about how poorly he had treated me for so long, and how much time we'd lost being estranged from each other. Part of me wanted to scream, "Where have you been and why has it taken you so long?" Yet, a bigger part of me appreciated how difficult it must have been for him to make these confessions, and how important it must have felt for him to convey them before he died.

"Thank you for saying all of this," I said. "You have no idea how much it means to me."

"I love you," he said.

"I love you, too."

+   +   +   +   +

On Yom Kippur, the Jewish Day of Atonement, we are supposed to apologize to those we have hurt in order to be inscribed for a blessing in the Book of Life. We are also supposed to forgive. We cannot conduct these exchanges through email, text messages, or phone calls. They must be face to face.

I have no doubt that Roy would have apologized to me in person if he could have. But he couldn't wait for me to get back to New York. And he most certainly didn't want to wait for Yom Kippur. He needed to apologize while he still he could.

My mother never apologized to me. It was only years after her death, when I had children of my own, that I gained an inkling of the challenges she had faced, and felt not just forgiveness but also gratitude for all that she'd given me: the support to become a writer, and her unstinting belief in me, especially when I did not believe in myself. I never thanked her for this. I never apologized, either. Now, it was too late. I wouldn't make this mistake twice. I cherished Roy's words. And I forgave him.

For the month after Roy's death, I said Kaddish, as I had done for Steven. On Yom Kippur, I lit a third yahrzeit candle alongside those that I lit for Steven and my mother, and prayed for their memories, all of them, to be a blessing.

ACKNOWLEDGMENTS

My deepest thanks go to Vanda Krefft, who championed this book long before it was a book, painstakingly pored over its earliest iteration, and provided spot-on critiques that moved it forward. I am forever grateful to Lila Pollak, my aunt, who patiently helped me assemble the puzzle pieces of my life. Thomas Yagoda, a pillar, believed in this book's relevance and assured me that it would find a home. Ellen Gomory's keen eye helped me shape and sharpen the text. I am blessed to have friends who lovingly plowed through the first draft: Myriam Barenbaum, Barbara Benedict, Elizabeth Campbell, Marcy Gray, Anita McGovern, and Julia Miller. Without Rabbi Billy Dreskin and Cantor Jonathan Gordon of Woodlands Community Temple, who helped me find my Jewish self, while inviting my questions and doubts, this memoir would not exist. My deep appreciation also goes to Eliot Wise, Blydyn Square Books' marketing director, who read my submission during the press's closed reading period, and whisked it over to managing editor Megan Skamwell, who, despite being knee-deep in manuscripts, took the time to keep me updated on its status. I am fortunate to have discovered Blydyn, whose publisher Tara Tomczyk has handled this project—and me—with great care; we have both reaped the benefits of her editorial expertise. Kyle

McGovern, Esq., was invaluable in helping me to navigate the nuances of book contracts. Throughout writing and rewriting, I leaned on the shoulders of Sophie Parens and Ben Parens, who insisted that I had a story worth telling. Loving them has infused my life with joy and meaning that I never imagined possible, just as I never dreamed I'd find a partner in love and life, Erik Parens, with whom to build a family. Erik's love and wisdom have sustained me through tumult and loss, as well as the writing of this book. His faith in me fills every page. He is my heart.

ABOUT THE AUTHOR

Andrea Kott earned her bachelor's degree from the University of California–Berkeley and her Master of Public Health degree from Columbia University's Mailman School of Public Health. She has spent her 40-year career straddling the worlds of creative nonfiction and public health journalism. In addition to publishing creative work in *The New York Times, Lilith Magazine, Journal of the American Medical Association,* and literary journals, she writes about public health for global and national nonprofits, public health schools, and academic medical centers. She also teaches English as a Second Language to immigrants and refugees, and participates in Hevra Torah Study at Woodlands Community Temple. She and husband Erik have two grown children, Sophie and Ben, and live in Sleepy Hollow, New York.